Inventing

Creating and Selling Your Ideas

Inventing

Creating and Selling Your Ideas
by Philip B. Knapp, Ph.D.

TAB BOOKS Inc.
Blue Ridge Summit, PA

FIRST EDITION
FIRST PRINTING

Copyright © 1989 by Philip B. Knapp, Ph.D.
Printed in the United States of America

Library of Congress Cataloging in Publication Data

Knapp, Philip B.
Inventing : creating and selling your ideas.

Includes index.
1. Inventions. 2. Patents. I. Title.
T339.K67 1989   608   88-35944
ISBN 0-8306-0284-4
ISBN 0-8306-3184-4 (pbk.)

TAB BOOKS Inc. offers software for
sale. For information and a catalog,
please contact TAB Software Department,
Blue Ridge Summit, PA 17294-0850.

Questions regarding the content of this book
should be addressed to:

Reader Inquiry Branch
TAB BOOKS Inc.
Blue Ridge Summit, PA 17294-0214

To Pasquale (Pat) Amendolia
without whom this book would
never have been started,

And to Harriet D. Knapp (my wife)
without whom this book would
never have been finished.

I would also like to thank Ed Manuel and Dan Weiss, both members of the New York Society of Professional Inventors, for their incredible patience and terrific help in pointing out the "good" parts as well as the bad.

"Tradition and ritual are great for passing on information, but they play hell with invention."

Contents

Preface

THIS BOOK IS FOR ANYONE WHO HAS EVER HAD AN IDEA. FROM THE PET ROCK to the Hula-hoop, from Sputnik to the Space Shuttle, from the creation of Monopoly to Dungeons and Dragons, people have ideas. Some of these ideas have been translated into reality, and some of these realities—hoops, rocks, games and new frontiers—have been translated into millions of dollars, creating incredible changes in our day-to-day lives and in the lives of the inventor.

Inventing: Creating and Selling Your Ideas is about the transformation from the idea to the actual. It takes the dream or fantasy, and turns it into a reality. It's for both the amateur and the professional. It explains in detail how to create and sell an invention—and it explains where these ideas come from in the first place. In the process of taking the idea from concept to development, I will identify the steps involved in turning the amateur or professional dream addict into a well-rewarded inventor, both emotionally and financially.

The most incredible thing that I discovered in writing this book is that the detailed techniques of creating an invention apply equally to any form of art or research and development project. For the first time there is a map into the mysteries of creativity. If you've ever wanted to paint a picture, write a book, do a sculpture, or if you have the stamina, make a machine, this book will show you how you go about it. It's for all those people who have ideas and have always dreamt of "doing something" but have never known how to go about it. It's also for all those brave people who have actually "made something" and are now wondering what's their next move. Where and to whom do you take it? How do you sell or license it? What kind of deal should you make?

The main theme of *Inventing* is to take a chance and do your thing. You might make money, but surely the satisfaction and glow of having "done it" is worth more than money.

Remember:

1. This book is what I believe and sometimes do.
2. No one says you have to do it my way.
3. In fact, I'll understand perfectly well if you do it your way.
4. That's what inventing is all about.

PBK

Acknowledgments

THROUGHOUT THIS BOOK I HAVE USED SEVERAL STORIES TO ILLUSTRATE VARIOUS points that I wished to emphasize. In most cases I do not know where these stories originated. I have assumed that because no author or attribution was ever mentioned by the teller of the tale, and because some of the stories were repeated by different people, that the stories were part of common lore and therefore in public domain.

Please understand that I have very strong feelings about the proprietorship of "intellectual property." I would have been more than happy to seek permission from the author to use the material, if the author were known to me.

Therefore, let me thank all those unknown (to me) authors of the stories retold in this book.

Chapter 1

Invention and Creativity

I BELIEVE THAT ALMOST ALL OF WHAT IS CALLED THE *PROCESS OF INVENTION* can be taught. I also believe that the process of invention is almost completely an analytical process, whether approached in an organized or haphazard manner.

That small part of invention called the *creative process* cannot be taught, not by present methods anyway. I have never heard of anyone coming away from a course in creativity and doing anything remotely creative.

I do not mean to disparage those honest investigators who are constantly trying to determine what creativity is, where it comes from, and what the characteristics of a creative person are. I strongly feel that the tiny twist that makes a person creative is an accumulation of a series of chance impacts that somehow reinforce each other until, like it or not, the person is creative. I don't think any noncreative person can understand the anguish and loneliness and sometimes overwhelming feeling of strangeness that a creative person feels, particularly in the growing years.

Regardless, the importance of that small part called creativity cannot be minimized; without it there is obviously no beginning.

The creation of an invention is not always a spontaneous act, however. At times, and under particular circumstances, it can be a completely analytical exercise.

No matter how an invention comes about, it is, in its simplest form, a

1

venture into the world of the "new." It is an awesome discovery of something unknown. Each time it teaches us that there is a vast universe of ignorance out there. To quote Daniel Boorstin, "The great obstacle to progress is not ignorance, but the illusion of knowledge."[1]

It's interesting to examine the effect of invention. It is seemingly a never-ending process of stimulation—a chain reaction that plays itself out. One invention follows another—all new, all contributing to the "art." Then a different area of interest emerges that channels all energy and thought away from the old. In each step forward, an inventor takes another small bite of the apple. And with each bite, the apple seems to grow bigger than it was before. It's only an inventor's innate conceit that convinces him that what he has done is definitive and is the final and best answer to a problem. After all, it's his solution, and in most cases, the only one he could think of. Therefore, how can anyone think of doing it better or differently? The inventor's ego won't let him think otherwise.

PHASES OF INVENTION

Invention has a logic and sequence that cannot be denied. The process follows a pattern of action, an analysis that has a life of its own. The pattern or logic is not compulsive in terms of which action or sequence follows which step in the invention process. It is compulsive, however, in that, like it or not, each step is covered by the time the invention is completed. It really makes very little difference whether these steps follow each other in a systematic or a haphazard fashion. That is one of the things this book is all about. *Inventing* takes all of these steps and puts them in order. The essential fact to remember is that when you are making an invention, the analytical logic works either through mental imagery, systematic planning, or the unconscious. An invention, as far as I'm concerned and contrary to the rules of the United States Patent Office, is not an invention until it is put to practice and actually works.

When examined carefully, there are only five major phases to the process of invention:

1. *The Motivation.* This can also be called desire, need, or compulsion.
2. *The Idea.* This is the result of stimulation and inspiration.
3. *The Analysis.* This requires a detailed examination, inspection, and functional review of the idea.
4. *The Construction.* This requires building a working prototype.
5. *The Selling.* Unless the invention is sold and put to use, there's no benefit to anyone, particularly the inventor.

---

[1]Daniel J. Boorstin, *The Discoverers: A History of Man's Search to Know His World and Himself* (New York: Random House, 1985).

Investigators in the field of creativity make a very serious error in not differentiating the various phases that comprise creativity. The need or desire to do something or to create anything—like a picture, a sculpture, or an invention—is the compulsive feeling of the first phase of *motivation*.

Seeing something that strikes the eye or mind, such as a beautiful woman, stimulates or inspires the inventor to move into the second phase of the idea, saying for example, "I want to make a picture (song, poem, sculpture) about that woman." This is the ability of the individual to use various bits and pieces of experience to see the woman as a potential picture. That's the *creative part* of it . . . the beginning, small segment, or "tiny part" of it all. It's that little bit I spoke of at the beginning of this chapter that embraces all of the experiences a person has accumulated on a conscious or unconscious level.

The ability to see that potential is the creative aspect of creativity.

In the third stage of analysis, the inventor plans the idea, putting together bits and pieces of information to form an entity. This is the *analytical part*. It takes a great deal of learned ability to segment and differentiate the parts and functions of each particular component of a work.

In the fourth phase of construction, the inventor carries out the plan in a manner that makes it work. This is really the hard experience portion of inventing. It's the part that must be learned over a period of time from various sources, the part that teaches the inventor what can or cannot be accomplished. It is the *technique portion* of inventing and must not be confused with the creative portion. (Though it is entirely possible, and also probable, that in carrying out this phase of the work, creativity also comes into play.)

Creativity has been described as being 1 percent inspiration and 99 percent perspiration.

The ability to put together those incredible little unconnected pieces to find a potential solution to a construction problem, to be innovative when the building takes place, is to be creative in construction. In the construction phase, however, you must differentiate between technical capability and creativity. These are often badly confused. Admittedly, the tricks of the trade and learned experiences of a good technician can make the difference between something that works or something that doesn't. But these are techniques, not creativity.

WHAT IS CREATIVITY?

What you must seriously consider is whether or not you think "desire" is creativity. Many people have a desire to write a great novel, to create a great invention, or to paint a great picture. They have the idea that they'd like to do it about a particular subject, but does that, in and of itself, speak of creativity? Doesn't the possibility strongly exist that without the necessary combination of forces—the desire, the ability to analyze, and some degree of technical capacity— creativity could not exist?

My argument is that the analytical ability and the technical capacity to invent can be taught. Where, then, does the learning process stop? Is it possible that the second phase of inventing—the idea—also can be taught? I sincerely hope that someone someday finds a way. Right now, however, I doubt it. I do know that I can't teach you how to get an idea, but I can teach you what to do with it to make it a reality.

I know many people with either extraordinary analytical or technical ability or a combination of both. Many of these people, however, simply do not have either the creative "spark" or the desire. Even when some of them have the desire, for some reason they lack the spark necessary to make something new. Others simply don't have the need to be creative.

Can something be judged creative or noncreative based on an evaluation of the techniques used in the analysis and construction? Is it fair to make that kind of differentiation? Are people being a little too hard-nosed about it? Isn't it a fact that someone who creates a bad piece of music is being just as creative as a person who writes a good piece of music? After all, it's still the making of a particular thing. The differentiation, I suppose, is the difference between technique and "original" thematic material.

I know people with great experience and technique who have tried and found it impossible to make a good piece of music. Therefore, before we become too judgmental about what is and what is not the result of creativity, we must first define what we consider creativity to be.

I, for one, am willing to accept any new thing as creativity. I don't care how bad a piece of work is; it is something that the person who designed and made it did out of his own needs and experiences. Therefore, from a very practical point of view, whether or not the work is accepted by others really makes very little difference. Creativity is really too personal a thing to be judged by other people.

Perhaps what really differentiates the creative person from the noncreative person is the fact that the creative person wants to make something. Indeed, most creative people I know feel compelled to constantly make something. Whether the result is good or bad is of little consequence, it's the desire to make something and then following through to actually make it that really counts. Having said all that, I must also state that the acceptance of a work by others generates a rather remarkable degree of satisfaction for the inventor.

Quality is a very relative subject. When you think about quality, you think about it in relation to life, art, or invention. What it really comes down to is that quality is judged on the basis of a person's experience and life-style.

What's Good and What's Bad

At the conclusion of a successful business trip to China, an English merchant was given a keg of tea by a Chinese merchant. This was considered a singular honor and, of course, most pleased the Englishman. The note that went with the gift said that the keg contained a rare tea of the finest quality.

When he returned to England, he served the tea only to his most important guests. Each time, he would tell his guests how he came to receive the tea and of its uniqueness and quality.

About a year later, the Chinese merchant arrived in England and was treated royally. At tea, the Englishman surprised his guest by making a great show of serving the tea without telling him where it came from. The Chinese merchant took one swallow of the tea and spit it out.

"My God, what was that?" he said, making a sour face.

"Why, that's the keg of tea you gave me as a gift," the Englishman replied.

The Chinese merchant was incredulous. "Can't be. Impossible!" he said.

At that, the Englishman had his servants bring the keg from the locked storeroom. The Chinese merchant looked at it in surprise. He reached into it, dug down to the center of the keg, and pulled out a small, beautifully lacquered box. The tea surrounding the box was packing.

The question is, what's good and what's bad?

WHEN IS AN INVENTION AN INVENTION?

When is an invention an invention? In my opinion, whether it be a novel, a painting, or a motor, it's not an invention until it is completed. You can't just say, "I have an idea for a book or a painting," and count it as a work of art. I don't believe that.

An invention must be completed in order for it to be something. Unless it can be communicated to others, it is not an invention. And it is not an invention unless it works.

An idea for an invention is only an idea and nothing else. It's not an invention. After that, it takes the learning and experience to make it one. It takes analytical ability, either consciously or unconsciously applied, and physical labor to put it together so that it works. Unless it is a finished work, it is nothing.

SOURCES OF INVENTIONS

Inventions come from individuals, company and government research and development (R & D) operations, and schools and universities. Many make contributions in terms of innovation, invention, and original theoretical research.

When you think about government and company research and development (R & D), you are talking about vast resources of money and teams of people. These people are supposedly capable of doing the "big things."

When you talk about the scientific community, the schools, etc., you are talking about individuals or groups working on various projects that are sponsored by either government or corporations. They get sponsorship (as grants) theoretically because they, as members of the scientific community, are able to take advantage of the prestige and clout of their institutions and the "good old boy" network. In reality, the "network" dictates who gets the grants. The people responsible for dispensing the grants usually come from the same institutions (alumni) into which the grants are directed. Unless you belong to the "club," the possibility of getting a grant is practically nil. To get a grant, the individual investigator must belong to an institution.

Corporate research and development operates in many different areas and on many different levels. It can range from an individual who does a bit of experimentation up to companies like 3M, General Electric, DuPont, and Westinghouse. These companies are so large and powerful and have so much money that they are capable of supporting large groups doing original scientific and theoretical research.

Most companies have not contributed anything to new products and new devices. Their primary thrust in research and development is in the area of product improvement. That is all they really care about. I'm sure that they would very quickly eliminate their entire research and development operation were it not for competitive needs. Personally, the only thing I envy about these people and their programs is that they have enough resources to experiment on multiple levels at the same time, and can afford to make mistakes without sinking projects.

Who Supports R & D?

Oddly enough, the great support system behind most research and development programs in the scientific and corporate worlds is the American government. Good old Uncle Sam supplies most of the money for a great many of these projects.

What is fascinating, however, is that most new products and a majority of new businesses started came from the efforts of independent inventors and entrepreneurs. A study conducted by the Massachusetts Institute of Technology revealed that in the Northeast almost 100 percent of new employment was created by small (20 employees or less) businesses and start-up operations. Nationally, the estimate was nearly 70 percent. The R & D money that went to major corporations to develop new jobs was a mistake. Most of the major corporations created very few new jobs, even in those rare cases when they actually developed new inventions. They usually filled their personnel needs from within the corporation.

The MIT study showed that the individual entrepreneur came and went with great frequency. There seemed to be a balance, however, in relation to the number of successes and failures that took place each year. The overall point to emphasize is that these entrepreneurs created most of the new jobs that took place in the United States.

It is shameful that the support given to the independent inventor is so minimal and that the thrust of R & D expenditures is primarily to corporations and universities. The amount of money that is spent just to keep the independent inventor at bay is amazing. If that amount of money was just spent in support of the independent inventor, rather than trying to keep him out of the way and not bother anybody, it would be more than enough to compensate for some of the marvelous things that could be produced by them.

The American government designates a small business or enterprise as a "company with up to 300 employees." Whoever thought this up was a genius at keeping the independent inventor at bay.

The people in government agencies that might have to deal with inventors are afraid to take a chance. If they allocate funds to a corporation with history and background, and if that company fails to properly deliver on the funded project, the money the government invested in the research and development or the new products goes down the drain. The government individual who made the decision to give them the grant in the first place can simply shrug his shoulders and say, "Well, it's not my fault." He's safe because he based his decision to award the grant on accepted stereotyped standards that imply that groups are safer and innovatively more productive than individuals. However, should he take a chance and make a grant to an independent inventor, he really puts his neck on the line. Supporting an individual requires judgment, both objective and subjective. Judgments, particularly in bureaucratic environments, are subject to further judgments and scrutiny by superiors. The golden rule they live by is "Keep your head down." That's the reality of government support today.

The inventor is effectively shut out. Government agencies set up specific conditions and designate departments to get the independent inventor out of the way. Similarly, many corporations employ individuals to handle new inventions or products that come in over the transom. They immediately send inventions right back and have nothing to do with inventors.

I have yet to hear of an independent inventor who has ever been able to get significant support from any governmental agencies. The government tries to convince independent inventors and the world at large that it is really interested in invention, innovation, and entrepreneurship, but it simply isn't so. The government has not, to my knowledge, ever significantly supported independent inventing. More often than not, it will point to "small" businesses of 200 to 500 people as examples of working with inventors. It isn't the same. In terms of support for an independent inventor . . . forget it. It is one of the great tragedies of American society that the independent inventor, the person who contributes so much to our excitement and standard of living, is so badly treated.

Remember that nearly all of the products we have in use today were not in use ten years ago. The continuous introduction of new and better devices, objects, and inventions are the result of constant pressures applied by independent inventors trying to make their own places in the world.

Small Business Innovation Research

I have noticed that every time I begin to rant and rave about inequities of one sort or another, and make very negative definitive statements about agencies, bureaucracies, and government in general, a program comes along that makes me eat my words. Such an exception is the Small Business Innovation Research (SBIR) program. And I do mean it's an exception to the general rule of ignoring the independent inventor.

The main point to remember about the program is that the inventor is not working on projects he develops but on projects others require and specify. If that doesn't bother you, the SBIR program might be for you. The program itself is not complex, as usual government programs are, but is too long to include in this book. You can get all the information you'll need from: Small Business Administration in Washington, D.C.

> Imperial Building
> 1441 L Street NW
> Washington, DC 20416
> 202-653-7561

Briefly, here's what it's all about. In 1982, Congress passed an act that stipulated that any federal agency with an "extramural" R & D in excess of $100 million is required to allocate a maximum of 1.25 percent of their annual budget to fund Small Business Innovation Research.

Before you're scared off by the "small business" aspect, let me review the eligibility factors.

☐ You have to be a company organized for profit. (This is no big deal. Many inventors have one-man companies. I have a subchapter S corporation that I primarily use for dealing with other companies for ordering material, getting information, negotiating, etc. It comes in very handy to operate company to company rather than individual to company. I bring in people to work for me as needed, depending on the project and the kind of help that I need.)

☐ At the time of award, but not at the time of application, the Principal Investigator's primary employment must be with the company. He must commit a minimum of 50 percent of his time to the project. (There is no reason why a company can't have more than one Principal Investigator.) The Award goes to a company, not an individual. A company can apply for as many projects as it can handle.

Now that you see that eligibility is not really a problem, here's how the program works. At present, there are eleven federal agencies that participate in this program. They are:

> Department of Defense
> Health and Human Services
> Department of Energy
> National Aeronautics and Space Administration
> National Science Foundation
> Department of Transportation
> Department of Agriculture
> Nuclear Regulatory Commission
> Environmental Protection Agency
> Department of Education
> Department of Commerce

Each of these agencies develop specifications of projects or devices that they need. The list of projects are published every three months. These lists are called "PreSolicitation Announcements." They contain due dates for each project; the number of awards to be made; and the name, address, and phone number of the agency representative to contact.

The program essentially works in the following manner:

1. After reviewing the presolicitation announcements, select those projects you feel you can do. Contact the representative to determine the actual specifications of the project. Ask for the bibliography of research that went into the development of the specifications.

2. Prepare your application based on the specifications, bibliography, and the concept you feel will contribute to the solution of the problem.

3. If your application is accepted for Phase I, you will receive $50,000 (sometimes more by the DOD) and six months to complete the task. The primary purpose of Phase I is to prove that your concept works. This does not require the building of a prototype.

4. If you complete Phase I successfully, you become eligible to apply for Phase II, which is the proposal for prototype development, research merit, and business prospects. Phase II provides between one and two years for completion and awards between $100,000 and $500,000 per project. You cannot apply for Phase II without first successfully completing Phase I. Both Phase I and Phase II are funded by the federal government.

5. Phase III requires commercial market development using private monies (nongovernment) for support. In Phase III, however, you can make application under the government procurement contract. Also, bear in mind that what you have completed is something the government wanted in the first place. Therefore, the probability is that, upon completion, you have a built-in market for your product.

Funding of each phase is discussed further in chapter 17. It's a good program. If it fits your needs look into it.

Chapter 2

Inventors

ONE OF THE THINGS I FIND MOST INTERESTING IN LIFE AS AN INVENTOR IS the stereotyped image people have of what inventors are like. I have come across several versions of these stereotypes. For example, most businessmen believe that all inventors are crackpots. The media have portrayed inventors as eccentrics, invariably picking the weirdest thing they can find to publicize. The serious inventions fall by the wayside; it is rare that you even hear about them.

Most inventors are really too ashamed to even use the term "inventor" when someone asks, "What do you do?" They'll make up all sorts of excuses. "Well, I design machinery," or "I make things," or "I make models of devices." It is rare that an individual who is a professional inventor will actually state to anyone who is interested, "I am an inventor."

Some businessmen so completely believe in the stereotyped image of the inventor as "absent-minded" that they refuse to accept the fact that many inventors are just as versed in business as they are. They treat the inventor as some sort of or idiot savant and are sure that the invention came about by some accident of fate. The inventor just happened to be present, somewhat like winning the lottery. All they want is for the inventor to turn the invention over to them, at which point they pat him on the head and send him away. After all, they know what they're doing and what's best and really don't want to be bothered by some stupid, childish, and possibly interfering

11

inventor. (This might be an advantageous position because it lets the clever inventor sit with businessmen and ask questions and make demands that would normally not be appropriate.)

TYPES OF INVENTORS

I differentiate six different types of inventors, or people who might call themselves inventors.

Suggestion Box Inventors

The first type of inventor is the kind who has a feeling that inventing is a lark. All he needs is a few part-time hours. He will have a brilliant idea, and his dreams of wealth and freedom and recognition will come true. This is the kind of inventor that very frequently will come up to you and say, "Hey, I have an idea . . . tell me how to go about getting somebody to buy it." And when you look at him askance and say, "It just doesn't work that way," he thinks you're withholding information from him because you don't want him to be successful.

For whatever reason, the suggestion box inventor will not recognize the amount of hard work that is needed to complete an invention. If he does get involved with the development of an idea, which is quite rare, he might then recognize the amount of work that is necessary. Then he usually gives up the idea of inventing and moves back into his dream world of being an inventor on the basis of "if only." He will talk about his ideas to anyone who will listen, but he always lacks "something" that prevents him from carrying through.

Casual Conversationalists

Then there is the second type of inventor. He is the one who will sidle up to you, almost whispering, and say, "Gee, I have a great idea. I haven't got the time or the know-how to do it, but you're an inventor. I'll tell the idea, you make it, and we'll share the profits."

Unfortunately, you can't always laugh at these people or dismiss them for their foolishness. Quite often, they are very serious people who simply have a very peculiar image of what an inventor is or does. Mostly they are casual conversationalists, creative people only in terms of having thought something up outside their usual area of concern. But beyond that, they are usually not very creative.

Concept-Only Inventors

The third type of inventor is the kind of person who will develop an idea or a concept but will never make a model or a prototype. He will work on the concept in excruciating detail, sometimes for a very long period of time, even years. It becomes an overwhelming subject of his fantasy world. Rarely will he tell anybody the concept. If he does, it will only be to someone he trusts implicitly, though he might discuss it with someone in order to overcome a hitch in the concept as he is working it out.

The concept-only inventor will go to fantastic extremes to put the idea down on paper and make drawings of it, but he will never take it beyond the concept or analytical stage. By taking it beyond that stage, he will face reality . . . and reality means determining whether it will work or not work. As long as he doesn't have to test reality, he can continue living with his dreams of recognition, freedom, wealth, and everything else that goes with the stereotypical version of what happens to a successful inventor.

Prototype-Only Inventors

The fourth type of inventor will take the concept and build a working prototype, but he will never make a conscientious effort to sell it. Even when offered help, he will make all sorts of excuses as to why the invention is not ready for show or sale. The most frequent reason is that he has an idea for improvement and wishes to incorporate it before anybody sees it. He is constantly saying, "Gee, this looks good, doesn't it? But I have a better version of it that I want to work on before I do anything with it."

These people suffer from the same fear as the concept-only inventor. Reality is what they fear. They can continue to dream and live in this marvelous fantasy world of theirs thinking what their invention will do for them. But they won't bring it to anyone who might be able to do something with it. They bask in a fantasy glory. And that is exactly where they want to stay. It would take more than an explosive force to get them to go beyond that point.

The prototype-only inventors are consistent in that they make all sorts of great efforts to perfect and work on their projects. They will never take them to fruition, however. I am not sure there is anything wrong with what they do, as long as it gives them pleasure and doesn't impose or interfere with other people's lives. But from my point of view, inventing something and not doing anything with it is a waste of time.

Ready to Sell, But Where?

The fifth type of inventor is in many ways the saddest of them all. He has taken up the creative challenge, plunged ahead, and made a working prototype. He has shown great perseverance and, in many cases, spent a great deal of money and time to complete the invention. He made it because it solved a problem, and he is sure (even positive) that it is valuable to someone somewhere.

Now what? What does he do with it? Where does he take it? To whom? He doesn't know. He's prime bait for all the charlatans out there who make it their business to prey on naive inventors with big dreams. Hopefully, this book will point the way. If it keeps one person from falling into crooked hands, it will have served its purpose.

The Successful Inventor

The sixth type of inventor has an idea and takes it to fruition. Fruition not only means working on it, building a prototype, and making the idea work, but doing the hardest part of inventing, which is bringing it to the attention of someone who can make it and sell it. Some inventors in this category are the entrepreneur types who will set up their own businesses and take their own risks to make and develop their inventions.

THE PERSISTENCE FACTOR

The difference between a successful inventor and an unsuccessful inventor is not so much what he has invented, but the amount of persistence he will expend after the invention is completed. You might have the best mousetrap in the whole, wide world, and still no one is going to beat a path to your door. I hope whoever coined that phrase made a great deal out of it, because it certainly is the most untrue, unrealistic statement that an inventor has to live with.

When you are a successful inventor, your success isn't really the invention. The primary difference between a successful inventor and a failed one is simply persistence, with a slight modification. As a human being you must know when to keep going and when it is realistic to give up.

Everyone has a fondness for the hero, the person who wins against all odds. You root for the person who practices until it hurts, who outwits the opposition, who survives under terrible circumstances, who comes up from last . . . the person who achieves under any circumstances. These kinds of people make you cheer and make you cry. They are the substance of every heroic book or play that has ever been written. They are the winners, and it is a winner, of course, that you want to be. As long as the novel, the play, the human drama, or the reality turns out to be winner, you'll remain loyal.

It is when you lose that life becomes very difficult and very depressing. It is during that point of loss, however, that you can distinguish between friends and opportunists. Particularly, you can establish and measure the stamina that you have in relation to persistence and perseverance.

There are inventors who have invented products of very minor importance. Whether or not these inventions existed would make very little difference to the world's scheme. Yet these inventors persisted and succeeded because their ideas, regardless of how insignificant, were going to provide them with their dream. They persisted and brought it off. Conversely, I have seen others fail with inventions that could make an important contribution to society—inventions that would make a difference in everyday life. They gave up because they had neither the stamina nor the know-how to get to first base.

Press On

I once came across a poem about persistence that was posted on the bulletin board of a small hotel in Canada. I was quite taken by the statement. It is something that many of you have surely seen because it has been around for a long time. But it was the first time that I had seen it. I have no idea who the author is, but it is almost as if it had been written specifically for inventors. It reads:

PRESS ON!

Nothing in the world can take the place of persistence.
Talent will not;
Nothing is more common than unsuccessful men with talent.
Genius will not;
Unrewarded genius is almost a proverb.
Education alone will not;
The world is full of educated derelicts.
Persistence and determination alone are omnipotent

When to persist and when to give up are equally important. There are no instructions or guidelines—only individual circumstances. There are inventors who abandon perfectly good inventions not because the invention does not work or is not marketable, but because they've thought of a new problem and want to pursue it. These inventors have so many ideas that they simply don't know what to do with them, so their inventions sit around and do nothing. Then there are the inventors with a single idea who pursue it to the bitter end. They either succeed or fail, but they stick with it. When to give up, when to keep going; these are very personal decisions that only you can answer.

Some inventions (see sidebar) take a long time to develop and a long time to get to work. They are new, dynamic, and of sufficient consequence for industries to be started around them. Therefore, they are considered great inventions of our time.

It is not that kind of invention that most inventors are faced with, however most are small inventions—small because they are not going to change the way you live. Most inventors have the kind of invention that provides some sort of service or convenience or saves on labor or costs. It is the inventors of these small products and inventions who must really dig deep within themselves to determine whether or not they are going to pursue their personal goals or give up.

Some Great Inventions

Some of the great success stories of inventing took an enormous amount of time.

*****

It took Chester Carlson 24 years to bring xerography from concept to financial success. He had been turned down by Radio Corporation of America, IBM, and General Electric. He was at wit's end and didn't know where to turn when rescue came from out of nowhere. A year or so after an article appeared about him and his invention, Dr. John H. Dessauer, Haloid's Company Director of Research, happened to read it. That led to the formation of Xerox. The rest is history.

*****

Nikola Tesla dug ditches to support himself rather than give up and continue to work for Thomas A. Edison. His invention changed the way we live. He received a million dollars from George Westinghouse for the patent rights. Tesla had invented the AC motor.

*****

Westinghouse's story is pretty good too. He invented a system of air brakes primarily for use on railroads. It was the same old story. None of the major lines would even listen to him. He finally found a small one that was willing to set up a test—nothing promised, just a test. During that test, however, the train succeeded in making an unexpected emergency stop to avoid hitting someone crossing the tracks. What better way to prove the worth of an invention than to have it work when it's supposed to?

It is my feeling that you keep going with your invention. Sell it or do whatever you possibly can with it without letting it interfere with your normal everyday life. Take every opportunity to present it to get someone interested. The only time that I would give up on an invention is when it has been produced and marketed and became unacceptable. At that point, the only thing to say is, "The world isn't ready for it yet, and it's their loss, not mine."

THE CREATIVE PERSONALITY

The point is often made that creativity is genetic. I disagree on the grounds that the average intelligent human being learns to be creative based on the circumstances of his upbringing, environment, and conditioning. It doesn't take a superintelligent person to be creative—an average intelligence is adequate. When you think of those people who have made a mark in an area of creativity, regardless of the form, each one is, in his own particular way, superintelligent or superknowledgeable in his chosen area of activity. I also suspect that one of the impacts that stirs a person's creative impulse and motivation has to be some form of simultaneous physical satisfaction and approval.

For example, the most important impact on my life involving my longtime desire to become a composer happened when I was eleven years old. I remember standing transfixed listening and watching as a family friend played the piano at a relative's home. I remember his fingers moving quickly across the keyboard and the sounds and rhythms he created. I stood there incredulous at the excitement it generated in me. Shortly after, when I expressed an interest in learning the piano and music, there was a great deal of family approval and assistance, which enabled me to build on this "impact" in my life.

It wasn't until many years later that I found that, despite my desire to write and create music (probably one of the strongest impulses in my life), I was technically unable to do so, therefore making it impossible for me to continue in music. It was when I became musically frustrated that I began to invent on a secret basis. And it wasn't until there was approval of my inventions that I finally realized this was an area in which I could function.

In spite of my intense desire to create and write great music, I could not do it even after a great deal of study and effort. I had something to fall back on, however. Over the years, I had learned mechanics of various kinds, including auto mechanics during my stay in the Army. I consider this my creativity in development.

In order to create, you must have the technical capability to create, or you must be able to invent the tools of creation.

This entire argument raises a very interesting issue. Why was it necessary for me to find some form of creativity to obtain satisfaction? I cannot answer that. I can only guess that this was my method of gaining approval from those around me. Or maybe it was to gain recognition and prove my worth. Because I received great approval for my pursuit of music, I sought the same kind of approval by becoming an inventor. What baffles me most about this argument is why some people require that kind of approval while others go through life very happily without it.

One factor about creativity that I must address is its compulsive demand. To this day, ideas spill from me in what seems to be a never-ending torrent. I feel that if I lived to be 5,000 years old, I still wouldn't have enough time to complete all the projects I presently have. When an idea occurs to me, I really can't let go of it until the problem is solved, even if it's only in my head. I've tried many devices to let go so that I could stop and rest, even for a short time. It doesn't work. I can be in a group, at a party, reading a book, watching TV, in a movie theater . . . it makes little difference. I suddenly realize that I haven't seen or heard a word—that I'm into the problem and can't let go. This, then, is one form of the compulsive nature of creativity.

There is another factor that contributes to the making of a creative individual. That factor is rebelliousness . . . not necessarily destructive rebelliousness, but constructive rebelliousness. It is the ability to keep questioning; the refusal by the creative individual to be confined by authority or by what preceded him; the refusal to answer or think in a particular manner. The creative person is continuously looking for freedom to expand, to go beyond what already exists. That is a rebel. In childhood, rebels are the most difficult of all people to deal with. In adulthood, they are continually questioning authority. They wish to go beyond the limits of what is now known in order to find methods of doing new things.

When the rebel in childhood starts out questioning the authority of his parents, teachers, and peers, he is continuously challenged. And the challenge creates a situation whereby he must, to justify the rebellion, devise an answer and a method for doing something differently than the way it is presently being done or the way authorities wish him to do it. He wants to do it the way he feels it should be done. These are not isolated situations; it goes on throughout his life. He becomes sensitized to putting together the bits and pieces of information that he accumulates throughout his daily life, assembling them during the period of crisis or challenge. And when he puts it together, it is new, it's different, it is creative.

Now consider how practiced this creative process becomes with him—how unconscious or even deliberate. He becomes very aware and sensitive to things around him—to observations, to feelings, to incidental things that other people would simply ignore. And then consider the moment of utilization: the moment he is challenged, he has to put it all together.

What I am saying is that the creative person does not spring up overnight. The creative person is simply not born with a particular talent or capability. The creative person is sensitized by a series of events that takes place around and with him, he then learns the techniques of reply by utilizing these little odd bits of information. He puts them together simply because that is the way he survives.

For the creative person, authority means confinement. Questioning means expansion or freedom. And freedom means being able to go beyond the limits of ignorance or knowledge that exist now.

There is still an awesomeness to creative discovery, however. Each time an invention or concept comes about, the inventor feels overwhelmed and awestruck by the knowledge that he made something new, something that has never been done before. All of this information suddenly came together to create something. How incredible a feeling it is to know that you made something and you don't know where it came from. You might rationally and intellectually know, but it doesn't make any difference. The point is, when it happens, it is the most intense, awesome and tremendous feeling in the world. It has often happened to me that after I have discovered something, I will stand back, look at it, mull over the idea that has flashed through my head and wonder how I was able to bring these bits and pieces together in the first place. How was I able to think of something like this? Why me?

Here is a summary of the psychological profile of the creative person:

- ☐ Explores an area that both stimulates excitement and provides physical satisfaction
- ☐ Receives approval and encouragement for the reaction
- ☐ Has a compulsive need to make something—anything—to create
- ☐ Constructively rebellious from the word go
- ☐ Feels authority and precedence equals confinement
- ☐ Feels questioning and exploring equals freedom
- ☐ Has incredible persistence in learning areas of interest
- ☐ Feels disbelief and awe when discovery comes together or when an idea is formed
- ☐ Feels extraordinary satisfaction when the project is finished and works
- ☐ Is pleased when someone buys it

THE INVENTOR'S OBLIGATIONS

The social impact of an invention and the inventor's obligations to it is an area that must be faced sooner or later. I have rarely seen an article or any discussion on this, except in very vague terms by historians who try to establish the changes in certain societies as related to various inventions (see sidebar). Today's society does not acknowledge either an invention's impact or an inventor's obligation.

Only recently, because of a lawsuit against the University of California by 17 farm workers and the California Agrarian Project, has the situation come to light in modern times. This lawsuit is indicative of the kind of situations that occur.

Case Study: The Tomato Harvester

In the agricultural field, the American government supports research through grants to agricultural university and extension programs and facilities. These facilities operate with government money to do product and machine research and development. They might work for years. When they successfully complete the development of a machine or product, it is thoroughly field-tested and made ready for the market. Then various companies in the field of agriculture might or might not pick it up for free, depending on whether or not they would consider it profitable to manufacture and market.

The University of California had developed and constructed two types of tomato harvesters: one for table tomatoes and one for processed nontable tomatoes. The University of California developed the machinery to harvest both types of tomatoes. In the case of the tomato harvester for processed tomatoes, they developed a machine that could go through the field and automatically pick up almost 60 to 70 percent of the tomatoes in one pass. This level of efficiency was good enough that it was not economical for the machine to go through the field a second time to pick up what was left. (There is an aside to this story. After developing the tomato harvester, it then took the inventor many years to develop a tomato with a tough enough skin to withstand the bruising that would take place as it was harvested!)

This machine not only substantially reduced the number of people required to harvest these tomatoes, but it greatly increased the productivity of those people who supported and tended the harvester as it picked up the tomatoes.

This harvester, according to the people in the lawsuit, put a great number of people out of work and, of course, increased the profitability of the farmers and the manufacturers of the machinery.

> *The contention: Did the government have the right to support such an enterprise that would eventually throw a number of people out of work?*

Now what is the obligation of the person who invented the machine and developed a tomato that could be harvested by this machine? What is the obligation of the government in supporting this? What are the moral and ethical issues involved in a project of this sort? Should the inventor lend himself to this kind of social disruption? And is this kind of social disruption good or bad? Does a mechanism of this kind, in fact, create greater problems than those that it solves? For example, it might increase the productivity, it might substantially reduce production costs, and therefore, it might reduce the cost to the consumer on an overall basis. But doesn't society have to do something about those people who were displaced by finding new jobs for them?

In an article in *Science* of March 30, 1984, the vice president of the University of California at Davis in an interview states: "We do not deny that the machines take the place of the workers." Then he goes on to say that it is society's role, not the inventor's, to compensate the workers. That says that the inventor has no obligation whatever in relation to society. The vice president adds that it is not society's right to impose restrictions on discovery.

I wholeheartedly agree that the inventor must be free to make whatever discoveries he wishes. All information, whether helpful or not at the particular moment of discovery, is an inquiry into the vast field of ignorance. However, it is the utilization of that information that raises moral and ethical questions. Somewhere, the inventor and society must establish their responsibilities.

Is it fair to say that it is society's role, not the inventor's, to compensate the workers? It's the inventor's invention that has created the difficulty in the first place. What is the responsibility of the government and private industry in utilizing the invention? There is a shared responsibility here, but it all starts with the inventor's idea of making something that is new and different that ends up disrupting society.

Case Study: The Cotton Harvester

What should be done when an invention not only throws masses of people out of work but is responsible for mass migration and disruption of society with an almost total demographic realignment? Such an invention occurred in our time, and the dust of upheaval has only recently begun to settle. The invention was the *cotton harvester*.

The Invention. Not too long after the end of World War II, the development of the cotton harvester became a reality. It had been the dream of agricultural inventors, ag extension programs, farm machinery manufacturers, and especially cotton farmers for many years. The promise was always on the horizon, but the machine seemed to be out of reach.

Think of it . . . a machine that could eliminate so many evils. Chopping cotton by hand is painful, labor-intensive, and backbreaking work. Men, women, and many children were pressed into labor. When paid, it was always minimal. Its greatest evil was sharecropping, a marginal existence at best. Well, the cotton harvester was going to cure all that.

What actually happened was that the landowners discovered that to use the harvester they needed large, unencumbered fields—the longer and bigger, the better. It was uneconomical to take time to turn the machine around at the end of each pass. The fewer turns, the longer the productive runs.

The Consequence. The sharecroppers had to go. Their fences were in the way. They were in the way. After all, they couldn't operate the machines—it took training that they didn't have. And the number of people now needed to plant and bring in the crop was miniscule compared to before harvester times.

Go they did. In probably one of the most shameful and cynical moves on the part of the landowners in the United States, the sharecroppers were forced off the land. (This was somewhat similar to the tenant farmers forced off the land in England to make way for sheep ranching.)

It soon became apparent that a very large body of unemployed was developing in the South. These people had to be dealt with, if in no other way than supplying some form of welfare. Someone thought up the diabolically brilliant idea of moving them to the North. The premise was that if "they" were not in your backyard, you didn't have to deal with them. But how to get a large, mostly untutored population to migrate voluntarily to an essentially strange and cold part of the country?

The solution was simple and clever. People were told that the North had plenty of high-paying jobs available to anyone who wanted to work. Not to worry about surviving until you got a job. Lists of northern cities with the amount of welfare provided by each city were distributed. The crowning touch was to provide one-way bus tickets. You all know of the upheaval that followed.

Where then is the inventor's responsibility?

Unless you have been in the field and know the backbreaking labor involved in using the short-handled hoe for thinning and weeding, you cannot comment on its benefits or ill effects. Some work is totally devastating. Using a short-handled hoe in the field is the most torturous type of work. Typically a foreman supervises about 150 people. When one person stands up to stretch, everyone must automatically do the same, at which point the foreman screams obscenities. Some invention could eliminate work that is this physically devastating. I am not sure what the obligation would be to those displaced by such an invention. However, because of the devastating nature of such work, I feel I would be morally sound in creating such an invention.

I have raised many questions about moral and social obligations without providing solutions. I am too deeply involved to be objective. By bringing such problems into the open, perhaps I can encourage someone who is capable of meeting these ethical and moral challenges.

Chapter 3
The Idea

MANY YEARS AGO, OR AS THE FAIRY TALES MIGHT SAY, IN ANCIENT TIMES, four blind men came across an elephant. Each of them touched a different part of the elephant—one the trunk, another the tail, the third the tusk, and the fourth a leg. As they examined the parts, they described to each other what they imagined the animal was and what it looked like. Each had a different interpretation based on what he felt. None came close to the reality of an elephant.

Does this mean that what the blind men described was wrong? I don't think so. The ancient interpretation of this story would be that if you can't see the whole picture, then you can't know what an object really is. It is my feeling, however, that sometimes it is possible to see only one small part, and not necessarily a crucial part, and then build the rest.

As an inventor and an intuitive human being, what you must deal with is what you can feel and what you can see. From that you can build your "elephant." And as long as it works, who's to say it's not an elephant. After all, intuition is nothing more than a direct perception of truths and facts; it is independent of any reasoning process. That is one interpretation. Another might be that it is an immediate cognition of an object, not inferred or determined by a previous cognition of the same object.

THE INTUITIVE MODE

The creative person has an enormous amount of creative absorption and a high degree of sensitivity to information and facts that usually go unnoticed by others. The creative person has developed an ability to remember, consciously or unconsciously, unrelated facts and information, integrating and applying them to what seems to be an unrelated entity. Then, in a flash, an idea takes place. "Ah, intuition!" you say.

Sometimes a solution to a problem escapes you. You just can't think of it. You forget about the problem for awhile when, suddenly, a flash occurs. The solution or idea is there, and the parts begin to fit. It is the same as the elephant—you can integrate all the individual parts you wish to, but you won't get a satisfying answer until that flash takes place and the entire entity (or picture) suddenly comes together.

Utilizing information is not necessarily sequential. Logic versus intuition—it doesn't really matter. The organization of it all is filed in your head; you can't tell what comes first. Perhaps you've picked up some information, remembered a particular part or machine. Or you've seen pictures of it in a magazine or in a newspaper. You've somehow put together a series of thoughts. Who cares if this method of thinking is practical or impractical? Who cares as long as it works.

Once you have this vision of a particular creation, device, or invention, you must decide whether to go with it or not. Is it worth working on? Why not develop it if it seems to be a good idea? At least take it to the next step. Does dollar value or satisfaction mean anything at that moment? Perhaps there is no way of really knowing if your idea is valuable. Does it matter? The fact is that, at this marvelous moment, you have solved a problem! And that, in and of itself, provides far more satisfaction than anything else that you could have done.

Studies have revealed, much to the surprise of everyone, that inventors are primarily interested in solving problems and are not really interested in making a million bucks. They derive a great deal of satisfaction from pulling together those lovely facets from all over and combining them into something new—it's a satisfaction that no money can buy.

But they pay a price for all of this—in loneliness—because, at that moment of conception, the paranoia of the inventor prevents them from sharing, to any great degree, the pleasure of their accomplishment. Who can they talk to? And can they ever really impart to anybody the enormous feelings of satisfaction that they felt when they originally solved the problem?

DISCOVERY

First comes discovery—of a problem, a need, a question of why something is done in a particular way. You feel that it can be done differently and, of course, better. You have been challenged, just as you were as a child by peers or authority figures. Now the challenge is to make something different than the way it is.

You deal with your reaction to the challenge with awe. Where did you get this spark? You've thought of something that is absolutely creative and has never been done by anybody else!

What happens next? Suddenly the discovery becomes a conceit. Yours is an original idea, therefore it has to be better than anybody else's. Even if your idea is not better, you're sure that it can be brought to market more successfully than anything that presently exists. You're ready to charge ahead, forgetting all the obstacles, if indeed you even think of obstacles at this time. You are on your way to realizing your great dream.

This is the *blinding dream factor*. Even though the primary satisfaction for an inventor is problem solving, there is always the underlying dreams of recognition, riches, power, and freedom. You don't consider reality because, at that insane moment, you are ready to plunge ahead from concept, to idea, to prototype without stopping to find out if your idea is saleable.

Enjoy your moment of discovery and, yes, your dreams of success. Then, if you want to, make them a reality by taking your idea further. Now you get to the hard part!

FORMULATING THE CONCEPT

I consider formulating the concept the hard part. You must look at what you have conceived to see if you really want to go ahead with it on realistic basis. You must be realistic or you will spend too much in terms of money, energy, and impact on your family and yourself. Failure at the end of such a great expenditure of effort is, in many ways, psychologically disastrous.

Let's start with what to do with this great idea of yours. To get the most out of this book, I suggest that you first apply the following steps to an existing product to understand how the procedures work. Then, apply the steps to develop an idea or concept that interests you, working on it step by step as outlined.

Example: For purposes of explanation, apparent simplicity, and because the device is well known, I will show how a marking pen might be developed as a concept.

Step 1. Analyze the Idea

The first thing to do is to write an analysis of where your idea comes from, how you arrived at it, whether it has any value, and to whom it might have some value. Most important, why do you want to work on it? Tell the truth because, after all, this is for you. You are trying to determine all of the factors relating to your idea for your own purposes, not for anybody else's. You don't have to convince yourself of anything, so be truthful.

Example: The idea occurred while reading a text and underlining key words and sections. Although the underlining worked, it was unsatisfactory because the information did not stand out clearly enough. I wanted something that would make each important word stand out so that when I returned to the page, those words would immediately hit me in the eye.

I think such a device would have value to any person trying to learn, specifically students, though I can visualize many professionals who do a lot of reading making use of it. I want to work on it because it can be useful to many people. They might be willing to buy it. I'll make a million bucks. I'll have made an invention no one else has thought of. (How clever of me.) Someone else might have thought of it, but who cares.

Step 2. Organize the Analysis

Next, organize this analysis in a preliminary manner. At this point, general statements are very acceptable. The analysis doesn't have to be in great detail—it doesn't even have to be accurate—but it must be in terms that you can understand. Think about what you want to do and perhaps (if you know) how you want to do it. Describe what your idea is, describe what it does, and then tell how it does it. Organize your thoughts in a reasonable way.

Example: At this point, all I know is that I want to make a device that will make important words stand out on the page. I want the words to be "highlighted" by some means other than underlining.
☐ How about a slightly tinted but clear plastic tape that comes out of a hand-held dispenser?
  • Sounds reasonable, but rejected. Too bulky and difficult to handle.
☐ How about just tinting with a small brush and bottle similar to liquid paper?
  • Rejected. Too easy to spill.
☐ Okay. How about tinting by some other means. Not bad, but how?
  • Crayon-type pencil
  • Wide-nib pen
  • Some type of ballpoint pen
  • A dispenser of some kind, such as a pen with a brush tip or some type of porous tip. How about felt?
☐ How about a felt-tipped pen dispensing tint or ink in a light enough wash so that the words can be easily read through the color?
☐ One more thing—the ink has to dry fast.

Step 3. List Similar Inventions

The next step is to list any items that already exist that do the same thing. This, of course, is a matter of judgment on your part. Frequently an inventor will be deceived by conceit. He might think that there is nothing in the world that does what he intends his invention to do. This is never true; there is always prior art. Even though it appears that your invention came out of the blue, the probability is that something exists that performs the function you want your invention to do.

Even if other things exist, at this time, write down why yours is better. The reason I want you to write all this down is that you can go back and review it afterwards to evaluate your progress.

Example: There might be something like it around, but I can't think of anything at this moment. (This means that this question must be left for future review.) More than likely, it also means that at this time I really DON'T want to spoil my pleasure by thinking of other devices. When the flush of excitement is over, however, think of it I must.

Step 4. Describe How Your Invention Is Different

The next step is not only to list why your invention is better but also how it is different. Review it in terms of its functions. Think about it in terms of how it works—why yours works one way, why someone else's works a different way, why yours performs a particular operation in a particular manner that is different from anybody else's. Describe the differences in function between your invention and what presently exists.

Example: It's time to be objective and realistic. My pen is different in the following ways:
- ☐ The ink does not obliterate the words. It makes them stand out.
- ☐ The ink does not smear the print or writing.
- ☐ The felt tip is large enough to cover a single letter or a word or line in a single stroke, unlike a thin point or ballpoint that requires several strokes.
- ☐ From a functional point of view, it might be necessary to hold the ink in a saturated reservoir rather than in a liquid state because of the size of the tip, the larger amount of ink required, and the need for even flow without dripping.

Step 5. Make a Concept Drawing

Next, draw your design. The drawing need not be a masterpiece, but it should communicate the idea. I have come across too many inventors who are terrified of making a drawing. What is so difficult about taking pencil to paper except, of course, crystallizing your thinking? Even if it is very badly drawn, at least you can use the drawing to communicate what your invention does. The drawing should only be a rough sketch; it doesn't have to be precise or to scale. This is only a concept drawing; drafting can be done later. Then you can divide your invention into a series of drawings, providing appropriate dimensions (none of which in itself will reveal your concept), and take them to one or more draftsmen.

Your drawing can be either two or three dimensional. A two-dimensional drawing can be done in pencil and paper, crayon and paper, or blackboard and chalk. (I personally find using a blackboard best because it's easiest to erase.) Make a three-dimensional drawing from cardboard, paper, or tin that is cut to shape to resemble your invention. Some people mistake a three-dimensional drawing as a "model." The difference is (in my opinion) that a model represents a scaled down, limited operating version of the invention, somewhat similar to a small pilot plant.

This step is very important. When you complete it and study the results, you can begin to lock in on relationships to some of the factors and functions of your invention.

Example:

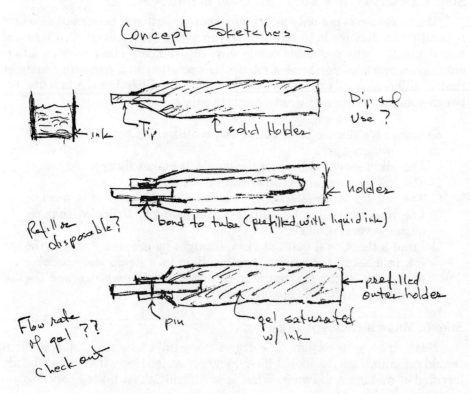

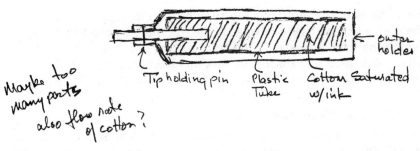

This is only a vague idea of how my invention will work and what it will look like. Exploration and experimentation (particularly with materials) is ongoing to determine the specifications of each part until the device works.

Step 6. List Functions to Be Tested

Try to determine the methods by which you can test various functions of the invention to see whether it works. List them on paper.

When describing a *function* of an invention, I mean how a part works, either alone or with other parts (*interfacing*). For example, one of the functions of the Magic Marker is that the ink must flow through the pen tip onto paper. The ink must flow evenly without overflowing or making blots. In this case, ink flow is the function I must list.

It is very important to begin to think about testing at this stage. Making something that works is a lot better than making something that doesn't! Try to figure out how to test your device. In fact, if the invention contains a series of separate components, test each component. This is the time to determine whether what you have has a chance of working.

Example: Tests of function that come to mind at this time are:
☐ The steady flow of ink from the reservoir to the tip.
☐ The steady flow of ink from the felt tip to paper.
☐ The ability to see the words clearly after they are covered by the ink.

These are but a few of the possible tests that can be performed. The point is to think of various methods of testing before construction so you will be sure that the finished product works.

Step 7. List the Interfacing Factors

The next step is to list the interfacing factors to consider. *Interfacing* describes how one part works with another part in your invention.

Example: Some of the interfacing factors for the marking pen:
☐ The device or part used to dispense the ink must be capable of absorbing ink from a reservoir and transporting it to the page.
☐ Whatever is used to transport the ink must not scratch, mar, or destroy the material being written on (for example, paper).

Step 8. List the Specifications

The next step is listing the specifications. *Specifications* include the actual material and physical characteristics of the device you are trying to make.

Example: Some of the specifications for the tip might be as follows:
☐ Need a fibrous nylon or plastic rod up to 1/8″ in diameter by any length.
☐ Thin metal tubing should have a wall thickness nominal .020″ with an inside diameter of approximately .050″.
☐ Each of the materials should be free flowing and corrosion-resistant.
☐ The material should be formable and shapable.

On a practical level, the same kind of "thinking out" must be applied to any invention that is being contemplated, regardless of the number of functions or factors that go into the invention. These eight steps will help you formulate the concept of your idea. Now you are ready to analyze your concept further.

Chapter 4
Analysis of the Concept

Y OU NOW HAVE AN IDEA. YOU HAVE DETERMINED THAT THE IDEA IS WORTH
pursuing. You have formulated the concept of your invention:

- ☐ What your invention is all about
- ☐ What the preliminary organization of your invention is
- ☐ How your invention compares to similar object, if such exist
- ☐ How your invention is different and better
- ☐ What your invention looks like, on a preliminary basis
- ☐ How you are going to test the functions of your invention
- ☐ How all parts of your invention interface
- ☐ What the specifications are for your invention

DETAILED ANALYSIS OF THE CONCEPT

Now it's time to look at your concept in more detail. At this point, you
are dealing with some of the most important aspects of making an invention.
You must keep this very, very much in mind: it is not essential that each of
the following steps described be followed sequentially. It is essential that you
cover every single one of them, so you can lock in on what you are doing and
make sure that, by the time you're finished, everything will work.

Step 1. List Details and Functions

First, outline how you expect each job to be done. List how you intend to go about putting your idea together. To make this list, you are going to separate each function, movement, or step in order to determine every single detail of your invention. You will list what parts are needed, what movements are going to take place, and every function and specification. Again, this is not a locked-in type of breakdown but something that will be added to as you think of things. You must remember to constantly make sure that each function, movement, or step is separated and described. Just be as sure as you can that you are describing every aspect of your idea as far as it can be broken down.

Example:

1. A plastic tube approximately 5.5″ long with a diameter of ⅝″.
2. Must find tip material that will permit the even flow of ink.
3. Find two types of ink—one that "highlights" and one that blocks out words completely. (Notice that I've added an additional use for the device.)
4. Determine a method of maintaining reservoir supply of ink.
5. Fit a cap to prevent accidental smudging with ink.
6. Simple preliminary test. Dip selected types of material tips into selected inks and apply to typed, printed, and written pages.

Step 2. Determine Human Interaction

After this list is completed, examine each of the separate factors to determine the compatibility of human interaction with each function. When your invention interacts with a human being, certain factors must be considered. Most important, there must be no interference on the part of the machinery with the human being who deals with it. You must also determine how human capabilities relate to each of the functions and areas involved—particularly to define the limitations. Thus, when construction begins, you can eliminate or modify those limitations that make it difficult for the interaction to take place.

Example:

1. Consider possible shapes for the marker and how it might be held in hand, particularly because it will be larger than an ordinary pen or pencil.
2. Consider the shape of the part held by the fingers and the shape of the reservoir.
3. Consider how you get the cap off and use the marker without getting ink all over you.
4. Consider how to store cap while marker is in use.

Step 3. Identify Problems

Next, you must identify any problems that might be related to each function that must be performed. As you mentally take your invention apart, ask questions like:

- ☐ What must be done?
- ☐ What wheel must touch another wheel?
- ☐ What gear must interface with another gear?
- ☐ What part of the formula must interact with another part of the formula?

Step 4. Determine Function Interaction

Regardless of what it is, you must be able to break it down into its smallest component parts in order to determine interaction. In addition, you must determine how each function interacts with the next function in the total operation of the device.

Example:
1. Bleed factor of tip
2. Potential of tip drying as exposed to air
3. Type of cap to protect drying of tip or leakage and how to prevent loss or misplacement of cap
4. Major problem—how to interface tip with reservoir so that flow of ink remains constant.

Step 5. Justify Each Function

Next, question the necessity and the justification for each function: why it must be done, and why it should be done in the manner selected. You don't want to build into inventions functions that are not essential. You only want functions to fulfill the prime objective: making something that works. (I will be repeating this statement frequently.) At this point, limit the functions in your invention only to those that are essential to making it work.

Step 6. List and Validate Specifications of Each Function

The next step is to determine and list the specifications of each function. This list is very important. In effect, you are saying, "Here is a function. here is what it must do. As it interfaces with the next function, here is what the next function must do." This exercise enables you to establish the specifications for each individual function.

Next, validate the specifications by visualizing the interaction between the functions. You can do it on paper, with a model, or any way that makes it easy for you to find out whether the functions will work and interact properly.

Example: The function of both the reservoir and the tip and how they interface so that ink is transported from the receiver to the tip in sufficient quantity during marker use.

☐ The tip must be long enough to protrude from the marker and at the same time sit deeply enough in the receiver to absorb ink.

☐ Reservoir is encased in a thin plastic membrane that keeps it from leaking.

☐ Need a means of getting ink from reservoir to tip.

In this step, eliminate all specifications that are not essential. This might sound difficult to do at this stage, but I have seen many inventions stall or not work at all (and at great expense) simply because specifications were included that were not essential. Very frequently, people build a tightness of fit into their specifications that is unnecessary in relation to the function of a particular item. I have seen people build in plus/minus thousandths inappropriately, which created difficulty in fabricating the unit.

Step 7. List Convenience Factors

The next step is to list separately the specifications of nonessential functions, convenience factors, or esthetics that make an invention more attractive. There is no reason that a device should not be attractive, but this list is for future reference *after* you are sure that your invention works. If you have ideas that will make it attractive, that will make it more convenient to use, or make it easier to use, list them now but don't work on them. Save these niceties to build into the device at the end.

Example:

☐ Include an advertising design on tube.

☐ Include a snap-on clip so that the marker can be attached to the book for easier use and greater accessibility . . . Nice, but not essential to making the marker itself work. (To be included after the marker works).

Step 8. Make Sure Functions Interface and Work

Your first priority is to make sure that the functions will interface and work. That is the key to building a successful invention. There is no way in the world that you can make an invention without knowing that each part is going to come together, each part is going to interact, and each part will work with another part. That is the first area that you must address. If you recognize a problem with interaction and interfacing, solve it before you go on to the next area.

Test each of these functional areas to see that it interfaces. If you find something that doesn't interface, stop until you can solve that problem. Otherwise, you might find yourself spending a great deal of money and time and ending up with a product that doesn't work.

REVIEW OF FUNCTIONS

The very first thing I must say at this stage is *stop*! Do something else. Think about what you have been doing. Do not work on your invention any further. After you have put all of the effort into it, the best thing to do is not do anything. Go play tennis. Go swim. Go fish. Go do anything you want to do but do not work on your invention for a period of time. It doesn't have to be a long period of time. I recommend a couple of days at minimum; a week would be better. But the main thing is to go do something else and then *think*. Then, come back and review each aspect of the project to determine again:

- ☐ Will it interface?
- ☐ Will it work?
- ☐ Is there an easier way to do the same thing?
- ☐ Is there a better way to do the same thing?

These aspects become extraordinarily important in making an invention because, more often than not, you will find that what you thought might work, doesn't. Often you will discover that you have found a slightly better way of doing it. Now is the time to look at the invention as objectively as possible to determine whether the functions interface, the parts interface, and the specifications fit each of the functions that you wish to perform.

Next, review the eight steps in "Detailed Analysis of the Concept." Now is the time to stop and do all of the things that are necessary. It is much too difficult to go on without knowing that you have a chance of success. Try to look at the project as if you were seeing it for the very first time—better still, as if it were your worst enemy's pet project and you want to do everything you possibly can to find its faults and weaknesses and why it won't work. You are going to take it apart and then put it back together again before you go on.

Too much work goes into an invention not to stop and critically review a concept at this stage in order to determine areas of weakness—functions that need to be strengthened or corrected. (Note that I did not mention strengths.) Solve the problems before you go on. This is the thinking stage, the analytical stage. Reexamine everything that you have done. I cannot overemphasize the importance of reviewing the functions, the specifications of the functions, and the interface factors of each specification and function.

Stop before you go any further.

After you have made all the corrections that were necessary, you can proceed with a reasonable degree of confidence that the invention has a chance of working.

I recognize that most inventions are far more complex than the examples I have presented and that most inventions have many more parts and interactions. Therefore, your list, analysis, justifications, and explanations will vary in length with the number of details and parts in your invention. Any shortcuts you take are at your own risk.

FINALIZE YOUR DRAWINGS AND DESCRIPTIONS

Now is the time to make a final draft of your preliminary two- or three-dimensional drawings. It is not necessary to do all of the final drafting yourself. Remember, it's all right to bring individual parts and segments to a draftsman; you need not give one draftsman all the parts. If you want to maintain secrecy, you can give various parts to different draftsmen.

Next, make a final copy of the description of your invention. Describe exactly what the invention is supposed to do and how it is supposed to do it. This is not an idle exercise. You will be using this information later when you are trying to sell the invention. Now is the time to start putting it together. You can change it later, but start it now.

This final draft need not be perfect. It is only essential that it communicate exactly what the device is so you can make it or have it made.

MATERIALS, PARTS, AND COSTS

The next step is to list all the parts and materials necessary to build your model, working prototype, or the finished product. This leads to extraordinary difficulties later if you do not now list every single part that goes into your invention. Take each function separately, the easiest ones first, though it really doesn't matter where you start. As you look at the sketches that you have made, you can breakdown each part that goes into it, comparing the parts to the specifications that you have been establishing. Most important, determine the parts that have to be made and the parts that can be purchased and how these parts will interact. You're determining the finished materials and raw materials you might have to obtain in order to make your model, working prototype, or finished product.

Example: For the marker, you need—
- [ ] Two types of plastic tubing—one for the outer shell and the other to hold the reservoir
- [ ] A round rod-like sponge that can be saturated with the selected ink, then encased in a tubular membrane to act as the marker reservoir.
- [ ] A felt rectangular rod to operate as the marker point. This will transfer the ink from the reservoir to the paper.
- [ ] A pin—specify length and diameter—to hold the felt in place. Might require some other type of plastic that could be used to shape the piece of felt in the head and hold it in place.

Justifying Your Choices

After you have listed each part you wish to incorporate into your invention, give the reason for selecting each part and/or material. Never mind that you already have determined that this is the part or material that you want in your invention. At this point, you must list the reasons for the selection of each particular part or type of material—particularly if more than one type of material or part can be used.

This doesn't mean that you should not use the material that you originally selected in your list. It simply means that if other parts or materials can be interchanged to perform the same functions, you should at least consider your choices. This is the time to look for comparisons. You want to make sure that you have a darn good reason for selecting the particular type of material or part that you did.

Research

Next, list very, very carefully (this is for you, not anyone else) what you know about the parts or the materials selected. Do you know their specifications? Do you know the technology behind them? Do you know how they work? What has to be done in order for them to work? Do you know any specialized information that is required in order to utilize these parts or materials? Is there any technique that you aren't familiar with that is needed?

These are the things to find out at this stage. You have to be very honest with yourself when answering this question: "Have you ever worked with these parts and materials before?" If you have not, you must honestly ask yourself, "Do I have all the information necessary?" If you don't, now is the time to get it.

> *Example:* Research the types of plastics available. Obtain the technical factors and specifications of the materials from commercial plastic manufacturers. Determine the ability to work the material. Your primary interest is the machinability of the material for the prototype. Consider that when the product is manufactured, the specifications and material might change when it goes from the machine shop into an injection molding operation. Therefore, you want to use the material most appropriate for injection molding.

This might sound silly, but many inventors (even experienced inventors) have little knowledge of the types of parts or materials that are best suited to meet their needs. Some experienced inventors know very little about the availability of certain materials or parts, but if they don't know, they find out. There are ways of determining whether specific parts or materials exist. It requires some research, consulting libraries and other sources of information.

At this point, you should try to determine how much information you need to help you obtain the parts and materials that fit your specifications. The information might be available through various associations or manufacturers' material and parts catalogs. Primarily, review the kinds of materials that might fit your needs. This review might make it possible for you to use a material in a manner that has never been used before. There is nothing wrong with material or parts experimentation. Before using any new materials or parts, however, you must first get the manufacturer's specifications to match them against the specifications you have established for your invention.

The method that I use is to review parts literature in libraries. I ask supply houses and manufacturers for catalogs covering the specification of the materials and parts. Some of the technical service departments in these companies are happy to provide you with information. If you describe what you're doing, and that your project might be using their product in a novel way, they might be more interested in giving you every assistance possible because your application might represent an expanded potential for their market. I would not hesitate in asking any manufacturer for the specifications of any materials or parts that he might be able to supply.

Look for Alternatives

The next question is very important—what do you intend to do if your needs cannot be satisfied? What if the materials or parts you need are not available, or the specifications for those that are available do not fit the particular functional needs?

There are alternatives. First, you might change the specifications. This might be the most difficult option. Second, you might look for different materials to perform according to the specifications you require. Third, you might change the design to include other materials that would more closely fit your needs.

Keep in mind that you are the inventor; you can make your device in any way you wish to make it. The most important thing in making any invention is to make sure that, regardless of what materials you use, what you are making works. The alteration of specifications, the modification of functions, and the selection of materials is entirely up to you. You as the individual inventor can pick and choose whatever is necessary, whatever contributes to the working success of the device.

List Your Costs

As you accumulate this information, begin to list your costs. Wherever possible, list the actual costs of every single bit of material or part that you're considering. If you can't get the actual cost, list the estimated cost, then check to see if that estimated cost is close to what you expect to spend.

CASE STUDY: A MUSIC BOX

Let's take a different approach to the problem of outlining invention objectives and methods of concept delineation. Let's say I am going to invent a music box, an ordinary tabletop wooden box with a hinged top that plays music when opened. I will describe every function and aspect needed for construction.

Concept. The box is approximately 5 inches high, 8 inches deep, and 12 inches long. The lid on the box is approximately 1 inch high by the same dimensions fitting the top; it is a closely fitted top, hinged to the bottom. In one inside corner of the box is a small music drum apparatus that turns the music on each time the lid is opened. In addition, there is a device that permits me to turn the music on or off when the lid is opened. A turnkey for winding the spring mechanism of the drum is available—or space for batteries and a small motor.

I have described what it is, what it does, and, in many ways, how it does it. For purposes of brevity, I will not go into listing several devices that do the same thing or why mine is or is not better. Instead, I will jump to the concept drawings.

Drawing. Drawing a box is not difficult. My drawing will show the inside of the box, where the batteries might go, and the windup mechanism for the music. If I wish, I can make a three-dimensional sketch of the music box by cutting up some cardboard and either gluing or taping it together. This will give an idea of what it is going to look like. I can also indicate any aesthetic design on the sides of the box—to marquetry (the inlay of small pieces of veneer to make a picture) or a piece of metal attached to the sides of the box, for example. You might even want to include a latch and a little lock on the box. These things can be considered as I go along.

Compare. I know that similar things have been made that work. Because I am not going to alter the design to any grat degree, I can be fairly sure mine will work also. After it is built, the test for the box is whether the lid fits and can open and close, whether it turns the music on and off, and whether I can lock the box after it is closed.

Human Factors. Now to determine human factors and interaction with each function. The lid has to be opened and closed, the switch has to be turned on and off, and objects can be put into and taken out of the box. I want to make sure that these things can be done.

Next, I want to determine the limitations of human capabilities, or how each function interacts with human use and demand. For the box, however, there aren't too many functional limitations. The human capabilities required with each function are "normal" in utilization. (There are, without question, inventions that impose limitations to human interaction, but not this one.)

Functions. The next step is to define each function that must be performed. Any problems I might have with the box are more in terms of how the box might be used than in terms of the functions that must be performed in using the box. Defining each problem and function that must be performed really means describing how the item works. For the box this means opening and closing it. It is this function that makes the box usable. The operation of the hinges must interface smoothly. The second function of the box is having the switch turn the music mechanism on and off. Those are the two primary functions we have established as necessary.

Suppose I want to partition the box. Each of the partitions will then permit the performance of another function, such as the storage of particular items. Therefore, I have increased the number of functions that are part of the box.

If I were to now change the design of the box, I would have to justify why, how, and what I was doing differently. If I was going to put handles on the box or indents into the sides so that the box could be lifted or transported easily, then I would have to justify these functions. (What if these utilitarian functions detracted from the overall design—are they then justifiable?)

Specifications. Next, to the nitty-gritty—the determination and listing of the specifications of each of these functions. Now I am beginning to lock in, though on a preliminary basis, the actual specifications of each function. I am going to examine the concept of the box and begin to determine the size, depth, type of wood, handles (if any), the size of the hinges, the switches, the size of the music mechanism and where it will be placed, the batteries or turn knob and where they will be placed, and the partitions. Each factor must now be determined in terms of size and position to each other. List them in relation to each of the functions and in relation to the physical specifications of the box itself.

The same is true for the magic marker. We analyze it in order to list each and every part. At this point, all we need to know about materials is their size and the way they interface.

Nonessentials. Next, eliminate any nonessential specifications. There does not appear to be many nonessential specifications. By listing all the specifications, however, you can review in an organized way more efficiently than relying on memory—particularly the specifications for parts that interface. Examine the specifications to decide whether anything is going to get in the way of making the original prototype or model.

List, then put aside for the moment, the convenience or esthetics factors. For example, you might list the marquetry or metal design that might be attached to the face or the top of the box as a separate item that could be added later on. Keep in mind that the first priority in building any invention is to make sure that it works; that is far more important right now than the esthetics or convenience.

Review. Next, go through and review the functions very carefully to determine whether the project will work. You are going to stop, you are going to think, you are going to do something else. Then, with a fresh mind, review the project to make sure that all parts will interface.

Materials, Parts, and Costs. Let's assume that the box is going to work. Now I must determine the materials, parts, and costs. Here I need the final draft of the preliminary description—the words that describe in detail how the concept will look and function. The same is true for the drawings. My drawings must be as close to what I want as possible.

I will list all the parts and materials necessary to build a model, a working prototype, or the finished product. If the item is complex, I recommend strongly that you build a working prototype first. For our example, however, I will go directly to the finished product because the box is so simple. I have the technical capability to make a finished product because it doesn't require extensive tooling or an extensive outlay of capital.

I have made a very detailed list of every item that goes into the building of my finished box. I've selected the kind and amount of wood to use and determined that two or three different thicknesses are required—one for the sides, another for the top and bottom, and possibly a third thickness for any partitions that might be included. I want to cover the internal portion of the box with some type of material after it has been constructed. The box will need hinges, either screws or nails to hold the hinges, and a latch and a lock.

These items must be listed. If I decide that, instead of cut-ins to the side of the box, I want to use metal or wooden handles, it must be listed. I might want handles on the box, some sort of design on the outside of the box, and some soft material on the bottom of the box so that it won't scratch furniture. Briefly, these are some of the factors relating to the materials and parts for the box.

For the magic marker, you might want to make a working prototype. You are certainly not going to go to the expense of having molds made and parts purchased for an injection molding operation in order to make a single working prototype, without knowing it works and is a useful and saleable product.

In essence, determining availability and costs for materials and parts for the box are not difficult. Catalogs and small quantities of materials or parts are available from manufacturers and supply houses. With fluctuations in manufacturing costs, the picture can change dramatically. A guide to places to look for parts and materials can be found in chapter 20.

Chapter 5
The Prototype

CHAPTER 5 WILL OUTLINE THE PROCEDURES FOR MAKING THE MODEL OR PROTO-type. The music box and the marker will continue to be used as examples.

ESTIMATING COSTS

The first step in estimating your costs is to list each *purchasable* part and the *quantity* of each part required. List only items you are *not* going to make. For example, for the music box list: music mechanism, two hinges, two handles, wood (type optional), and the dimensions and quantity of raw wood required. For the marker: the reservoir sponge or cotton ball, the plastic tubing of the marker itself, the plastic sheathing that will hold the reservoir, and the felt for the tip of the marker. This then is your shopping list, which includes the quantities of parts and materials required to make the prototype. Next, list the sources of supply for each part and, where possible, estimate the costs of each purchase. Although the examples deal with rather simple pieces, the more complex the invention, the more important it is to use an outline method. Some inventions might require extensive parts lists.

Tools. The next step is to review your available tools. List the lead time and the cost for the tools that you do *NOT* have. For example, you might require a miter box or a carbide-tipped saw in order to make accurate finished wood cuts for the box. This is the time to make sure that you can afford what tools you need.

This is a trap that people often fall into in building an invention. They suddenly find that they need some esoteric or rare tool to make their prototype. Because the tool costs too much, or they don't have the knowledge required to utilize the tool, they can not complete their invention.

This might be the case for the marker. Though the marker looks simple, it has possible complications. For example, the tubing that holds the reservoir is tapered at the end to hold the cap. The cap itself is similarly tapered inside. The top of the tubing that holds the felt tip is also tapered so that there is a snug fit between the cap and the top of the marker that protects the felt. The back of the marker has the same taper. If you are going to make a prototype of the marker, you must have some type of tapered tooling and a lathe to cut or shape the end of the tubing to taper it. This implies not only that you have a lathe but that you have the training to operate it at the proper speeds. You will also need the tools required to cut the materials you're considering (which again implies that you have selected the kind of material that lends itself to this type of machining).

Sometimes, there is a way out of this mess. You can redesign the invention to conform to your tools and ability to use them. It might also be that the design is wrong and requires redoing. Many inventors lose much time and expend unnecessary effort wearing blinders. They get locked into a methodology and find it difficult to see alternatives. Or, as once happened to me, I built a machine that wouldn't work properly. I tried every kind of fix I could think of, rather than recognizing that the basic design was wrong and that the machine required dismantling and rebuilding. When, after much agony, this was finally done, the machine worked like a charm. That's why I recommend stepping back occasionally and then coming back to the project with a fresh mind . . . particularly when you get stuck.

Inside or Outside Help. Now, list all the parts of the project that you can do yourself. For example, if you don't have a lathe, you can't make the Magic Marker prototype; or you don't have the saws, you can't make the parts for the box prototype. Study this list to see exactly what you can do yourself; then list all the parts of the project that require outside help.

Getting outside help is a difficult area because of the paranoia inherent in the development of an invention. To protect yourself (or to indulge your paranoia) requires you to prepare detailed instructions, drawings, and specifications for those sections to be farmed out. To get somebody to make the thing, you have to specify what you want accurately and completely. If you don't, you won't get back what you're looking for. If you don't do this properly, you risk wasting a great deal of money, effort, and time. It is not part of an outside vendor's job to try and guess what you want.

Flowchart. Next, prepare a flowchart so that you can coordinate lead time and parts priority. Include actual or estimated time for making each part and the time required for parts assembly. If an extensive period of time is involved, you certainly want to know it. You want to identify the parts that are going to take longer to make. You want to plan the project so that the parts all come together in a reasonable manner. You also want to deal with all of the parts as they come in to make sure that they are exactly as you specified (and adjust them if necessary to make them work).

FEASIBILITY EVALUATION

The feasibility evaluation is probably the hardest study you have to make because it requires honest, nondelusionary self-evaluation. You are going to make an evaluation of your ability—not someone else's ability, but your own ability to do things.

You must know what you can do and what others must do for you. The worst thing you can do at this time is to assume that you can do things that you really cannot do. There is nothing wrong with trying to do something new, but if it doesn't work, who do you blame? The concept? Or the fact that you don't have the capability of making the thing as it should be made. Many good concepts often go by the board simply because the inventor does not have the technical capability of making a particular part.

At this stage, you must be totally honest with yourself. You can try to make a part, but make sure that the piece works and that the part interfaces properly. If it doesn't, recognize your lack of capability in this area and have somebody make it for you.

Consultants, Technicians, and Assistants

If you need *consultants*, define exactly what help you want from them, how much they are going to cost (they're expensive—that's the reason for the list, it saves costly time), and how long you intend to use them. (How big is your budget?) In my opinion, the utilization of knowledgeable outside help can be extraordinarily time-saving and make the difference between success or failure.

It is important to recognize that you do not know everything. It is appropriate to sit back occasionally and say, "I don't know," and call in a consultant to help you—an expert in a field that you know very little about. If the information is essential to make your invention work, call in a consultant. You don't have to accept everything that he says. You must incorporate the information, think about it, and use it in accordance with your best judgement. Do not be overwhelmed by consultants (or, for that matter, by anybody else); use your brain. You wouldn't have reached this point without intelligence. Consider the consultant(s) advise; keep what you believe is useful and discard the rest.

The same applies to *technicians* and *assistants*. This is the time to evaluate what kind of help you are going to need and how much it is going to cost.

You might not need a consultant; you might only need an assistant to hold the other end of a piece of wood while you are cutting it. In this case, you might need a carpenter or a cabinetmaker. Or you might need someone who knows how to machine plastics.

What Are the Total Costs?

Having made your evaluation and listed all the requirements, your next step is to estimate the total costs for:

1. Materials and parts
2. Making of any parts that must be made
3. Assembly of these parts
4. Time and effort required for everyone,
   including yourself.

It might not be necessary for you to put a dollar figure on your own efforts. It might be helpful later on, however, when you are trying to evaluate what the invention actually cost you.

Should You Continue?

After you have thoroughly reviewed and determined the feasibility of making either a working prototype, a model, or a detailed outline in drawings, you reach the place between the hammer and the anvil—determining whether you should continue with the project or drop it. You might have an invention that costs far more than you can spend at this time. You either drop the project or raise the money with which to continue.

I do not believe in being self-destructive about any particular invention. If you are an inventor, you probably have many other inventions under your cap. If you can make an invention reasonably without killing yourself, then go ahead with it.

If you come to this stage, however, and find that completing the project might be financially damaging to you without any immediate reward, or that you are gambling a disproportionate amount of your resources to complete the project, or that you are stressing yourself to a degree that jeopardizes your well-being, you should seriously consider whether or not you should go on with the project. If you reach such a point where the finances and other needs are so taxing that you can't complete the project by yourself, consider putting your project together in the form of a proposal that outlines the specifications. Then raise the money that will enable you to complete your invention.

MAKING THE PROTOTYPE: SOME THOUGHTS

By this time, you have evaluated enough of the planning and cost information to indicate whether the project is a go. Here are some thoughts on how to proceed to make your prototype.

The plans for your work are laid out so that the most crucial parts can be made first. The way I work is to follow my chart. Everything has been put down. I know where I am. I know what my potential costs are. I know which parts are to be made first. And I know which are the crucial parts.

It's no use making the easy parts before the crucial ones (the parts that have to interface). Making the crucial parts first assures you that they will work and interface with other parts. Therefore, make a flowchart and follow it, but make sure to make the important parts first.

Wherever possible, *test as you go.* Do not go on unless the crucial parts mesh, interface, or do whatever they are supposed to do. It is no use kidding yourself. Make these parts one at a time and make sure that each works before you go on to the next part or step.

Buy only what is absolutely needed at each stage of construction.

Do not buy all the material and parts needed for the entire project at one time. Your evaluation might be wrong or optimistic. Your project might not work because some of the crucial parts don't fit. You don't want to be stuck with a lot of expensive parts and materials!

Be a little patient. Take the project one step at a time to make sure that everything works when assembled.

When you have parts made outside, test and measure each part immediately upon receipt to make sure that it is exactly what you ordered. It's your invention, and outside vendors are going to build it to your specs (maybe), but make sure they have done it to your specs. *Do not wait* until you are ready to use the part; test it immediately as it comes in. By the time you are ready to use it, it might be too late to go back to the vendor and say, "Hey, you made this wrong," or "This doesn't fit," or "It's made of the wrong material," etc. By then, it's usually too late to complain.

The moment a part comes in the door, check it, test it, and make sure it's what you ordered.

My feeling about any prototype is first make it work. And I mean that in caps: First MAKE IT WORK! Forget about making it pretty; you can always make a thing look pretty later on. Make it work! If it works, you've got something. If it doesn't work, there is no use in trying to make it pretty.

Now you get into an area that many inventors find tricky—stick to your design. Try very hard not to change ("improve") your design in midstream. Unless a change is essential, don't make it. Stay with what you have as long as it works. Again and again: first make it work, then you can improve it *if you have the time to do so.*

If it works, now is the time to sit back and enjoy it—and enjoy it thoroughly! For myself, it is a time of great pleasure to admire with awe and veneration the part or the invention itself. I sit and enjoy it to the utmost because that enjoyment might not last very long. In that microcosm of time, however, I believe that I have accomplished something that no one else has done.

TWO PERSONAL CREDOS

Let's go back to two areas that I have already covered. I consider them important enough to be covered in greater detail.

My first credo is: *First, make it work; pretty comes later.* Other inventors might not agree with this, but this is my personal credo. I believe that it is the job of the inventor to make a product work—and that is it. Beyond that, it is up to someone else, such as a value engineer, to take over the product and redesign it to reduce its cost. It is up to an industrial designer to make it look pretty. It is up to a packaging designer to make an appealing package for the product. It is up to marketing to determine how to sell it, what to sell it for, and where to sell it.

In my opinion, it is not up to the inventor to make anything except a working prototype to prove that the concept works. It is up to the manufacturing people to do the rest. You can't be an expert in every field. I am thankful that I know enough to get my inventions to work.

My second credo is: *Don't play with it.* This is the kind of activity that many inventors indulge in because they don't want to finish their inventions. They like to deal with the fantasies inherent in the process of invention. (This failing is not reserved just for inventors.) I do not know of a single inventor who doesn't "play" with his invention—to try to make it better, to change the design, or to do something else with it.

Too Much "Playing"

I had an invention that was presold. I was to be paid $100,000 within thirty days after a third-party report came through certifying that the invention worked as specified. This was all part of a guaranteed royalty agreement that had been concluded prior to the building of the invention itself. Included in the arrangement was what would happen if I did not meet the deadline.

As it turned out, I didn't meet the deadline—not because I hadn't finished the invention, but because I was "playing" with it. Indeed, I somehow decided that I had another month to go, so I took a vacation.

After much hunting, the client found me in Maine. His message was, "Where's the invention I paid for?" Because I thought I had exctly six months in which to deliver the invention, I was shocked when he called. I hadn't kept track of the time.

I called him back and said, "I have another month to go."

He replied, "Well, why don't you count the months?" (You must understand that counting is not my forte.)

I counted the months, and he was quite right: I had missed the deadline.

I immediately called my patent attorney asking, "What should we do?" (with the emphasis on "we").

"Well," he said, "Before *you* do anything, call back and find out if the client still wants your invention. If he still wants it, get him to agree to a postdated extension of time."

The client gave me a thirty-day extension (not even post-dated) so that I could get Battelle Labs to test the product, certify that it worked, and then turn it over to him.

*****

I had done the same thing that a lot of inventors do: I had kept playing with my inventions. I had the entire thing done, completed, tested; as far as I was concerned, it worked. I had all the test data. I had test data coming out of my ears to show that it worked. But I had another idea on how to do it and got hung up with it.

You can get hung up with your invention. You enjoy getting involved, seeing dials going every which way, or paper coming out of the recorder. An invention you made is working! That's what it is all about. It's when you make money on an invention, however, that you know you have something—if nothing more than a means of keeping score. I recommend very strongly: *Avoid "playing" with the invention!*

Chapter 6

The Total Concept Invention

IN REREADING CHAPTERS 3, 4, AND 5, I CAME TO THE CONCLUSION THAT further explanation might be helpful. To to this, I will explain two different kinds of inventions: the evolutionary invention and the total concept invention. Both are valid, but they are approached and developed in very different ways.

With a *total concept invention*, when the idea strikes, it comes all at once. The moment you think of your idea, you see it in its entirety—every part, every facet is completely revealed. The second type, the *evolutionary invention*, starts with an objective—the desire to solve a particular problem. As you solve your problem, your invention "evolves" or takes shape.

It is not my intention to imply that these two inventions are without variations or shadings. On the contrary, the mix is infinite. The two types combine and recombine *in toto* and in working parts. For example, while working on an invention, you might come up with a "concept flash" for a particular segment, but you might have to research, experiment, and try repeatedly to find the solution to the next segment.

Because it is easier to explain, I'll discuss the total concept invention here in chapter 6. I'll discuss the evolutionary invention in chapter 7.

Remember that a total concept invention is a sudden inspiration. You see your invention in its entirety. It is now only a matter of getting your thoughts down on paper and actually building it. The parts, materials, and plans are all in your head. All you have to do is follow what's there. This does not necessarily mean that a total concept invention is simple. On the contrary, they are sometimes very complex and contain a multiplicity of parts and crucial interfacings.

To illustrate how a total concept invention might come into being, I will use a personal example. I will take you through my thought processes, stressing the steps you learned in the preceding chapters.

CASE STUDY: A LIQUID METERING AND DISPENSING DEVICE

Although the concept for this invention came to me in a flash, it took almost six months to complete and test. Very little changed in the invention from the original concept to the finished product. I knew from the very beginning what had to be done and simply went forward, step by step, to completion.

The problem was to invent a device that would dispense one liquid into the stream of another liquid. The dispensing rate of the injected liquid had to be accurate in terms of ppm (parts per million) over the total period of dispensing, and have a range of 35 ppm to 5000 ppm—for example, be able to dispense insecticides into a stream of water at the rate of 175 ppm.

Another specification was that the ppm should not vary if the water pressure varied. In other words, as the flow and amount of water increased or decreased, the amount of insecticide would always remain proportional and in direct relation to the amount of water flow. In addition, it was necessary that different insecticides also be dispensed at the ppm rate prescribed for each.

Another specification was to contain the insecticide (or liquid to be injected) in a prefilled disposable cartridge. These cartridges would be filled with various insecticides at the manufacturer's plant. Also, the user would be able to use different insecticide cartridges with the same dispenser and be able to safely recap and store, for later use, any unused portion of insecticide remaining in the cartridge.

My solution was to utilize the vapor pressure area of a cavitating venturi. As you can see, the water enters the upstream end of the venturi. The pressure there is equal to the pressure in the outer container of the dispenser, where it exerts pressure against a flexible bag (the cartridge) filled with the material (insecticide) to be dispensed. This pressure pushes the material in the cartridge through an orifice at the tip of the bag into the stream of water at the downstream end of the venturi throat. The size of the orifice can be varied to provide the ppm rate that is prescribed for the particular insecticide. The exit nozzle or orifice at the downstream end of the venturi is directly related and proportional to the throat of the venturi. Therefore, the pressure relationships in all parts are constant in relation to each other, regardless of any changes in the incoming water pressure. Because the vapor

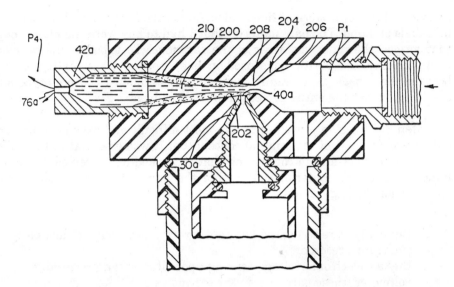

pressure area of the venturi operates at one quarter of one percent of atmosphere, no liquid in the cartridge is or can be siphoned through it's orifice. Only the incoming pressure on the flexible bag within the cartridge permits the release of its ingredients.

The only specification that I could not work out in advance was the nozzle orifices required for each different insecticide. The cartridge tip would vary for each ppm rate. However, the remaining development and testing proceeded as originally conceived.

In general, the steps in development were as follows:

Step 1. A rough concept drawing. No details, just a means of getting the concept down on paper.

Step 2. A review of the concept to see if there was anything that needed to be added or eliminated (to the concept).

Step 3. Preliminary detailed drawings of each functional area and a review to make sure that each area would work as desired. In addition, interface factors were considered.

Step 4. Detailed drawings of each part, with particular attention to those parts that would interface. These drawings included size specifications and a listing of potential materials.

Step 5. Review and select materials for each part, including an estimate of the costs of the materials and sources where they might be obtained (after a review of my own store of materials). As it turned out, I had most of the materials on hand. The only material that I had to buy were the plastic bags that formed the inner container of the cartridge. To expedite the development, I purchased plastic bags used in baby bottles. As a matter of fact, becasue these bags were readily available, I established the prototype size specifications for the entire project around those bags.

Step 6. This step proved to be the most difficult and expensive to work out. It was not part of the original concept, but it was essential in the building of the product and in confirming that it worked as conceived. To determine methods and materials for testing the ppm rates for various orifice openings for the bag, I had to:

- ☐ Build an entire test stand and rent a very precise balance and electronic tape recorder.
- ☐ Buy an electronic voltage sensing apparatus and a precise digital voltmeter (these parts were very expensive).
- ☐ Buy microdrill bits ranging in sizes from .002 to .0135 inch in diameter. They came in packets of ten and cost from $3.00 to $4.50 per drill bit. The bits alone cost well over $1000, and they broke very easily.
- ☐ Buy a very sensitive microdrill stand (an unexpected expense), a microscope, and a fibre optics lamp that could focus light onto the part being worked on.
- ☐ Make an X-Y apparatus for the drill stand so I could precisely position the cartridge nozzle for drilling the orifice.

All of the drilling had to be done under the microscope because everything was too small to be seen accurately by the naked eye. For example, without the microscope I wouldn't know when the drill bit (running at super high speed) touched the material to be drilled.

Nozzle design is no easy task to begin with, but when working in brass under a microscope, the task became horrendous. I found that it was first necessary to machine a cuplike insert that would fit into the main body of the nozzle. The cup was machined from 3/16th inch brass stock down to .1225 inch with a drilled inside diameter of .104 inch and a thickness at the base of .020 inch. The cup was inverted and press fitted into the nozzle.

This process made it easier to experiment in nozzle design and orifice size. The orifice was drilled into the flat section of the inverted cup. If what was made was inappropriate, the "cup" insert could be knocked out and a new one inserted.

The only material I found suitable for testing as a substitute for insecticides (I flatly refused to handle actual insecticides) turned out to be kosher salt. It is the only pure salt readily available on the market; all other salts have additives (to keep them flowing in damp weather).

I had to plan step 6 with as much precision as any part of an important invention. The costs for testing proved to be far greater than the cost estimated for building the prototype, and more difficult to determine. Each piece of equipment had to be reviewed to determine its accuracy and precise fit, and evaluated for a make, rent, or buy decision. Each item was listed and relisted, evaluated and reevaluated. The methodology was constantly reviewed to make sure that the testing would give me the answers I was looking for with the accuracy required to satisfy an independent testing lab.

Step 7. The very first problem that had to be solved was *how to determine the accuracy of the ppm rate*. My solution and procedure was to carefully weigh both the salt and water, mix them thoroughly (the mixing was crucial because all the salt had to be dissolved), then measure the solution's precise conductivity. You can see the reasons for obtaining both an accurate balance and a very good digital voltmeter.

The next problem was *building nozzles*. Once I had a precise voltage readout for several different ppm solutions of salt and water, I could use the data to measure against the downstream flow of mix as it left the dispenser. As is obvious, I compared the voltage to the test data chart and graph and was able to know the ppm as related to nozzle orifice. By experimenting, I was able to build nozzles to precisely fit the dispensing rate requirements of various insecticides.

My next problem, in building the test stand, was to *confirm ppm with a backup procedure*, which included a water flow meter, pressure regulator, pressure and temperature readouts (incoming and outgoing), a micro ohm, and a series of directional valves. All of these connected to both the digital voltage readout and a chart recording tape for a hard copy of each experiment.

Another aspect that had to be considered was *safety*. I'm a fanatic about safety. Because I was measuring flow at various levels of water pressure, I had to build a test chamber that both allowed the dispenser and the cartridge to be observed during operation and provided protection in case the dispenser container exploded from too much water pressure. (Please note that thus far the design and construction of the dispenser and cartridge have not been included in the above.)

A few problems also arose in the *construction of the cavitating venturi*. For example, because I wanted to observe the flow of water and injected material in the prototype, I had to make it out of some sort of transparent material rather than stainless steel, brass, or aluminum. Machining it out of plexiglass or Lexon would have been reasonable, but even fine cutting would leave tool marks, requiring that the inside be polished in order to see through the material. This would have been long and tedious. In addition, it would have required making special tools to conform to the inner shapes. I therefore decided on casting acrylic. (My assumption was that if successful, the manufacturer could always have the part injection-molded or cast in brass or aluminum.)

To use the acrylic, it was first necessary to *machine a "positive" of the cavitating venturi*, which included the positives for the injected inflow holes and the water inflow and outflow holes. The mold had to be made as a series of highly polished, interlocking parts so that each could be removed from the acrylic after it cured. As you can see from the earlier drawing, it was a tricky business.

One other important detail was the needed—to build a vacuum stand. This would remove the bubbles from the material immediately after the pour so that the cast would be clear.

Step 8. Once the testing procedures and equipment was decided, the rest was just a matter of carrying out the plans, making the prototype, building and setting up the test stand, and testing the completed prototype. (Sure does sound easy.)

This, of course, meant laying out a planning chart to make the parts sequentially as related to interface factors. I should stress that all of the applicable procedures described in chapter 4 were diligently followed.

Even when everything you want to do seems perfectly sequential and logical "in your head," paper planning is a must. It makes you justify your moves before you make them. I have found that it has saved me from many costly hidden and obvious mistakes.

Chapter 7
The Evolutionary Invention

T HE EVOLUTIONARY INVENTION STARTS WITH AN OBJECTIVE—THE DESIRE TO solve a particular problem. You might not have any idea how to go about solving that problem, but the solution becomes the primary objective of the creative process.

The process starts with researching and understanding the dynamics of the problem itself. After the problem is understood, the potential solution often becomes apparent. At that point, the potential solution becomes the objective of the invention.

To make an evolutionary invention, then, requires step-by-step research and testing to solve each step of the objective before going on to the next. Many times, when one step has been solved, a new problem arises that demands solution before the original invention is completed. In this type of invention, you must bring together many diverse disciplines. The ever-present objective is to solve the original problem. You hope and pray that you're on the right track, but the methodology is always the same—research, trying, and testing . . . persistently trying and testing one excruciating step at a time.

The evolutionary invention demands extraordinary patience.

CASE STUDY: ENVIRONMENTAL SEED CELL

Ever since man began to farm, he has dreamed of the possibility of placing one seed where he wanted one plant to grow and not touching it until harvest. This dream becomes more desperate as farm field labor becomes more expensive and scarce in our society. (It's mostly backbreaking work.)

The problem starts with the seeds. The ones I'm talking about range in size from this period "." (and smaller) to this asterisk "*" (and possibly somewhat larger, but not much). These seeds are extraordinarily difficult to handle not only because of their size but also because of their varied shapes. Some of them are aerodynamic; some are irregular; none (even the same type) are ever exactly the same. They vary in weight, shape, and size within the same species. For example, a lettuce seed looks like a flattened miniature banana, one end rounded and the other end very pointed—an extremely aerodynamic seed. Small seeds are used by vegetable, tobacco, and flower farmers.

Until recently, the vegetable farmer dribbled the seeds in great quantities into the growing beds. This practice required that the emerging plants be thinned or removed by cutting out all the plants between those that the farmer want to remain. Unless a plant has enough room to grow unhindered by other plants, it will not reach its full growth. Thinning is extremely backbreaking work, requiring the use of a short-handled hoe—one of the great torture instruments of our time. In addition, thinning usually damages the roots of the remaining plants, resulting in uneven growth and an uneven harvest.

If a way could be found to place one tiny seed where you wanted one plant to grow, many benefits would accrue. The most important benefit would be uniform growth and greater yield at harvest.

For many years inventors all over the world had been trying to find a solution to this problem. The solutions ranged from placing a seed in a small clay ball to placing the seeds on a water-penetrable or dispersible paper or plastic strip. Other solutions included constructing planters theoretically capable of dispensing one seed at a time and properly spaced. None of these solutions were satisfactory.

This then was the problem I started with:

My Objective:

☐ To develop a mechanical means by which a farmer could plant a single seed where he wanted one plant to grow to best market size without further touching the plant beyond the need for water, fertilizer, and weeding.

☐ In addition, to provide a means of optimum spacing and depth of each planted seed with the further objective of uniform harvest preferably by a mechanical harvester.

The solution took seven and one half years.

Research

My first job was research. I had to find out for myself what the problems were. I had to understand what was involved in planting and growing small seeds. How did the farmer get his seeds? What kind of machinery did he use? What was the level of labor and supervisory intelligence? What were the prejudices and superstitions that prevailed? What had been done up to now to solve this problem? Why did none of the solutions prove satisfactory? Most important, what path should I take in searching for a solution?

In gathering information, I used both primary and secondary sources. The research, which took several months, became the basis of further development. The research effort took as much planning and preparation as the development of the invention.

As is obvious from the above description I ended up working with vegetables. I got there by secondary source research into small seed acreage and dollar volume associated with each species. I chose vegetables for three reasons:

1. Dollar volume and acreage were highest.
2. We discovered that Union Carbide, through a subsidiary, was experimenting with the manufacture and marketing of "seed tape". This was a water-redispersible material made in the form of tape. The tape was approximately one-half inch wide folded onto itself with a seed placed in the center of the fold every few inches. In planting, the tape was unrolled from a large spool.

   I felt that if Union Carbide was interested in the vegetable market, that was a good place to start looking too. I wasn't stuck-up.
3. Also, fortunately, at the time the research was to begin, there was field labor agitation going on in California. In addition, the federal government passed new regulations pertaining to the use of immigrant labor from Mexico by California farmers. The same problems were true for Arizona and Texas.

These facts helped establish the area direction of my research. I began by developing a working list of the type of people I wished to interview — Department of Agriculture, ag extension services, ag schools, and farmers. I also developed a preliminary list of topics to be discussed with each respondent. These lists were continuously refined and sharpened as the research proceeded. Most respondents were able to guide me to the next level of information I sought. As I asked more questions, I discovered the "right and appropriate" questions to ask. In other words I got smarter and smarter as the research progressed. Everything I did was recorded. At the end of each interview, I diligently wrote down every bit of information I could remember that wasn't recorded during the interview. When the research was completed a full and comprehensive report was written and summarized.

Two primary directional pathways emerged from the study:

1. The primary market for any product that resulted were vegetable growers.
2. The primary product would be lettuce.

Understanding Lettuce Seeds

If ever a single seed incorporated every conceivable obstacle to handling, it is the lettuce seed. Nature, in its infinite wisdom, constructed the lettuce seed for natural handling. The seed in its natural state is meant to be carried to its next growing site by the wind. It is beautifully aerodynamic: not only can it be carried by the wind, but its shape makes it possible for the seed to land in the soil in the most favorable position. In addition, nature fixed it so that not all the seeds are ready for growing at the same time. This is a precautionary measure to make sure that the seed survives. A portion of the seeds is not ready for growing until the second season has begun.

Nature never meant for the seed to be handled by man. She made this painfully clear every step of the development. It was almost as if she were saying, "Leave my work alone."

From my point of view there were three things I had to learn about lettuce:

1. The light needed for uniform germination.
2. The factors that contribute to increasing the percentage of germination.
3. The physical characteristics of the seed

Again, I used the inventor's methodology: listing and analyzing every fact that I could find in each of these areas, summarizing the information in terms of actions required, and planning and carrying out those actions in a specific time frame. The results were as follows:

1. Experiments with light spectrum filters indicated that the seed's ability to germinate could be turned on and off at will. However, this proved to be one of those times when I did not carry the research far enough. If I had, it would have saved me much time and money. After I had completed my experiments, I found out that seed growers always light-treat their seed.
2. By research and experimentation, I found that the higher the density (weight) of the seed, the higher was its percentage of germination (representative samples of various seed were germinated in

petri dishes under time-controlled lights.) I ended up using only the top five percent by weight of any seed available. I made a deal with a seed grower and supplier to select only the high-density seed. Out of every hundred pounds of seed, I received five pounds. The winnowing was done by dropping the seed into a stream of air and then separating the seed in relation to the distance they were carried and fell from the nozzle of the blower. The heaviest seed fell closest, and the lightest seed traveled furthest. Using the high density seed gave me seed with an unheard of germination rate of 99.9 percent.

3. To determine the physical characteristics of the seed, the seed had to be studied under a microscope and sketched. Many seeds were studied and many sketches were made before a final decision was made on a set of average dimensions—$\frac{3}{64}$ inch thick, $\frac{1}{4}$ inch long, $\frac{1}{16}$ wide—it looked like an elongated, flat banana with longitudinal airfoils. The model was 32 times as large (8 inches long).

Establishing the Product's Specifications and Criteria

I knew the following about any invention that was to be created:

1. Machinery to plant the naked seed directly in the field was definitely out. The machinery would not be able to withstand the dust, dirt, mud, and moisture. (It should be noted that the farmer usually plants 16 rows at one time.) Many people had tried this technique, and they all failed for the same reason. Their machines would work under lab conditions but always broke down very quickly in the field.

2. Paper or plastic tape was out. Tape requires a lot of water for it to dissolve or disintegrate before the water can get to the seed. In addition, when the soil in the field was relatively clumpy, the tape would stretch between the clumps, the water would dissolve the tape, and the seed would fall to a nonuniform depth between the clumps. Another problem that occurred with the tape was that, every once in a while, a portion of the tape was left exposed during planting; when that happened, birds would get hold of it and pull out an entire line.

3. A single seed had to be incorporated into some matrix so that it could be easily transported and handled relatively roughly in the field—possibly with existing planters, but if necessary, with a new, durable type of planter.

The Critical Step—Developing and Testing the Concept

Consider that the direction has been loosely dictated by both the research and evaluation of the various methodologies that had been tried in the past. (Included, but not listed above, were various methods of coating seeds that will be reviewed as I proceed.) Therefore, this became the brainstorming step. Each of the potential methods of creating a matrix around the seed was listed—all of the methods I could find out about or think up myself. Each was listed and examined, evaluated, reviewed, and everything was written down. Here are some examples of the ideas that were considered.

Honeycomb Matrix. Make strips of honeycomb out of paper, kraft, or plastic. Fill the cells half full, deposit a seed in the cell, and fill the cell the rest of the way. Cover both flat sides of the honeycomb with thin paper whose function would simply be to hold the material and seed in the cell. The comb would be ridged and might be approximately 3 inches wide and 2 feet long. Transport the sheets of comb to the field and punch out each cell with a planter built for the operation. Construct the planter to space the drops at prescribed intervals. This spacing could be adjusted in the field.

Rejected. The mechanism required to place a single seed in each cell and then test to determine if only one seed were present was considered too complex. Consider that it did no good at all if the cell contained no seed or contained more than one seed. In addition, how many misses or doubles could be tolerated per sheet of comb? If the answer was none, then how would you go about correcting those cells that were faulty? If two or more seeds were planted from a single cell, they would require "finger thinning" to remove the unwanted plants so that the remaining plant could properly grow.

Enlargement By Coating. Coating the seed by enlarging it had been tried many times without complete success. It consisted of placing the seed in a rotating drum and either adding material by placing the additive in the drum with the seed or by spraying the additive into the drum while the drum rotated. The seed became larger as the additive dried around it. The more coatings, the larger the seed.

Rejected. Even though planters were already in the field that were capable of using this type of enlarged seed, the process was rejected. The primary reason was that there was no way of telling whether the pellet contained a seed or more than one seed. In addition, because it was always uncertain whether the pellet could be wetted enough for the seed to germinate and emerge, the spacing in the field called for a minimum of four pellets per foot, which was really taking a gamble that all other conditions were just right. Most plantings were done at a minimum of six seeds per foot. The drawback here was that when, all was done, thinning was still required.

Tableting. The first attempt at placing a seed in the center of a tablet had very limited success. It was done by a vermiculite salesman in California whose motive was to sell more vermiculite. Regardless, he had the makings of a good idea. He turned the idea over to Bill Harriet, at the University of Arizona, who developed, made, and tested tablets made out of vermiculite.

Prior to the salesman and Harriet, various people had made some tablets by hand and conducted some experimentation, but very little is known of them. I suspect they were independent inventors who never carried their work to completion.

In any case, it was Harriet who did the initial development work. Harriet placed a single seed in the center of vermiculite that had adhesive added to it, and then compressed the material; he let it dry and had himself a tablet. He made enough tablets to conduct several test plantings. Vermiculite stratifies when compressed. (Vermiculite is exfoliated mica and is made up of a series of small plates. When these plates are compressed, they lie flat against each other . . . called stratification. Also it is a rather hard, though brittle substance.)

It was necessary to plant the tablets on end so that the emerging seed could work its way out of the tablet. It should be noted that all of these tests were made by hand planting. Harriet also found that too much pressure during compression would kill the seed. He also found that too much adhesive would prevent the seed from emerging and that the optimum amount made for a weak tablet. The tablet size was ¾ inch in diameter by ¼ inch thick.

The idea was picked up by the people at The FMC Corporation. They modified the tablet by compressing each half of the tablet separately. Each half was made with a concave depression in the center into which a seed was placed; both halves were then glued together. The poor seed had a terrible time getting out even if the tablet was planted perfectly on its side. They next tried placing just three small drops of glue between the sides before they were joined so that the seed could find its way out. The tablet had to be planted vertically or the seed would not emerge. The emerging seedling sometimes did not have the kinetic energy to push its way through the compressed vermiculite plates.

After much consideration I felt that *tableting* was a viable path. I felt that other materials, forms, and methods could be found that would enable the seed not only to have a suitable home in which to germinate but also one that permitted easy emergence from any direction.

Little did I realize how long it would take . . .

- ☐ To find the right combination of materials and tablet construction design
- ☐ To invent all the machinery to make the finished tablet automatically
- ☐ To invent a suitable planter

At this point,

☐ A problem existed that needed solution.
☐ The direction of the solution (or pathway) was unknown.
☐ Research indicated prior attempts (all unsuccessful) to solve the problem, data for in-depth understanding of the problem area, and potential pathway direction.
☐ Analysis of many potential pathways leads to the selection of a single pathway and direction based on estimates of feasibility and process of elimination.

The Invention

Now, for the first time since the project started, I knew what kind of invention I must try to make. The following are some of the major problems that had to be solved in order to make the Seed Tablet (later named the Environmental Seed Cell).

What is important to remember is that as one problem was solved, another would crop up or be indicated by the previous solution. In looking for the right material for the matrix, I had to first look for material, then pH, then only one kind of vermiculite, then particle size, then the proper type of lime, then the kind and quantity of water-redispersible adhesive, then the maximum amount of pressure to be used in compressing the tablet, then the best shape of the tablet, then the coating of the tablet. And, in the midst of all of this, I needed to find a dry but thoroughly water-soluble material that could act as a protective blanket during compression so that greater pressure could be applied to the tablet. For example:

Matrix Material Selection. Based on the accumulated research data, many grow materials were individually tested to select the materials that were finally used. The test consisted of simply filling a small paper cup with the material, placing 25 seeds in the material, and then counting the emergence rate. The cups were placed in a controlled environment. These tests were repeated several times to make sure that the results were not accidental.

pH. One factor that led to the need for many such tests was the pH (acidity-alkalinity) requirements of the seed. A pH of about 5.5 was needed for best environmental conditions. A pH of 7 is neutral. Peat moss (a favored material because of its water-holding and expandability characteristics) has an average pH of 2.5 to 3, which is so acidic it would burn the seed. So peat moss had to be mixed with lime as a buffer, which therefore required additional tests of each mix contemplated. Vermiculite, another favored material, also required much testing. It turned out that there was only one source in the entire world (controlled by an American company) where horticultural vermiculite of the proper pH could be obtained.

Particle Size of Matrix Material. Each material that showed promise was tested to determine its best particle size. If the particles were too large, they penetrated the seed during compression into a tablet. If they were too small, they suffocated the seed when watered by clogging the seed pores and preventing oxygen access, which resulted in rotting. The best size turned out to be approximately 40 mesh. Mesh sizes from 10 to 200 were tested. The tests were conducted in the same manner as above and repeated many times.

Obtaining the proper mesh sizes for testing and later for production, turned out to be one of those subsidiary problems that are sometimes more of a headache than the original problem. It necessitated researching and purchasing a high-speed variable screen chopper, which in turn required the set-up of a separate chopping room. (The dust and dirt became intense each time the machine was in operation. It was also dangerous to operate not only because of potential kickback and care of fingers in feeding but primarily in breathing the dust. Every protective precaution was taken in the selection and use of proper masks.)

Mix Development. After these tests were completed, various combinations of materials were made and tested until a mix was found that proved satisfactory. The logic behind the mix development and determination was as follows.

Although vermiculite stratified because of its platelike structure, it had other attributes that made it a very desirable material—its ability to compress and then expand with water, and its ability to absorb and hold water like a sponge. To be used, a method had to be found to overcome the stratification. That method proved to be the use of chopped and sized peat moss (also compressible and expandable in water and also an excellent water holder). The particles of peat moss prevented the vermiculite from stratifying. The problem with peat moss was its pH factor. To solve that problem, lime was added to the peat moss to buffer it and thereby bring its pH up to a desirable level. Next, a particalized fiber was added to assist adhesive binding. Once that was all done, the decision was made to add nutriments and trace elements.

Detailed records and observations were diligently kept every step of the way.

Compression Problems and Solution. Concurrent with the search for the right matrix mix was the search and experimentation of a solution to the problems of compression. Once the mix had been determined, concentration was directed toward some means of compressing a tablet sufficiently to make it strong enough to withstand handling, transportation, and planting without falling apart. The major problem was that the seed centered in the mix could not withstand pressures greater than 100 psi. The less the pressure, the better the seed fared. However, pressure was definitely needed to compress the mix to make the tablet hold together.

Adhesives. Adhesives were researched; they were included in the mix as a means of assisting the binding. The specifications that developed called for an adhesive that was nontoxic, would not physically affect the seed, was water redispersible,and required very little water to activate.

This factor of water to activate became another of those horrible subsidiary problems. Too little water and the mix would not hold together; too much water and all sorts of unwanted things happened, such as premature germination of the seed, mix sticking to the tablet punches, and tablet weakness until the adhesive dried and held.

Tablet Punches. The tablet punches were the most difficult to deal with. At one point I thought that the problem had no solution. I tried plating and polishing, and making the tips out of teflon and other plastics. The mix material would abrade the tips and then begin to stick. The solution turned out to be a combination of several factors. The best tip material was a form of impregnated nylon.

Moisture. The next factor was that the moisture content of the mix had to be carefully controlled. This was done by adding the water, permitting the mix to stand for a minimum of two days to let the moisture permeate, then testing it to determine if the moisture content was at the right level for tableting without sticking to the punches. You would be amazed at the number of devices that exist to measure moisture that don't work. I found that the only way that worked was the "Margot" method. This consisted of Margot, the woman in charge of the mixing department, sticking her arm deeply into a barrel of mix, grabbing a handful, and saying if it was "ready" or "not ready." She was infallible. Without her, the project would have fallen apart.

Tablet Design. The next three steps completed the solution to the problem. All three came as "Flashes." The first was the physical redesign of the tablet. Up until this point the tablet was made as a simple slug of material that was ½ inch in diameter by ¼ inch thick. I changed the dimensions to ⅝ inch in diameter and maintained the ¼ inch thickness. But in doing so, I redesigned the punches so that they now contained an outer ring that was ¹⁄₁₆ inch wide and a concave inner portion in the form of an inverted flattened half circle. When compression took place a tablet was made that looked like the planet Saturn flattened at the poles. The advantage was that the outer ring, which was away from the seed, was able to take far more compression then the center and was, therefore, hard enough to act as a protective barrier for the entire tablet.

The Protective Blanket. The next "flash" came from remembering (whatever the stimulation was I don't know) that water cannot easily be compressed and that any applied pressure was equally distributed throughout the entire mass. My reasoning was that if I could find a way of placing the seed in some protective water type of environment, I could apply greater pressure to the tablet by equalizing the pressure on the seed and indeed protecting it from any possible damage from the matrix.

The idea worked like a charm. I was able to apply far more pressure to the tablet, which not only resulted in a better tablet but also resulted in the matrix material not sticking to the punches.

However, finding that water type of material to surround the seed with was no easy matter. First, it had to be nontoxic; second, its particle size had to be small enough to act like water; third, it had to wash away completely, during irrigation, so that the small particles would not interfere with the seed's ability to breathe.

The search ended with Sorbitol, a synthetic sweetner. It had all the right characteristics. The finest particle size flowed like water (it was very moisture-sensitive and had to be stored dry); it was compressible; when wetted, it dissolved very rapidly; and best of all, when it dissolved, its molecular size was compatible with the pore openings of the seed and did not interfere with the seed's breathing or water intake. This area of the tablet was called the *Blanket*.

Protective Coating. Although I now had a pretty good tablet, I felt it still wasn't good enough. When handled roughly, the tablet had a tendency to abrade and flake. It needed a coating of some kind. I tried the standard methods used by the pharmaceutical industry to coat tablets; that is, spraying them with a coating solution as they tumbled in a rotary bin. The solution usually contained a mixture of chloroform and alcohol plus some coater such as methocel. I found this type of operation much too dangerous, particularly after a container dropped, burst, and spilled all over the place, sending my assistant to the hospital and making me very sick from the fumes.

It was shortly after that, while searching for some other means of coating, that the third "flash" occurred. I won't even try to describe where the thought came from. I don't think I know, except that it had a lot to do with *Shake* and *Bake*.

The idea was to shake the tablets in a finely powered dry shellac, coat them, and then drop them through a flame chute, where the shellac would melt around the tablet forming a coating. Because shellac is water soluble and redispersible, it would not interfere with the tablet's performance in the field. Once I found out how long and how hot the chute had to be, it worked fine.

It was a fine product. Whenever I wanted to show off, I'd place an ESC in a saucer, add a bit of water, and let everyone watch it expand to its former uncompressed size. It at least proved how water absorbent the matrix was.

Automated Machinery

Not related to the invention of the ESC, but in many ways part of the development, was the concurrent development and invention of the automatic machinery necessary to produce the finished product in profitable quantities. In addition, I also needed to develop and construct a suitable planter.

A few of the primary problems in the development of the machinery were:

☐ Picking up a single seed
☐ Depositing the single seed onto the center of each tablet
☐ Redesigning a standard two-layer tableting machine into a five-layer machine
☐ Integrating the machine with seed pickup and transfer mechanisms (which were invented for this purpose)
☐ Developing electronics to determine that only one seed was deposited in each tablet and rejecting any tablet that contained more than one seed or no seed, (all at high speed).

The process of inventing is really the ability to recognize, rank, grade, and solve problems as they occur until the project works.

(The rest of this book assumes that the "invention" works and that a successful prototype has been built.)

Chapter 8

Selling an
Invention That Works

AT THIS POINT YOU HAVE COMPLETED A SUCCESSFUL PROTOTYPE OR DEVICE
that proves your invention works. The question is: what do you do with
it? Should you sell it, license it, set up your own business to manufacture it?
What?

This is a difficult time for an inventor—not just because you must make
a decision, but because you now must leave the shelter of your cave and live
in the real world. You can't be a loner any more; you must deal with people
who might or might not be very interested in your great new achievement.
You must find someone who might be interested—someone who will at least
take the time to listen to your presentation—and sell yourself and your invention.

SALESMANSHIP

You face two basic problems: the first is finding the right company and
person; the second is selling. Because most inventors that I have met have
the greatest difficulty in selling, I'll take that first. However, before I do, just
one word about the "who" factor.

An inventor usually has a rough idea of the identity of companies that
either are his competition or might benefit from his achievement. If he makes
contact with one of these companies and "sells them," he's lucked out, and
that's great. If he doesn't luck out and stops, he's being shortsighted. By do-

67

ing some simple research, he can usually develop a pretty decent list of additional companies to approach. In other words,

Do not limit yourself and your opportunities.

Now to selling. I have never met what I would consider a professional salesperson. I have met people who appear to believe in what they are doing sufficiently to give other people confidence in their product. Some people do this magnificently. They are instinctively attuned to what other people want. The key to their presentation (or "pitch," if you prefer) is their sincerity and knowledge of their product.

Be Sincere and Straightforward

I believe that you can make a presentation and sell your own product. No one has to teach you how to be sincere about your own invention. After all, it's your baby, and sincerity comes with the territory. You don't have to be flashy. You don't have to be "on" (pumped up with the artificial enthusiasm of the stereotypical salesman). It's your product; you know how it works; you know what it does; you know not only why it's good, but also why it's better than anything else. Therefore, let's assume that you are correct, and it is better. (It might not be the best in the whole wide world, but then again, it might!) So just tell it like it is. If you were describing it to a friend, you would have no difficulty telling him what you thought about your product, why it works, and why it's better than anything else.

During a workshop on invention that I conducted, I discussed writing a proposal letter to manufacturers about a new invention. The most important thing that came out of the workshop was:

If you're going to write a proposal letter, do it in everyday language.

Don't be fancy, don't exaggerate; you don't have to. Don't tell the other person his business; he knows his business. Don't tell him how to sell it because you'll antagonize him. Don't tell him what he knows and what he doesn't know. Tell him what you know about the product as sincerely, as honestly, as clearly as you possibly can.

The same hold true if making a personal presentation. Wear a suit and tie and look professional. Present your product in the best light without exaggeration, without distortion, without dishonesty. That to me is salesmanship.

Find the Right Person

In trying to make a deal with a major company, it is equally important that you find the *right person* within the company for your presentation. In my opinion, sending a proposal letter to the president is usually a waste of time, unless you happen to know the president. Sending a letter to the vice president of manufacturing, unless you have something that directly relates to what he is doing, is also a waste of time. Sending a letter to the head of research and development is even a bigger waste of time because most of the time you are directly competing with what he's supposed to be doing.

You must analyze who within the company would be the most interested audience for your invention presentation. If the company is sales oriented, the man you want to see is the vice president of marketing. If it is production oriented, then contact the vice president of production.

Many of the major companies operate with product managers or directors. If this applies to the company you wish to approach, then in all probability, the person you want is the product director in the field of your invention. For example, if you had an appliance and were contacting a major multidivision company, you would contact the division dealing with either outdoor appliances or indoor appliances. To bring an outdoor appliance to the indoor appliance director is useless—most of the time he will do nothing about it. Just because a product is to be sold in a department store doesn't mean you can pitch it to any buyer in the store. It doesn't work that way. There are different buyers in the housewares department and in the hardware department.

The same thing happens within a corporation; there are different areas of responsibility. It is easy enough to pick up the telephone and find out whose area of responsibility covers your device. Sometimes the people are listed in corporate directories.

It comes down to this: you must find and get to the right person. This assumes that you have, first, found the right company and, second, were able to identify the right person. Call him. Be persistent. Don't be insulted if he doesn't return your calls. Remember, he doesn't yet know what you want. Never give long explanations to secretaries. It usually doesn't help and, most of the time, creates confusion. Simply state why you want to see the boss. The time for detailed explanations is during your meeting, not before. Avoid lengthy explanations before you meet.

In addition to those telephone calls, however, you might now send him a short letter asking for or confirming an appointment. Follow up the letter, after a reasonable period of time, with telephone calls. Don't get mad; get an appointment.

MAKING MONEY ON INVENTIONS

There are five methods by which you can make money on an invention other than—and I want to emphasize this—starting your own production company (see chapter 9).

Own the Product, but Vend Out the Manufacturing

The first is a method used by a friend of mine, which I consider absolutely terrific. It can be very rewarding, if you can do it. Although my friend did not invent the method, he has used it to perfection to present his products.

My friend takes a device that he has invented and has the various parts made by as many vendors as appropriate, including the setup of an assembly line. Then he sells the device as a finished product to a company who can use it to increase the sales of their existing product line. He presents his invention as a compatible and complementary product.

For example, my friend invented a method for increasing the use of a food wrap commonly used in both the home and in commercial establishments. With his device, the user pulls the wrap out of the container with both hands and brings it down. A blade comes out and cuts the material off; the wrap falls and lies flat on the table so that wrapping is fast and easy. It's very fast, safe, efficient, and automatic—a beautiful product.

Now my friend's methodology was as follows: he took his invention concept to various vendors and had the parts made. Because he invented and designed it, he knew exactly what needed to be done. He had the molds, blades, and all the parts made, and had it completely assembled, packaged, and ready to ship. He set it up so that the production and assembly people would make a fair profit doing their part.

He then went to the various wrapper manufacturers and essentially said, "You make wrap. Here is my product for use with your product. It makes your product easier to use and sell." He then offered the company a finished product to sell in conjunction with their product. By this method he expanded his own sales capability with a sales staff of perhaps 1,000 salesmen all over the world.

What he has done is rather remarkable. Suppose he were to take this same product and licensed it to the same corporation to manufacture and sell it for him, for which he would collect a royalty. If the royalty were 5 percent, he would earn $.25 per unit if the manufacturer's selling price was $5.00 per unit. By getting the product made (and letting the various vendors who manufactured and assembled it also make a profit), and by acting as his own salesman, he could sell the product to the corporation for $5.00 per unit. Instead of $.25, he would make $2.50 per unit (assuming that the total cost of manufacturing, etc. is $2.50 per unit). That, I think, is a very profitable way of doing things.

But the *methodology* is what counts here. That methodology enabled my friend to invent a device and get it made by investing in it himself (and if necessary, getting other investors). The method is based on the preplanned intention of having vendors make it for him. He owns the product. He doesn't own the manufacturing facilities. He doesn't own the sales facilities. He doesn't own anything except the product. And it is totally his. That is one great method of dealing with a product—if you can do it. Not everyone can afford to do it, nor does every product lend itself to that method, but I think it is a marvelous method of profiting from an invention.

Consider the method again: he owns the product, he gets it made, he sells it himself to another company, which resells it because it fits in. This is the most important part—it fits directly into the company's own product line. It enhances and is very compatible with their product line. If your invention can be handled in this way, you should consider this method.

The method implies four things:

1. Having the capacity to get the product made—and made properly
2. Having the money or being able to raise the money to get it made
3. Having the know-how to get it made to your requirements at the best price so that everybody makes a profit on it
4. Once it's made, being able to find your customers and sell it to them.

Shoestring Method

The shoestring method was outlined in a talk given to the New York Society of Professional Inventors. The speaker had a unique method of dealing with his inventions. He would make a working prototype of his invention, then set up a small manufacturing facility in his garage. He would do whatever was necessary to start a minuscule enterprise—very small money, very small potatoes, very small everything. He would make the product and sell the product, either acting as his own salesman or with other salesmen.

His purpose was to establish a small but strong market for the product to prove that there was a market for the product. What better proof could there be than that the product was selling—and being reordered? The most important point in his entire operation was that reordering was a reality.

At that stage, and not before, he would try to sell or license the entire operation to someone else. He would not just make a prototype and say, "Hey, I have this marvelous invention. Please license it, buy it, or do something with it." With his setup, he could show that customers wanted it and bought it. On the basis of his limited investment, and proof that a market existed, he was able to sell the product and the entire operation, either as a company or a licensing deal.

This method has one major disadvantage. If the product has national or general distribution potential and is to be considered by a major company, the product's market exposure might be thought of as premature. Many companies try to keep their new product marketing strategies as secret as possible in order not to alert competition. In addition, many of these companies wish to conduct extensive research to determine the best method and direction of marketing. A premature and misdirected marketing approach can make redirection of the marketing effort extremely costly and difficult.

Licensing

Licensing gives a company the right to manufacture and sell your product. In return, licensing gives you up-front money (hopefully) and guaranteed royalties for a period of years, then regular royalties (based on the selling price) for the remaining life of the patent.

Selling

Selling the product and patent rights directly and completely is another way to make money on your invention. This is a complete sale. You're out. You've sold it for "X" number of dollars, and you're through with the product from that point on. Other people own it and can do whatever they please with it, including just sitting on it.

Start-up Company Method

There are two primary methods for starting a new company based on a new invention. The first is doing it yourself (see chapter 9). The second is letting someone else start up a company based on your invention.

When someone else starts up a company, you either participate in or stay out of the organization. You might own a piece of the company and perhaps receive some royalties. As an employee, you might make a contribution in terms of taking the invention from the prototype stage to the manufacturing stage.

There aren't many people around who have that kind of capability. It takes a great deal of know-how to take an invention from prototype to production. I know of products that worked just beautifully in the laboratory. My colleagues and I could make them one at a time like crazy. But it took us six months to set up a pilot plant that would make a product in quantity that worked. We had both major and minor problems of the kind we never dreamed would occur.

In one case we used giant ribbon blenders to mix our ingredients. One of the employees, while cleaning it, dropped a steel tape measure (the kind you wear on your belt) into one of the blenders. He pulled out most of it, but some of the chewed-up parts remained in the out-going valve, then stuck in some of the pumps beneath the blender. We, who knew nothing of what had happened, couldn't figure out why the pumps jammed until another employee said, "Hey, I know what the trouble is." We nearly lynched the person who dropped the tape measure in—not for dropping it in, but for not telling us about it.

The point I am making here is not so much to alert you that even the best employees make mistakes, but to emphasize that somewhere along the line you must have the know-how to check things as they are done. You must recognize when something is going wrong and not be so busy that you have no time left to check on crucial components going into your invention. This is part of the process of taking an invention from prototype to the successful production stage.

In this method of starting a company, more so than in the other methods, know-how is essential. The person who sets up a company must be capable of doing it and must be someone who knows business. He might not know his elbow from anything else about invention, but he has to know how to put together a corporation and how to hire and supervise the people who do the work. I don't know many inventors who have that kind of capability.

I believe that sometimes it really doesn't make any difference whether or not you have the businessman's capability of operating a business. Dealing with your own invention is difficult as it is, but dealing with it in the business arena is extraordinarily difficult. You have to become practically schizophrenic in order to be successful—to make believe that the invention really isn't yours but that the business is.

A Point to Remember

In dealing with any of these methods, let me emphasize one vital detail—who to deal with. It's worth it to take the time to find the right person. Unfortunately, one of the problems that inventors sometimes have is tunnel vision. They think in terms of one particular area and get locked in. They rarely spend the necessary time researching potential opportunities. I sometimes believe that inventors as a group are the most easily dissuaded and easily discouraged people in the world.

You must be able to pinpoint those people who are *capable of dealing with you* in any one of these methods. Define precisely who your buyer is. Keep in mind that all you want is one company to license or sell your invention—one company, one operation. In reality, the probability is that you're not going to be able to license your invention to more than one group unless you have the most fabulous invention that every came down the pike.

PREPARATION OF PRESENTATION

The first and most important thing that you must understand in preparing a presentation is that *you need a new analysis* of the invention now that it has been completed and a working prototype exists. Start your analysis with:

1. What your product does and why it is so good at doing it. This list is created for your own needs and as future reference.
2. Why it is better than competing products.

Write these things down. They are not ideas to keep in your head.

The second thing your presentation needs is *a new functional review* of every single aspect of the invention. This means listing every function and why each of the functions is better than anything else that exists. Again, write these things down. Do not leave them to memory.

The third area is to list *the benefits* of your invention—what it does that no other product does. These factors are extremely important. After listing them, put them in order of priority. Then, if you want to talk about them or write a letter or a written proposal, you will know which of these factors to plug in and in what sequence.

It is important to organize your thoughts about your own invention so that you can write or talk about it persuasively. Very frequently, inventors are not capable of coherently analyzing and discussing their own inventions, particularly in formatting a proper presentation. Sometimes an invention (or concept) is easily understood and sometimes it is not. I am not capable of doing it with my own inventions all the time. I always think I can, but in reality, I have sometimes had to find other people, such as analytical engineers, to take my invention apart, analyze it completely, put it back together again, and then give me an analysis so that I could present my invention more intelligently. At times inventors become so ego-involved with their inventions that they are unaware that their presentation lacks proper prospective. Objectivity is difficult to achieve; sometimes third-party review can be very helpful in reaching clarity.

Your written list is now completely prepared: you have your analysis, functional review, and list of the benefits your invention provides. Now put it aside and decide who you need to contact. Remember, getting to the right company is important, but getting to the right person—the decision maker within the right company—is twice as important.

Patent Applications

The assumption for the remainder of this chapter is that you are going to either license or sell your invention. You therefore need to make a presentation.

My feeling, however, is that you should at least have a patent application in the works before you show anything to anyone. With a patent application in the works you can speak a bit more freely about how your device works without revealing all of the details. The application gives you a modicum of protection; it tells the person you are making the presentation to that you have taken protective measures, both for yourself and for him.

Many inventors and some patent attorneys feel that before applying for a patent, you should at least have a patent search done. Not all attorneys agree with this, however. Many attorneys contend that a patent search is a waste of time because the patent office automatically does one to determine whether your invention infringes on any prior art. Therefore, they feel that submission of an application is sufficient, and a patent search is not necessary.

Other inventors and patent attorneys feel that a minimum search is essential to determine whether you're reinventing the wheel or if your device is different from prior art. They feel, and perhaps rightly so, that the patent office might not dig up everything that is pertinent; if anyone in the future challenges their patent, the challenger's case might be strengthened by that unrevealed patent. They also feel that every bit of prior art they find and cite strengthens their arguments to the patent examiner and eventually results in tighter and stronger claims. (In a patent application, it is necessary to cite prior art claims and then show why your claims are different.)

If you have done a patent search and applied for a patent you can tell your company contact, if appropriate. This lets the company know that you are going through with the total process of protection. You might wish to show a working model of your invention. Doing so is very, very controversial, however. You have to carefully weigh the possibilities about the company that you are dealing with. Be sure that you are not getting yourself into a position where what you describe or show can be taken from you without too much difficulty.

> *Always remember they have more money clout than you do, and if push came to shove, they could use it to take what they want. You could sue, but suing costs a great deal of money.*

Leaving a Presentation Package

Another possibility is leaving behind a presentation package for the person to review. This depends on how many meetings you have had, how much interest there is, and where you are. I am not entirely sure that leaving a film or a tape or pictures of an invention is appropriate. It's a matter of judgment. Although the final decision is yours, at least discuss this with other inventors, with a patent attorney, or with knowledgeable individuals who can alert you to any dangers they perceive in your current negotiations. Also, much depends on the type of invention you're presenting. I have no objections to giving a description of the product itself—not how it works, but what it does and how it does it (if you can describe how it does it without revealing how it works).

You might want to give any market data you have that is valid. I wouldn't press the point except to state its availability. Generally speaking, the people that you are selling to know more about the market than you do. If you know any of the manufacturing costs or can estimate the cost of the finished item, then you should state them and possibly include that information in your package. You might also include a statement about the patent status.

I wouldn't include much more in a presentation package unless you feel confident that you might have a deal. This means you have studied the situation and the people that you are dealing with and have a reasonable basis for leaving semiconfidential information behind without it coming back to haunt you later. The greatest danger in any form of negotiations is making a series of assumptions as to what the opposition thinks and feels without having concrete evidence about their true intentions.

How Much Should You Reveal?

I feel very strongly that you should review the legalities section of this book (chapters 18 and 19) before you make your presentation. I personally do not conduct a patent search or make a patent application before the preliminary presentation. This is my personal practice and I am not recommending that everyone follow it. My feeling is that if there is interest on the part of the potential purchaser in the item that I have to show, then I will make a patent application. My statement to them will normally be that an application "is in process." This, I hope, conveys the meaning that all of the information is in the hands of my attorney, who is in the process of making a patent application. This indicates to the purchaser that movement is being made in the right direction.

Patents and patent searches are so expensive that, in my opinion, they are only necessary when you have something that is really worthwhile, saleable, or licensable. Only then do you spend the money necessary to protect yourself.

THE N.I.H. FACTOR

People often ask why the N.I.H. (Not Invented Here) factor exists. It exists because every time you present a new product to a company that has its own new product department or research and development operation, you are stepping on people's toes. They believe that you're showing the boss that they haven't been doing their job. Therefore, they are going to take any swipe they can take at you. Reconcile yourself to the fact that this type of behavior exists and must be dealt with.

Always remember when presenting: it is much easier and safer for people to say no than to say yes.

Most people can give you a thousand reasons why something will not work rather than think up a single way to make it work. This is a fact of life, which you must consider when dealing with some companies. You run up against a negativity that is inherent in the N.I.H. factor. It is embodied in the personality of the sharpshooters or devil's advocates or whatever you want to call the nay sayers.

In dealing with any particular company or situation, it is worth your while to handle this factor. The best way that I know how (it doesn't always work, but it's worth trying) is to direct the conversation at the person who is the key individual within the group, and away from the nay sayers. In addition, be extraordinarily patient and very understated with the people who are being critical. You might address the criticisms if you wish to, but sometimes it is worthwhile to simply ignore the criticisms and go on with what you have to say. You must rely on your own judgment at the time that you make your presentation.

It might be desirable to make the first presentation by yourself. If you do, speak only in general terms, without committing yourself to anything. If you go beyond a first presentation, however, I would carefully consider bringing an attorney along, if for no other reason than to keep you from saying too much. One of the major problems with inventors making presentations is that they tend to talk too much and give away too much by trying to show off too much.

What if you can't deal with the N.I.H. factor? You will run across it. If you can't deal with it, you're up against a situation beyond your control. I strongly suggest, then, that you find another customer. That's what I do.

METHODS OF EXPOSURE

There are a lot of people in this world ready to take money from an inventor. Many people consider the inventor stupid and eccentric. There are a number of companies that consider the inventor nothing more than a sucker —someone to take advantage of. They promise to show him how to market his product, to make models of it, to do this and that. The truth of the matter is that they will take money from him and that's it. The inventor is their market . . . . not his invention. That's the way they operate.

One of the things that you must remember, and I will shout it from the rooftops over and over again, is this:

If anybody wants money from you for exploiting, marketing, or evaluating your invention, RUN in the opposite direction!

Trade Shows

Are trade shows any good? Should you show your invention at a trade show?

I think inventor trade shows are rip-offs. Inventors are the most easily preyed upon people I have ever come across in my life. Scavenger organizations send you letters saying they will make you rich, and some inventors want to be rich so badly that they lose their capacity to think. Because they think that every invention they have is going to be worth a zillion dollars, they are ready to lay out any money or do anything the promoters want.

Let me repeat my most important rule: the moment anybody wants money from you, run . . . don't walk, run! Get away from him as fast as you possibly can. If he is willing to put *his money* and effort into your invention, then talk to him. But don't ever, ever get involved with anybody who wants you to put up ten cents much less thousands of dollars.

Inventor trade shows are an abomination, particularly the trade shows that have news coverage. The news coverage is always about "crackpot" exhibitors. Therefore, if you are in that show, the general consensus of the people that you might want to sell your invention to is automatically that you are also a crackpot. However, it is sometimes helpful in negotiations to be thought of as a crackpot. Most businessmen think that inventors are stupid, and sometimes it is helpful to let them think you are. But that's for later.

In all fairness, I must say that there are many inventors (I don't know if they are professionals) who feel that trade shows provide exposure that would be otherwise unavailable to the inventor. My only comment about this attitude is the following question: Has anyone ever sold or licensed an invention as a result of one of these shows? I think not. And if they did, what was the deal like. Also, what percentage of the inventions shown ended in sales or licensing agreements. In other words, does the lottery give better odds?

There is something else that's wrong with trade shows that's far more subtle. Most knowledgeable manufacturers don't want their competitors to know which direction they are headed in, both in terms of new products and methods. When an invention appears at a trade show, it's public. In addition, in a patent pending situation, you might endanger your ability to obtain a foreign patent on the basis that the invention has been publicly presented. The rules for foreign patents are tricky. Before I exposed an invention in that way, I would at least check out my position with a patent attorney.

Agents: The Good and the Horrible

I have heard of new product agents or invention agents through my travels and travails. The only ones that I have ever heard of that are any good are in the toy industry. I have heard rumors to the effect that there are agents outside of the toy industry. In all of my years of experience, however, I have not come across a single one. I have found that those who purport to be agents, and advertise as such, and claim that they will help you market your product are the very horrible ones. If you can get an agent to represent you and your product to a manufacturer, if you don't have to put down up-front money, and if you don't have to tie yourself up forever with that agent . . . then you might think about it rather carefully, and maybe take a chance with him.

alties to a good agent who could take the problems of marketing my invention out of my hands and just let me do my inventing. I can think of nothing better than making my thing work, then turning it over to him to market. I would be more than happy to give up the 50 percent; however, I just haven't found anyone legitimate.

Advertising Your Patent

I've seen patent advertising by inventors (advertising inventions in a newspaper business section) every once in a while. I have never tried to do it myself, and I am not sure that it can do any good or any harm. Neither I nor any of my friends in the New York Society of Professional Inventors (that I know of) have had any experience in this area.

There are many outfits around that, for a fee, will list your patent to manufacturers. Some state agencies will also do this without charge. Each will list your invention and its availability. I have never tried them and personally don't think that they are particularly good or that anything can come of it. (I'd love to be proven wrong.) In my opinion, any manufacturer worth his salt who is interested in new inventions would certainly be a subscriber to the Patent Gazette. It is a United States government publication that lists and describes patents as they are issued.

Data Bases

The newest type of exposure are the various data bases. A data base might be able to help and might be as worthwhile as patent advertising. Your invention is classified, described, and listed in the data bank where someone who is looking for an invention in your category would be able to find it. The primary advantage is that a great deal of information, including pictures, can be shown. The United States Patent Office operates a data base that enables a computer patent search of prior art.

Is There an Ideal Way?

There is another aspect of all of this: Does exposure hurt? Can a trade show hurt? Can advertising hurt? Can a data base hurt? Yes, I think they can under certain conditions. If a company is looking for a highly competitive invention, and your's is it, they sure don't want anyone to know that they are interested or involved in it. Nor do they want that invention exposed and possibly shopped around. They want to know that they (the manufacturer) have it on an exclusive and secret basis until they are ready to bring it to market.

I think the ideal way of getting exposure is to find both a specific company and a specific person within that company that might be able to use your product. Deal with that person exclusively.

WRITING A PROPOSAL

The primary purpose of writing a proposal is to communicate your ideas to your reader. Do not use words and phrases that make you sound like a hotshot intellectual or a creative freak. You want to persuade your reader that your invention is worthwhile and should be pursued; the rest is an ego trip.

Communication is extraordinarily difficult. Do not be flowery. Be as precise as you possibly can. Take pains to communicate to the best of your ability. When you have finished writing your proposal, bounce it off other people to make sure that what you are saying is understandable.

Subheads of a Proposal

I will discuss several areas to include in a proposal (see appendix B). Which of these areas you include is a matter of judgment on your part. Just because I have listed all of these areas doesn't mean you have to use them. Include only what will best present the information that you wish to communicate. You want to convince somebody that what you have is worthwhile so that both of you can go on with negotiations and take them to a fruitful conclusion.

Communication is the key factor.

Detailed List. The first area of the proposal is a detailed list and description of what the invention does—*not* how it does it. I have mentioned this in discussing your description of your invention. When you are writing a proposal, however, you describe in specific detail exactly what your invention does and why it does it so well, but *not* how it does it.

Specifications. This establishes the specifications of the invention as completely as you can (again, without revealing anything about how the invention works). Say what it does in terms of its specifications—for example, its size and the types of materials that go into it. Include all specifications that you can define.

Manufacturing. Discuss where your invention might be manufactured. If you can, also describe how it might be manufactured and under what conditions. Don't include it if you are not absolutely sure about the information.

Estimated Costs. Where possible, estimate the costs of materials, manufacturing, advertising, marketing, etc. Emphasize that these are estimated costs, that they might very well change under particular conditions, and that you are not to be held to these costs, if and when the subject ever comes up. You are only giving them ballpark figures.

Estimated Selling Price. Where possible, estimate the selling price. Because of your experience and background, you might have a pretty good idea of what the selling price of the product should be. Rely more on the manufacturer than on yourself for this figure, however. The manufacturer can estimate what it might cost him and knows his markups and overhead costs. Therefore, be careful about including an estimated costs. Qualify to be on the safe side: for example, "This is my best guess as to what the estimated costs, selling price, etc., might be."

Materials and Alternatives. List the type of materials or potential alternative materials that can be used. This consideration is particularly important to manufacturers who might not be too familiar with new types of materials. Even engineers who are not familiar with value engineering require information. I have made objects out of stainless steel because stainless steel happened to be available at the time and I didn't feel like buying aluminum or plastic or whatever material was really appropriate. The same thing is true in making an invention. You happen to have a material on hand, it works well, you can cut it and shape it and do whatever is necessary with it; therefore, you use it because it's handy. But that's in your prototype. In your proposal, you say that, although your object is made out of a specific material, the probability is . . . and then you list the other materials that it might be made from and how the proposed materials might increase or decrease the cost of production.

Prototype Availability. State the availability of a working prototype. Certainly, you are not going to try to sell your invention without having a working prototype, but there are exceptions. For example, I have sold concepts to a potential buyer. The consequences of success or failure were then written into an agreement. However, that was a different type of setup and took a different type of proposal. What you are dealing with here is stating in your proposal that you have a working prototype on hand. Somewhere down the line, after you have done some negotiating and had a couple of meetings, it might be appropriate to show it to potential buyer.

The Buyer Will Make It Pretty. Make it clear to the buyer that he will have the responsibility of making the product "pretty." That's not the responsibility of the inventor. The manufacturer can hire industrial designers who are trained to take a product and make it not only look good but also fit a particular market.

Third-Party Verification—Conditions. This states that the invention works. When I sold concepts, I stated what the potential invention would do (not how it would do it) and the specifications. Then I would take on the project with a small down payment to cover sincerity costs. If the object worked according to my previously established specifications, I would receive my money, and the licensing deal would go into effect. One of the key factors of this concept proposal was that a mutually acceptable third party would verify the invention's ability to work according to the accepted specifications. In one situation, the buyer and I agreed to use Battelle Laboratories of Columbus, Ohio. Once Battelle verified that the invention worked as specified, the deal automatically went into effect. Everything (prototype, notes, test results, etc.) were then turned over to the licensee.

The Competitive Edge. Do not send out too many proposals. Maintain your competitive edge by not revealing the details of how the invention works before the deal is negotiated and signed. If you shop your invention around to several people, and somebody figures out how the thing works before a deal is signed, you might very well lose it. It's as simple as that. Also, people somehow get to know if it has been shopped around, and your invention might get a "shopworn reputation."

First Look. Your proposal can indicate when the buyer is going to see the invention. Essentially it's a matter of judgment on your part, depending on the circumstances:

1. He doesn't see it until you feel reasonably protected and a deal has been or is in the final stages of being made. *A deal is not a deal until everything has been signed.*

2. How much of a gamble, in terms of trust, you are willing to take based on your judgment and "gut feeling."

I certainly wouldn't let him see it until I've had a few personal contacts with him and checked his reputation. In addition, I'd review probabilities of loss with my patent attorney before I showed anything to anybody I hadn't made a deal with.

After Verification. Review the possibilities of making a deal based on the invention being able to satisfy a set of mutually established specifications. Then, after some sort of a deal has been negotiated, you can show the buyer or a verifying third party the invention. You can indicate that after the deal goes into effect, you'd be ready and willing to turn everything over to them. In fact, after the deal has gone into effect, it is to your benefit to give them everything that you possibly can. It makes it easier for them to go with your project. It is not until they start manufacturing and selling your product that you are going to make any money on it.

Patents. Never mention patents in a proposal. If you just applied for a patent, you don't know whether or not you will indeed receive a patent. There is no way you can outguess the Patent Office. You might find yourself in a position where you have made promises that cannot be kept. You will be much better off not mentioning patents in your proposal.

If you do have related patents, then of course mention them. In fact, if you have patents on your invention, you are in a totally different position about how much you can reveal. My suggestion is that without patents, first meet with your patent attorney. Together you can decide how much you can safely reveal, depending on the reliability of the people you are dealing with.

Specifications Alterations

After you have submitted the proposal, what happens if the buyer alters the specifications? Generally good things. Changes in the specifications might substantially increase the amount of time permissible for you to fulfill your obligations if you make a deal. They also open up all the financial considerations of the deal. Proposed changes indicate that things are going well, that the buyer is not only considering your proposal but is now interested in it enough to want to tailor the specifications to his needs. It probably also means that you have him hooked and can therefore gently press for more favorable terms.

Just remember one thing. Any changes, no matter how small or trivial, should be *agreed upon in writing*. Never, never, never rely on their memory or yours. If nothing else, then at least write and date a memo for both your files. It's not the best way, but at minimum, it's a record of the changes from the original agreement. If the changes relate to the invention only, then in all probability, a simple exchange of memos with the authorized person in the client company is sufficient.

If those changes affect the deal, by all means, hasten to your attorney to discuss the implications. Under no circumstances should you agree to any changes regardless of how minute they appear to the deal without first conferring with your attorney. You can always say to your client, "It seems okay with me, but before it's binding, I want to review it with my attorney." Don't be rushed into anything. If time is so precious, then at the very least, use the telephone to confer with your attorney. Law and accepted practices pertaining to licensing and sales agreements involving inventions or patents are so complex and have so many *hidden* ramifications that ONLY a competent patent/licensing attorney can guide you through the maze.

Deadlines

In one of my agreements, the licensee and I spelled out what would happen if I did not meet the deadline of producing a *working* prototype. We agreed that I would turn over to them *all* the plans, drawings, information, test results and materials, and all the parts that had been made up to that point. The licensee could then make a decision as to whether they wanted to go on with the project themselves or give me more time to work on it. If they took it over and went on with it themselves, I would still end up with the credit for and ownership of the basic invention. The basic invention would still be mine, even though somebody else might complete it.

One of my arguments in these negotiations was as follows. I can get to a point where the invention basically works but not satisfactorily enough. Somebody could come along and turn a knob in a particular direction, make an adjustment or something, and all of a sudden the thing would snap to and work. I said that if that happened, I wouldn't want to lose out on everything that I had worked on thus far. (See sidebar.)

Don't give up on something that you have worked on as a concept or as a machine if you feel your thinking was logical and sound. Don't give it all away simply because you failed to bring it to the final point of making it work. Drop it, if you can, for a period of time, then come back to it. But in a deadline situation, by all means, protect yourself from loosing it all, whenever possible.

NEGOTIATING A DEAL

Presumably you have found the key person with whom you are going to negotiate. By this time, you must know backwards, forwards, upside down, and inside out, what the deal is going to be about and who with. You must know whether you want to license you product, sell it, or use your invention to raise money to start a company. It really doesn't matter in terms of negotiations. What matters is that you must absolutely know, in advance, what you are looking for. You must know the kind of deal you want to structure, what your bottom line is, how far you are willing to go, and how much you are

Dead Lines

One of the first big machines that I built was a singulator, a device that picked up individual particles one at a time at a rate of between 8,000 and 10,000 units per minute. This was only the prototype, which was to be used to package vitamins, pills, etc. It was so fast that the only way you could see what was going on was by using a strobe at the output end, hooked up to an electronic counter.

We worked on this thing for well over a year. When it was finished, it wouldn't work. It just wouldn't work. At one point we were using navy beans for test runs (they were the cheapest). They flew all over the place. In addition, they burst as they came out of the machine. Until the day we moved, we found navy beans all over my shop.

Then we bought small plastic balls for the tests. The balls, a little over ⅜ inch in diameter, were meant to be used for a pocket deodorant device that never sold, so we bought them. They had a bounce return of almost 90 percent. (We still have plastic balls left over from those tests). When the machine was turned on, the plastic balls (like the navy beans,) flew all over the place. It was absolutely horrendous. We were standing there being showered by plastic balls and the machine wouldn't work.

Everyone was standing around the machine—my kids, my wife, my friends—all waiting for the singulator to work. My oldest son, who was then about thirteen, kept looking at the machine and saying, "I know what's wrong." I said, "Listen, please leave me alone. Don't bother me now." This kept up for about a half hour. He kept repeating, "I know what's wrong." And we, my assistants and I, the smart ones, continued to tinker. All us experts, hovered over the machine like drones attending a queen bee, adjusting this and trying that, with no success.

Finally, my wife said, "Listen. What have you got to lose?" So we listened to him. And he said, "It's missing over here." And we made the one adjustment that only this kid saw because he was faster at seeing things than anybody else standing around there.

It worked like a charm. It worked from that point on and there was never any doubt as to the ability of the machine to function as conceived.

You have to protect yourself from the "close miss." A machine is a complex mechanism, and this singulator had over 6,000 parts to it.

willing to give up before you start to negotiate. In knowing this, you not only strengthen your hand, but can negotiate with greater confidence and less uncertainty.

Normally, in negotiating a deal you are outnumbered. If possible, you should always bring somebody with you, usually a patent attorney who has licensing or selling experience. Keep in mind that it is you that are making the deal; the attorney is there to assist you, not negotiate the deal for you. The most important thing that the attorney can do is to keep you from talking too much when you are supposed to be quiet and listen. Establish your signals with your attorney before you go into a meeting.

Know the Value of Your Invention

Before you go into a meeting, you must have an estimate of the value of your invention. Find out approximately what you think it is worth and determine what you're going to ask for, such as the number of dollars up front, a guaranteed royalty deal, or both. Know exactly what you are going to shoot for and what you want before you go in. Also know what you're willing to settle for.

There are many factors to consider in estimating the value of an invention. How much (dollars) have you invested in it? How long have you worked on it? How much time have you put in on it? How much do you estimate it is going to bring in? What is its value in terms of production and profit? Mostly, the consideration reduces to what the market value is—how big is the market, how much money can people make on it, and how really valuable is it, and how protected is it in terms of being copied.

Know your bottom line.

Know exactly what you are willing to give up—the minimum beyond which you are not willing to go. If you are negotiating way above your bottom line, you can argue and give here and there, and know that you have more to go. You can feel comfortable with a deal that is settled above your bottom line.

Don't Get Desperate

The most important thing to remember in negotiating a deal is DON'T GET DESPERATE. Don't show that you are desperate. Don't even hint that you are desperate. As the TV commercial says, "Whatever you do, don't let them see you sweat."

If you do get desperate, try to postpone the negotiations. Do anything you can to get yourself out of that particular position. Remember, even though you might not think so at the time, there are other people who might be interested in your invention, even if they are hard to find. If you find it very difficult to be anything but tense during the negotiations, let somebody else carry the ball if necessary. Once you begin to show desperation, you lose a good deal of the advantage that you started with.

In a tense and delicate negotiating session, I try to forget what I want and try to understand what the buyer wants. What are they looking for, how far they are willing to go, where do they want to go. I watch their body language and listen to their words. I ask questions, I try to probe; if I can't probe, I try to get my attorney to probe. I find any detail that I can possibly work with, any kind of hint or foot in the door that gives me a clue to what *their* bottom line is (or their top line, which is just as important). In other words, what are their parameters. It's a pretty foolish feeling to settle for less and then find out that they were willing to go much higher in making the deal. On the other hand, it's pretty stupid to misread a situation and end up with no deal.

When you are involved in negotiations, you are in a high stakes poker game. Take it easy. Do what you would do in a poker game and do it well. "Read" your opponent as much as you possibly can to determine how far you might be able to push a point. If you gain one thing, push for another. If you gain that, push for a third. Don't push your way out of a deal, but keep pushing until you have to stop. As you can find out more of what they want, keep in mind where *you* want to go and where *they* want to go. Understanding what they want and how far they are willing to go is as important as knowing what your bottom line is.

Watch Out for Brain Drainers

In any negotiating deal, watch out for "brain drainers." These are people who will pick your brains, try to find out everything they possibly can, and then say "Thank you." They always want to think about what you have said. They rarely get back to you, and you can never seem to reach them again. Be very careful how much you give away. If you suspect them to be brain drainers, leave as quickly as possible. You have nothing to gain and a great deal to lose.

Don't Make a Snap Decision

It is not essential for you to make an immediate decision. If your potential buyers are sincere and really want your product, they will give you time to think and to talk to associates or friends. They want to make a good deal just as much as you do. Do not make an immediate decision unless you consider that it is very much to your advantage. Think about your decision. Again, if they are sincere, they will give you the time to think about it.

Don't Talk Patents

Don't talk about patentability in any negotiating session. The only thing that you might mention about patents is the fact that either you have the application in process, that the patent has been applied for, or that the patent has been granted. Even if it has been granted, don't talk about the strength of the patent. If it hasn't been granted, don't say that it will be granted. Remember there is no way of outguessing the Patent Office, and you can get yourself into trouble by trying to do so. In addition, by promising the buyer that the object is patentable, you make yourself vulnerable to being sued for fraud if a patent isn't issued.

Let's Talk Money

Who talks first in a negotiation session? That's a matter of feel. I am not talking about who begins the conversation. I am talking about who really gets down to the nitty-gritty first about the kind of deal to consider. If they are sharp, they are going to turn to you and say, "What do you want?" If you are sharp, you are going to turn back to them and say, "Listen, how do you normally work? What do you want to do? If you are interested in this, what are you offering?"

Sooner or later you get to money. How much do you ask for? The question leads to how much your invention is worth and whether or not what you want is in their ballpark.

Some companies are absolutely against paying up-front money. If you feel that there is a possibility of getting up-front money, certainly shoot for it. If you think there is very little possibility of getting up front money, structure your deal in a different way so that essentially you get your money using up-front money as a bargaining bit. You can say, "All right, if there is no up-front money, then I want to increase my royalties and the length of the guarantee of those royalties." Instead of having guaranteed royalties for three years, ask for five years. Instead of settling for 7 percent royalty, ask for 10 percent royalties. If they are willing to give you up-front money, you might lower the amount of the royalty arrangement to whatever seems appropriate, and you might reduce the number of years that the minimum royalties would be guaranteed.

You have to decide what you want to shoot for and how much you want to get. There is no average figure for royalties. You are playing percentages, which you determine in relation to the value of the product and how much it might sell for.

Whenever you license anything, base the royalties on the *manufacturer's selling price*—not the final retail selling price. You want the price the manufacturer gets when it leaves his premises. Make sure that the licensee is not selling it to himself (or to a subsidiary organization) at a low fixed price, with the subsidiary organization then doing the real selling at a higher price.

Guarantees

I feel that there should be protection of a number of years for guarantees. Establish how much royalty you want and what the minimum guarantees should be—whether it be $10,000 or $100,000 a year. With guarantees you get income regardless of whether the product sells or doesn't sell.

The main purpose of getting guaranteed royalties paid to you for a specific number of years is to make sure that the manufacturer does not sit on your product and do nothing. These minimum guaranteed royalties are deducted from the royalties as they do come in for that year only and are never subject to return.

For example, you have a guaranteed royalty of $100,000. If the manufacturer sells enough products to warrant a $120,000 in royalties, all he has to give you at the end of the year is $20,000. Presumably you have already received the $100,000.

The easiest way to deal with guaranteed royalties is to have them paid quarterly. If you can have them paid monthly, that's even better. Try very hard not to have them paid at the end of the year or at the end of six months. Part of your agreement should include a mechanism for verification of sales and royalties due.

License or Sell?

I would rather license a product rather than sell it, unless I am offered an extraordinary amount of money for the invention on a final sale basis. Keep in mind that once it is sold, you are completely out of the picture. (Unless, of course, you can include a consulting agreement with the buyer.) But with a licensing deal, if sales take off, you have an opportunity to make a lot of money from your invention.

Whether to license or sell depends on how you feel about your invention. There are some inventors who want to just sell the invention and get rid of it—they do not want anything further to do with it. This is something you must decide. It also depends on how much money you need and how fast you can get it.

I know of very few companies that will buy a really good invention and pay its true price up front without batting an eye. Most companies will buy it outright only if they can get it at a very, very low price. It seems to me that those companies who buy an invention do it in order to get the inventor out of their hair. They consider inventors a nuisance, and the quicker they get him out of the way, the better.

Lawyers and Other Aids

Good lawyers can make a substantial contribution to negotiations. If they are not good, they can hinder you. I feel very strongly that it is my invention, it is my deal, it is my ball and my game, and therefore, it is my negotiation. I want the lawyer there to assist me—not to lead me, not to guide me, not to take over from me, but to assist me. I would like to bounce ideas around with him beforehand. I would like to deal with the clients people with him at my side.

In any negotiations, it is good to have backup. If you have an experienced businessman with you, particularly if he is mature and has negotiated deals, he can be just as good if not better than any lawyer. Regardless of how big your army is, remember that it's your war and that you have to call the shots.

The object of any negotiation is to conclude the deal.

This isn't the time for your lawyer to show off how smart he is. Harping on some insignificant point or changing something just to prove he is working for you can jeopardize the deal.

This is the time to conclude a deal. A good lawyer is smart enough to recognize that some "minor" detail in the deal must be kept in and some other must come out. A good lawyer will take you aside to discuss these points with you so that you understand their significance before you argue them.

Trust

In every deal there is a matter of mutual trust. There is no way in the world that you can get everything into a legal document to protect yourself completely. You want to agree on points that are mutually beneficial; that is the purpose of any kind of negotiation. If it is at all possible, try to establish those points as the basis of the relationship. It is very beneficial to establish a rapport with a potential buyer. Let him know that you can be reasonably honest with each other.

Chapter 9

Going into Business Yourself

PEOPLE WHO START THEIR OWN COMPANIES ARE EITHER VERY BRAVE OR VERY stupid. In all my experience, I have met perhaps three inventors who had enough know-how to start their own companies. I know of no one right now who has started his own company and is still with it.

Consider what you must know as an individual entrepreneur in order to start your own company. Having natural smarts is not enough. You have to have extensive experience in a number of areas—handling money, the ability to borrow money, marketing and sales, production, quality control, and dealing with lawyers.

I know very few inventors who have these capacities or enough business experience to run a business and deal with employees, much less the ability to set up a new company in the first place. I have known vice presidents of marketing in major corporations who have started their own companies and failed. They were great marketing managers in a large corporation, but they did not know enough about selling—and there is a big difference between marketing and selling.

There is a huge difference between being vice president of production and being your own foreman on a production line. When you start your own company, you often act as a foreman, as well as sweep the floor if that is necessary to save money and keep the company going. When the president of Long Island Lighting Company (LILCO) started his own company, he used to act as his own porter after everyone else had left for the day. Few people these days have that kind of dedication.

BEFORE YOU START A BUSINESS

Before you start a business, do your homework. Find out what running a company involves. For example, although some members of my workshop on the "Process Of Invention" were professionals, not one of them knew what a pro forma is. I doubt that there are many inventors who know. There are probably even fewer who know how to prepare one, particularly a start-up pro forma (see chapter 12, *The Pro Forma*). If you lack the ability to put together your own pro forma and business plan, you should not go into business yourself.

Measure carefully how "small" you have to be for a successful start. Don't let your ego get in the way of your judgment. If you can make enough of your product by hand to start selling, that's the way to start. You can always "back order" a new product. It is not the happiest situation for the customer, but it's the safest situation for you. And it's a lot better than having surplus capacity eat up a hunk of your reserves waiting for sales to catch up.

Learn from every source you can. If you still insist on being an entrepreneur, the least you can do, for your sake and for the people who depend on you (particularly your family), is to start learning. Take nothing for granted. If you're an inventor, you have reasoning power; use it to full capacity.

Never mind how people in large corporations do things. When you're a large corporation, then you too can hire the same experts. For now, learn from books and people who have applied business principles successfully to small businesses.

Conserve every penny you can. Hoard your assets. If you run short of money, you might lose the company.

Grow only when you're sure growth is essential. Capacity growth is anxiety ridden . . . but also a source of pleasure and pride.

The worst mistake you can make is running short of *capital*. Using your cash reserves and building a plant with surplus capacity in anticipation of future sales can be dangerous.

But if the situation demands it, think big. Having said all that, I must add that, if the situation demands it (double-check to make sure that the situation really demands it), start *big* "Big" is a relative term. The logic of the business, not your ego, must determine the size of the start-up.

WHY GO INTO BUSINESS?

I have done my best to discourage you from going into business yourself. If you insist on going ahead, however, this section might increase the odds for success. If you follow the suggestions, particularly if they apply to your unique situation, your chances of survival might be better.

I have mentioned that I consider anybody going into business for himself either very courageous or very foolhardy. To quote Daniel Boorstin, "The illusion of knowledge is the enemy of discovery."[1] To paraphrase that, "The illusion of know-how in starting a business can only end in failure."

In starting a business, it is absolutely essential that you delineate your areas of know-how. It cannot be emphasized or stressed too strongly:

Before you do anything, you must be honest with yourself.

List the areas that you think you know and the areas that you know you know. (The areas that you don't know could fill a library so leave them alone.)

This section covers most of the areas that are required in a business. Tick off on your list those areas that apply to the business you wish to start. Pay special attention to those areas you know nothing about. Then collect the relevant information in those areas and study them. Inadequate or misapplied experience is a guaranteed road to disaster (for example, someone in marketing thinking he can handle sales or somebody in engineering development thinking he can run the production department). Remember, be truthful to yourself about your know-how.

Self-discipline is essential to the entrepreneur. If you can't take orders or directions, you shouldn't go into business. If you can't be a self-starter, organize your time, preplan, anticipate, be prepared to work longer hours than employees, be your own porter, or most of all, be patient with customers, don't start a business.

Why do people go into business? First, for money and power—and I consider these to be reasonable motivation. So is greed. Although these motives are acceptable, they would be far better if supported by other reasons, such as wanting to create and build a new entity.

Motives make the difference between success and failure. Dig deep for your real reasons for going into business. It is disastrous to go on an ego trip that can never be satisfied. The best motivation is the inner urge to build something; money and power are means of keeping score. Sometimes there is no way of getting something done except by going into business yourself. This is particularly true if you have a new idea or a new concept or a new product. Often there is no other way to feel personally satisfied except to go into business yourself; either no one else will do what you want to do or you believe that you can do it much better than anybody else.

It is important to learn as much as you can about the principles of the major business disciplines—production, marketing, and finance—and understand thoroughly how each of these areas work. To be successful in business,

---

[1]Daniel J. Boorstin, *The Discoverers: A History of Man's Search to Know His World and Himself* (New York: Random House, 1985).

you must also understand operational areas ranging from quality control to shipping and receiving, as they apply to your enterprise.

Never stop learning. You don't have to be an expert in everything, but it helps to have some knowledge and understanding of many areas. When an inventor wants to do something badly enough, he learns how to do it!

One of the things that you must continuously be aware of is the *fallacy of trust*. When you're in business, trust your own judgment. Do not trust anyone else—consultants, lawyers, accountants, vendors, salespeople, employees. Regardless of who gives you information or advice, you are the one who is totally responsible. Listen patiently, without interrupting. Check what you hear. Absorb everything you can get. Operate on a basis of inclusion rather than exclusion because in that way you will get more to base your decision on. Use this input to make your own judgment, but always reserve the right to use or disregard any advice that is given to you.

PLANNING

If you plan properly, you can anticipate the problems that might occur and take preventive action. Don't make impulsive decisions; think about them. It might be very satisfying to bawl someone out, but does it achieve some objective or just give you ego satisfaction?

Be deliberate. Plan what you want to do and constantly keep your eye on your objectives.

When you are in business for yourself, you wear many hats. If anything goes wrong, the blame is yours. You are the one who will be held responsible by yourself, by your employees, by your investors, and most of all, by your family. It is your job to make sure that everything goes right.

When you start a business, people (particularly investors) expect you to be familiar with finances, organization, management, marketing, purchasing, production, and personnel relations. They assume that you'll be working 200 hours per week and, in your spare time, save money by being the company porter. In other words, you're expected to keep on top of every aspect of the operation.

Size of Start-up

When you start up an operation, how big should it be? How much money should you go for? The business plan, especially the pro forma, will help you find the answer to these questions and a lot of others. The suggestions in this section will enable to discover what you know and what you don't know, how big you should be when you start up, and how much money you need.

To survive in business, you must carefully control the growth of your company. Your plan should include contingency funds to cover mistakes. Don't overreach. Be safe. Be sure. Keep your expenses as low as possible. In the beginning, if you pay yourself as little as possible, you have some justification for keeping salaries low for your employees. When you are making money, be as generous as you can afford. But when every dollar counts, be stingy.

Ethics

Now to the matter of ethics. I firmly believe that you do not have to be dishonest in any business relationship. I know many people who have made it who have been very decent and fair in their business operation. People liked to work with these ethical businessmen because they could be trusted.

Implicit in the slogan "Let the buyer beware!" is that sellers are permitted to act unethically. "You weren't looking, so I put one over on you." I consider that dishonesty and totally unnecessary. Vendors should supply the very best product they possibly can. Making a product that is inexpensive does not necessarily mean that the product has to be or should be shoddy. By making an honest product less expensively than the competitor's, a seller can carve out a niche for himself in the marketplace.

Success based on the utilization of dangerous materials or on the manufacture of harmful products is unforgivable. You as the inventor know whether the materials or the product can be dangerous, and you are the one who will be held responsible for whatever happens. Pleading innocence after the fact is unacceptable.

Now I come to a more pleasant subject—the rewards of being an entrepreneur: the satisfaction of having created a corporate entity that is capable of growth. The ultimate satisfaction is that you have established a business that other people can build with you.

You end up with money, with power, with influence, but most of all, you end up with something that is even more precious—independence. You have enough to do what you want, when you want to, as you want to on a self-sustaining basis.

A BRIEF LOOK AT A PRO FORMA

I will now briefly describe some of the factors that go into the pro forma. A *pro forma* is a summary document of all the time and money aspects of your business.

Forecasting Sales. The most important aspect of your pro forma. In the beginning, you must be able to project, even if only to an approximate level, your potential sales and refine this forecast as you proceed. Orders and reorders from customers are what count. Promises don't count. In determining the sales potential of your product, remember: interest is one thing, but it's orders that make up sales.

Identify Your Market. Who are your customers? First you identify your market by industry, then by company, and finally by the individual buyer. You might find that the buyer is not necessarily the same individual or the person who makes the decision about the purchase; in other words, the purchasing agent is not always the buyer. In most cases the purchasing agent operates on the basis of specifications established by other people in the company. He is instructed to purchase a product within a particular price range; he might evaluate various products whose specifications approximate the specifications established for him. In order to make a reasonable forecast, you must know who is actually responsible for the purchase decisions in your product area.

Identify Competitive or Comparable Products. These are products that perform the same functional service as your product—*and their market.* Take into consideration function, design, and price. Don't develop a car that you propose to sell for $500, and then forecast a potential market of 20,000 cars per year for Rolls Royces. The forecast must be tailored to your product, not another product.

SIC. By identifying the industry and competitive products in your market, you have achieved an important milestone because you are now able to *establish the Standard Industrial Classifications (SIC) numbers* for your product and for competing products (see chapter 22). Use the SIC numbers to identify not only the industry as a whole (in total potential market), but also the companies in that industry (how big they are, how much they sell). An enormous amount of statistical data is available through the Department of Commerce (state and federal governments) and numerous other sources.

Research. When you start to do research, you will learn that the problem with information accumulation in the United States is that there is so much of it. There are no secrets, industrial or otherwise. There is only the amount of lead time before someone finds the same data (see sidebar).

There Are No Secrets

The story is told that during World War II, Albert Einstein wrote President Franklin Roosevelt a letter outlining the importance of the atomic research being carried on by the Germans and how that research could lead to their developing an atom bomb. He felt it imperative that the United States not only destroy the German research capacity but quickly intensify our own research to build our own bomb.

President Roosevelt called a meeting of the Joint Chiefs of Staff and reviewed Einstein's letter with them. One of the Generals quietly turned to his aide and asked, "What's atomic energy." The aide passed the question down the line until it reached a second lieutenant. The lieutenant went to the local library, looked up everything he could find on the subject, and wrote a report. The moment the general read the report, he stamped it, "top secret."

If you do secondary source research in such places as libraries, etc., you can probably find exactly what you want if you keep your eye on your objectives. If you do not, you will be swamped. As you go deeper and deeper into your subject, you will discover more and more peripheral information. I call information that is interesting, but not useful, "curiosity" information. Many questionnaires for market research include a number of superfluous questions because the person who developed the questionnaire was looking for information he had no use for. He did not ask himself the one pertinent question that he should have: "What am I going to use the information for when I get it?"

It takes a great deal of effort and time to develop a pro forma for your business. Therefore, I urge you to be as specific as you possibly can. Check your library to see whether they have a computer tie-in to any of the computer data bases. If they do, it will make it much easier for you to get the information you need—for example, determining the size of the industry as related to your particular product.

Selling Price. This is related to the price of the competing products that are functionally the same as yours. If you come up with something bigger, better, "sweeter," you will be able to charge a higher price for it, but that price will not be set without some basis. The price will be based on what people are presently paying for that particular function. Therefore, there are limitations. For example:

A wholesale distributor in Texas decided that he was not going to sell his product in the usual way. His commodities—ashtrays, cigarette lighters, lamps, salt and pepper shakers, etc.—were sold in the housewares department of five-and-dime stores. His products were standard, inexpensive products sold mostly on the basis of price. This man hired some designers and told them to review the manufacturing process by which these products were made and then redesign the products. On the basis of the redesign, he was able to sell those products for ten times the amount of the standard product because it was sold on the design, rather than its price. It cost him exactly the same to make the new ashtrays as it did the old ashtrays.

The point is that unless you are making a unique product, you will have to compete within the existing price range. Even if redesigning the product, you have to consider the existing price structure—the price set by the high and low end of the market range. You can price products made out of precious materials, such as silver or gold, differently because the materials themselves contribute to and affect the final price of the product. When a product is made from a base material, such as clay or glass, and the cost of the manufacturing process and materials are essentially stable, it is the design of the product that contributes to the price level.

Estimate the Size of Your Initial Market. Remember, what you can't reach, don't count. Your national market might be 11 billion dollars, but if you are limited to selling your product in the Bronx, your total market might be only 50 dollars. Market forecasts are made more realistically on a short-term basis than on a long-term basis because of the number of variables to consider. Making a forecast for one month is much easier than making a forecast for six months. Making a forecast for any longer than a year is not realistic. Keep your forecast in the world of reality. Keep in mind that you will be updating your forecast periodically to see how well you're doing and how closely you're following the business plan (see chapter 13).

The Pro Forma. If you do not have a computer program available, you will need standard columnar accounting paper (item section followed by 13 columns). This paper usually comes in a pad and can be purchased in most stationery stores.

The pro forma lists every item (macro and micro) that is going to cost you money or time: everything, from the plant you are going to operate to nails you might have to purchase. It includes the time when you will purchase the material and the time when the material will be used. The sales forecast is a major portion of the pro forma. It includes the time when you make sales and the time when you receive money for the sales (usually different). Some businesses operate on progress payments; for example, if you contract to build a device or machine, you would receive one-third as down payment when you got the contract, one-third upon ordering parts and materials, and one-third upon final delivery.

The pro forma will show what monies are available and when money is anticipated to be received. It is a planning document that is continually updated as you operate.

If you do not have a cushion of operating capital, you might find yourself with a lot of orders on hand, a facility to fill those orders, but not enough money to buy the materials you need to fill those orders. You're hung up; you know you're going to receive "X" number of dollars in three weeks to a month (if your customer pays on time), but your supplier won't ship materials without being paid; that is, until you've established a credit base. Cash flow is one of the areas that create crucial problems for new businesses. A proper pro forma takes this factor into account.

Chapter 10
Forecasting

THE ABILITY TO FORECAST ANYTHING IS VITAL TO THE SUCCESS AND growth of any business. Forecasting applies to many areas of business. With the pro forma, you are forecasting when someone will join your company, how much you will pay for parts, when you are going to pay for machinery, when you are going to produce product, when you are going to deliver your product, and on and on. In addition to forecasting anticipated sales and revenues from the potential market, you are forecasting profits and, most important to survival, cash flow.

To repeat a point, honest objectivity is the key to success. In forecasting, promises are as useless (and harmful) as is wishful thinking. Orders count; promised orders can be considered as long as they are realistic, but what really count are locked in orders and reorders. When you get reorders from a customer, that is reality.

INDENTIFY YOUR PRODUCT'S INDUSTRY

The first essential step in forecasting is to identify your product's place in its industry. What is it? Who makes it besides you, or who makes something similar to it? What category within the industry does it belong in? What other products out there are like yours? What are you going to be competing against that is functionally similar to your product or service?

If you have sized up your competition, you know the generic name of the product category and have identified its SIC (Standard Industrial Classifica-

98

tion) number. The SIC numbers start with two digits; each additional digit represents a more detailed identification of the industry, the company, and the product. This analysis is done by the United States Department of Commerce, Bureau of Census, and is listed in the *Census of Manufactures*. If you can't find it in your local library, look for it in the local office of the Department of Commerce.

Another reference that you might consult to identify your product is the *Thomas Register of American Manufactures*. Dun and Bradstreet publications are crammed full of important industry and company data, and they also use SIC numbers. Your state's own register of industry and products (each state has one; many major cities also have one) also can be used as a means of identifying the SIC number for your product or service. There is even an identifying category called Not Elsewhere Classified (NEC). The NEC category lists an enormous number of products from a particulr industry that are not large enough, in terms of sales and production, to warrant giving them separate SIC numbers.

In any research that you do with SIC numbers, read the directions in the source books carefully. Directions for each directory might vary, and the changes can affect the meaning of the information.

Another source of information is the *Encyclopedia of Associations*, which lists practically every active association—a pharmaceutical association, a philatelic association, a race car association, a horse breeders association. Most of these associations welcome your requests for information in their area of interest. The Petroleum Institute will gladly send you volumes of data on the petroleum industry.

Essentially you want to learn how much of your product and comparable products (in units and dollars) is made and who makes it. By using the sources discussed above, you can generally figure out how much of the product a competing company makes and how much their sales are in particular geographical areas. You can use the data to develop formulas for later use.

MARKET RESEARCH

A main objective is to learn what competitive products sell for. How big is the total market? What share of this market can you plan to capture? From the SIC data and the other sources, you can break down your market by geographical areas and decide whether you should restrict your marketing effort (at least to start with) to a particular market segment or geographical area.

One of the ways to gather pertinent data is through *market research*—going into the field and interviewing knowledgeable people. The problem is that you can get just as lost doing market research as when you do conventional (secondary source) library research. You must constantly keep in mind what you are looking for and what you are going to do with the information once you get it. In gathering information, you must beware of being side-tracked onto peripheral pathways. This type of information, although interesting, can lead you away from your objective, resulting in loss of time and direction.

It is extraordinarily easy to interview people. You call them up, identify yourself, and say you are doing a study on a particular subject. Nine out of ten times you will be able to make appointments. The problem with interviewing people is that they talk too much. Most people want to show you how much they know. Generally, you'll be looking for specific information: the prices per unit of comparable products, the price range (very important), the discount structure, and the return policy.

You might have to look in several places to get the data you need. Trade magazines and periodicals cover every area of business interests—manufacturers, representatives, pricing structures, discounts, etc. (The *Harvard Business Review* is especially valuable for management subjects).

ESTIMATING SELLING PRICE

After you have projected the total potential market for your product, your next step is to estimate the selling price of your product in relation to its quality and the price range that prevails in the industry for competing products. For example, the film industry in the United States is dominated by Eastman Kodak. The price that they sell their 35-mm film for is the top price, the *umbrella price*. Some companies might sell their film at a higher price, but most will sell it at either the same price or for less. Of course, if you provide something different or more extraordinary than Eastman provides, you can sell your film for a higher price. More often than not, the umbrella price gives you a ballpark market price for your product.

IDENTIFYING YOUR MARKET

In the first part of this forecast procedure, you learned how to identify the industry in which your product belonged. Next, you will learn how to identify your market. Who will buy your product? What industries will you sell to?

You can use SIC numbers to identify the total potential market for your product, to analyze your market by geographic area, and even to list potential customer companies. The source you use for your market research (Dun and Bradstreet, the *Thomas Register*, etc.) might or might not list the company's SIC numbers, but they do list the products that each company is producing. Often, a major company might have products in a number of SIC categories. You work back and forth on the listing. For example, if you're looking for companies that make toasters, note the companies listed that manufacture appliances; then find out whether they make toasters (if necessary, by calling them). Their major product lines will usually be listed by the names you use to identify them. For example, the *Thomas Register* would directly list the names of companies that manufacture toasters, where these companies are located, and the size of the companies. You can then estimate the position of each product in the total market for that product.

If your product is seasonal, how do the seasons affect buying? I know of a small company with excellent potential that failed because it missed the customer's buying season. The buying period was September, October, and half of November. Delivery would be in the last weeks of March and in April. Selling to the public would start in May, depending on the weather, and continue through June, July, and August. The company had purchased some machinery that did not work properly. It had to hold back sales because it was not sure it would be able to deliver the product on time. As a result, they missed the buying period for their product. They lost a whole year. It is essential to know not only the time of the buying season but also the time of the selling season.

Where are your potential customers located? How do they buy (price, service, quantity, quality, reliability, etc.)? How do they pay? This is very important for your pro forma. What is the lag time, or the time between date of purchase and date of payment? What is the lead time, or the time between orders? Who within that company makes the buying decisions?

You are not going to get the answers to all these questions from the library alone. After you have identified your customers and buyers, you might call up some of them and set up interviews with them in order to learn how they operate. When you call, try to set a specific date and time for the appointment. Dress appropriately when you go. Make up a questionnaire beforehand and be sure to take notes. You don't need many interviews to get an overall view of industry. Find the appropriate industry association, then call to get the name of a member who is within your geographic area. Ask the person you interview whether they can recommend someone else who can supply the information you're looking for. As you go from one person to the next, ask each of them who else they recommend.

What you are looking for is a consensus. All this information is essential to the construction of your pro forma; for example, the importance of the seasonal factors. It is useless to forecast and include in your pro forma that you will be ready to sell your product in December if nobody wants to buy it in December.

SELLING YOUR PRODUCT

One of the questions you must explore is who sells your product. Do you sell it? Do your salesmen sell it? Do you contact manufacturers' representatives? How many people do you need to sell your product? How is selling done in the rest of the industry?

These are the kinds of questions you should ask the people you interview. How do they buy? Do they buy directly from the manufacturing company? Do they buy from a manufacturer's representative or from a distributor? How are they serviced? In other words, what are the channels of distribution in your industry? All of these questions need answers.

Each fact that you collect provides you with a means of formulating information for your pro forma. For example, if yours is a single product line, you might have a serious problem. It is very difficult to justify the cost of a sales force when you have only one product in your product line. By evaluating the data you accumulate, you will decide whether or not to use a manufacturer's representative. Regardless of how you decide to sell, you should be able to forecast your sales costs for your pro forma.

In your research, you are looking for a breakdown of the geographical selling areas and the size of each area. You want to determine the effective number of sales calls required per day (week, month) per person within the area. If your potential customers are spread all over the map, you might have a problem; every call that your salesman makes must be very effective because it costs so much to go from one potential customer to the next. Some of the major companies on the West Coast supply their salesmen with planes to get them from place to place. For this category, you want to know how much to include for travel expenses in the selling cost.

Next, you have to estimate the number of units each of your customers might purchase from you and your competitors. During your research interviews you might ask buyers how much of any particular product they buy. This is a case of talking about one thing, while looking for information about another. It is a legitimate way of conducting an interview, but be careful not to outsmart yourself. Here you'd like to learn how many units the buyer already has on order from other sources, and how many units he can order from you at one time. In other words, what is the normal size of the orders this buyer generally places? Then you discuss your product with other potential customers to get an estimate of the amount of units they might purchase.

Now you can determine the purchase pattern: what the usage is, what the function is, what the price is. Finally you can forecast how much these customers might purchase and when. This includes data on quantity prices, introductory and regular prices, and discounts requested and offered.

Before you put together your questionnaire, think about what you want to do with the information you will obtain. Remember, you are not just looking for information in relation to sizes, but also patterns. You need that information for your business plan. It will show your potential investor how well you know your industry, your market, your business. You want as many numbers as you can possibly get. Think out your questions before you ask them. Try them out on someone else to make sure they understand the meaning of the questions. People do not always understand a question as you understand it. Make sure that the words that you are using have the same meaning to them as they have to you.

YOUR FORECAST

To recap: what you can't reach, don't count. If you're selling in a particular area because that is the only area you can reach, then so be it, that's the area you count. This does not necessarily mean a geographic area. It might mean selling your product to a very specific industrial area (using "industrial" loosely). The customer industry you're selling to might be very specific, but can be geographically widespread. You count the number of customers in a specific industrial category. Your forecast includes:

☐ The industry your product belongs to
☐ The market you sell to
☐ The individual companies you sell to, their size, and their location
☐ The number of customers you can realistically reach and when you can reach them
☐ The number of units you might sell to each customer
☐ When you will sell and in what quantities
☐ The dollar value of your sales
☐ The probable dates of customer payment

This list implies that you have forecast what your unit sales will be in relation to various price levels—how much you are going to sell one unit for, ten units for, 100 units for—and what quantity lots you are going to offer your customers. I urge you to carefully calculate the discount structure and what the price is per unit for quantity purchases. You can offer a price break to your customers only after you have learned how they buy from other people. Some customers will buy your product only in quantity. Presumably, your unit price will be different for 10 units and 100 units because your cost per unit will vary in relation to the number of units sold per order.

Always remember, short-term forecasting is more reliable than long term forecasting. The shorter the period covered, the more accurate the forecast. To me, "long term" means a year. The forecast in your pro forma should be updated periodically during the year. The forecast is based on target figures; updating with actual figures.

There are a number of computer programs designed for forecasting. Be careful that the one you adopt fits your needs.

You can base your forecast on data provided by salesmen. Take their sales estimates with a grain of salt, however.

In working with sales estimates, consider three types: best case, worst case, and most probable. For a start-up operation, which is probably what yours is going to be, first determine your total market, then estimate your share of that market. It might be that you are going to have to expand your share of the market to break even or even in order to make it. But if you expand your market, you are implying that you are expanding your expenses to reach that market. So, you might have to go back and forth with your estimates to achieve a balance. Your best forecast will be based on a list of the customers you can reach and on an estimate of their purchases by units and dollars.

Forecasts are educated guesses at best. If you let wishful thinking prevail over reality, you're asking for trouble. Make your estimates realistic.

Chapter 11
Pricing Policy: An Overview

UNDERSTANDING PRICING WILL, AT THE VERY LEAST, CONTRIBUTE TO A MORE professional pro forma and, at best, enhance the prospects for profits. This chapter gives an overview of pricing policies and methods.

A *pricing policy* establishes the guidelines used to determine prices at various levels of business activity. Pricing is one of the tools used in implementing an overall marketing strategy that covers new product introduction, competition, general and specific business conditions, and government regulations. The price of a product or service is not the primary basis for a purchase decision. More often than not it is the third reason; the first reason is reliability (both of the seller and of the product), and the second reason is service (something goes wrong, the buyer is confident that you will back up your product). However, no one ever made money by selling at a loss.

TYPES OF PRICING

When you introduce a new product, try to include quick recovery of your development costs in the price. This initial price can serve as the basis for a future discount structure. If this is inappropriate for whatever reason, such as competition, at least include recovery as part of your price planning. Don't assume that you'll make it up in volume.

Competitive Pricing

Your prices will be related to the prices of competing products. Regardless of how you set your prices, however, never set them below cost.

There is only one exception to that rule as far as I am concerned: if you have a large inventory of product sitting in the warehouse doing nothing. Rather than dumping it to get rid of it, sell it for whatever price you can to get some of your money back. Even this move must be made cautiously because dumping can hurt any other products you might have on the market.

The only other possible reason for setting prices below cost is quick market entry at the largest possible volume. This is a very dangerous move. Raising prices is a lot more difficult than lowering them. If you plan to use this strategy, remember to count the difference (the amount below cost) in your negative cash flow.

Psychological Pricing

When you price psychologically, you try to sell your product on an emotional rather than a rational basis. A price of $.99 rather than $1.00 implies a psychological benefit; the buyer thinks he's getting a bargain.

It works in the opposite direction too. Often consumers feel that the higher the price, the better the product. (The sidebar stories illustrate this point.)

I suppose some brilliant psychologist can explain people's purchasing suspicions in scientific terms. Personally, I think consumers around the world have experienced "Buyer Beware," and therefore have a tendency to react according to their own myths, such as the more it costs, the better it is, or you can't get anything for nothing.

Traditional Pricing

Traditional pricing is based on customer expectations. For many years you couldn't price a chocolate bar for more than five cents because that's what a Hershey bar cost and that was the price people expected to pay for a chocolate bar. Chewing gum fell into the same category of consumer price expectation. With chewing gum, however, the profit margin was so generous that they did not have to worry about raising the price.

To compensate for this, the manufacturer would change the package and the size of the package, but never the price. For a long time, they made the candy bars smaller and smaller, but they didn't change the price. It was not until recent years that the psychological pricing related to these products was overcome.

Prestige Pricing

Prestige pricing is based on high customer expectations, not merely the quality of the product. You might very well end up with a quality product,

The Higher the Price . . .

An inventor that I know developed a method of coloring soft lenses that made it possible for the wearer to appear as if the color of his eyes had changed. The effect and coloration were so natural that it would take an expert to discern that the color was the result of a soft lens. Wearers could literally change the color of their eyes to fit their mood.

The way the story was told to me, the manufacturer introduced the product to the marketplace at a low nominal price in anticipation that the low price (around $150.00) would attract users to take a chance and try the product. After all, the coloration was just another means of satisfying an already ego-sensitive market. Therefore, it was reasoned, any additional cost to the consumer would make acceptance more difficult. Sales were just so so. Marketing assumed all sorts of reasons for the slow consumer acceptance.

As it happened, a new president came aboard at about this time and, after reviewing company marketing strategies and products, suggested that the price of the colored soft lenses be tripled to $450.00, accompanied by a proper promotional campaign. Needless to say, the product took off.

*****

In another story, a management consultant was called in by a shoe manufacturer who sold his product through his own chain of shoe stores. He wanted a general review of his operation with the primary objective being "to raise the consumers perception of the brand's prestige level, thereby increasing prices and profits." The consultant visited several of the stores, all of which were located in excellent neighborhoods, and then had the manufacturer carry out the following marketing experiment in one of his stores.

He had one of the clerks prominently display two pair of shoes in the store window. Both pair were exactly alike . . . absolutely no differences. Both were the same color, size, style, and product number, and both pairs ordinarily sold for exactly the same price of $40.00. Although placed side by side in the window, however, he had one pair show a price tag of $40.00 and the second pair show a price tag of $80.00. The sales clerks were instructed to tell any inquiring customer that both pair of shoes were exactly alike even to the extent of comparing product numbers.

You guessed it. Nearly every single customer insisted on taking the higher priced shoes. Convinced that the higher price somehow made for a better shoe and that the sales clerk was somehow withholding something.

but that is not the reason you are paying such an exorbitant price for it. The high price of a Mercedes, for instance, was the result of a deliberate marketing decision to make the car a prestige product.

Some people don't really care what they pay for some products; a low price would reduce the prestige value of owning that product. Some companies use price as a means of product differentiation; they set different price levels for essentially the same product in a product line.

For example, a famous watch company sells a number of different watches. The watch that sold for approximately $55 to $99 at the low end of the range was practically the same as the watch that sold for up to $10,000 at the high end of the range. The only difference was the case and the hand. When you sent a watch back for repairs, the company took the movement out of the case, threw it away, and put another one in. It was less expensive to replace the movement than to repair it.

Shoes, men's suits, and other personal items are often subject to prestige pricing. The products are sold in a prestige location or brand name outlets. Not too long ago, there was a lot of publicity about a men's suit being sold by Brooks Brothers and Saks Fifth Avenue at three or four times what it sold for at some bargain-type stores. Cosmetics are typical examples of prestige pricing. There is a plant in metropolitan New York that makes many of the cosmetics sold by major cosmetic companies. The plant makes big batches of the cosmetics and packages them to the specifications of any distributor. The cosmetics are essentially the same, but they are named and packaged differently for each distributor and sold at widely different prices.

Professional Pricing

Doctors, consultants, and lawyers at one time observed fee schedules set by their professional associations. Many associations in the past have achieved notoriety for this practice.

Loss-Leader Pricing

Loss-leader pricing is the method of pricing a product below its market value, but not at a loss. The objective is to lure customers into the store in the expectation of purchasing the item at a bargain price. The merchant hopes that, once inside, they will buy other products that are more profitable. Indeed, the consumer will sometimes find that the prices of other items in the store are either at full list price or have been increased above list. Because the consumer, once in the store, has little opportunity to compare the prices with those of other establishments, the probability of the consumer purchasing other products at a much higher price is in the store's favor. The loss in revenue resulting from the price differential of the loss leader can be considered advertising expense. In many cases, however, this so-called "loss" is insignificant in comparison to the profit generated by the purchase of the higher priced items.

Special Event Pricing

Special events provide the seller opportunities to generate sales at prices that are lower than normal. Hence you have company anniversary sales, holiday sales, trade shows, etc.

Superficial Discounting

Deceptive markdowns are unethical. This happens when a seller places a phony price tag of $100 on a product that truly lists for $59, then offers it as a bargain at $59 (reduced from $100). It's superficial discounting—and dishonest.

Product Improvement or Breakthrough Production Pricing

Value engineering provides a basis for breakthrough pricing. By chance and by brilliance, you might find a way of making your product much less expensively than any competitor without impairing the product's function or aesthetic value. You have a breakthrough.

Many years ago, a pump manufacturer tore the entire submersible pump market completely apart. They made a submersible pump out of cast teflon. The manufacturing process was so much cheaper than brass casting that they were able to sell their pumps at well below the market price of competing pumps. They used the established market price as an umbrella for their price. They made a handsome profit because of technological improvement and value engineering.

A technological value-added breakthrough can be used to expand your market share before competition catches up. It is easier to hang onto an increased share of market than to acquire it in the first place.

Trade Discounts

You can offer many types of discounts (incentive discounts, advertising discounts, etc.) to many types of customers, such as distributors, chain stores, and manufacturers' representatives. The discounts are inducements to buy your product without changing the base price of the product. You want the customers to move your product. *Advertisting discounts* represent a means of buying advertising without an out-of-pocket expenditure; the payment comes out of the lowered cost of the purchase. *Quantity discounting* offers different price levels for different quantities of product purchased. You also can offer *cash discounts*; for example, "2-10" or "1-10 net 30" means if the buyer pays your bill within 10 days, he can deduct 2 percent of the bill, but if he pays 30 days or more later, he must pay the full amount of the bill. Cash discounts are also used as a means of selling a product without lowering your price.

Factors

Because cash flow is so important to the survival of a company, use any legitimate practice to get paid as quickly as possible. Let me give you an example of the kind of thing you might be faced with.

Suppose you sell your product to a major department store. They now owe you $100,000, but you know that you won't be paid for at least 60 to 90 days. You need your money right now. A *factor* (an individual or company with liquid funds) will give you money immediately, using your receivables as collateral.

Factors operate somewhat differently in different parts of the country. Many states have regulations as to the limit of interest a factor can charge. Banks also fund receivables but usually demand that you have a track record before they'll consider it.

In essence, a factor will provide you with up to 80 percent of the value of the receivables and charge you a monthly or semimonthly interest fee for the money. These conditions vary considerably. Check things out very carefully before you get involved with a factor. Try to make any kind of reasonable deal with your customers for quick payment before going to a factor.

Cash Discounts

Cash discounts are, of course, also used as a means of selling product without lowering your price.

Seasonal Discounts

Seasonal discounts can be used in two ways. It can be a means of stimulating sales in slack periods, or it can be a good excuse for having a sale.

Allowances

Allowances provide a means of selling a product without reducing the price by taking back a trade-in. For example, when you buy a new car, you can trade in your old one. In a situation like that, the buyer suffers in two ways: a trade-in is usually accepted at a figure that is far below its market value, and the car bought is priced at its highest level. The seller ends up doing well on both counts.

More often than not, trade-ins can be considered mathematical sleight of hand. The consumer would usually do much better if he sold the trade-in item himself, then negotiated the price of the new item.

Geographic Pricing

Geographic pricing is usually based on shipping costs. Sometimes it is based on how much it would cost you to get somebody out there to do a job.

For example, suppose you are dealing with a product, such as a heavy machine, that requires application engineering. The customer buys it, but you have to set it up so that he can use it. You must send engineers to his plant to make sure that the setup is done correctly and that the machine works. This cost is reflected in the price.

Point-of-Origin Pricing

Point-of-origin pricing generally includes factory price plus cost of shipping from factory to customer destination. This is generally known as *F.O.B. Factory*.

PRICING METHODS

The formula that is used to establish selling price is determined by product cost. This includes *all* the costs pertaining to the product—materials, labor, manufacturing, marketing, sales, advertising, general and administrative, etc—and, equally as important, a predetermined and desired profit margin.

When talking about product costs here is something to think about. Many companies are lazy, and some simply don't know on a day-to-day, month-to-month, or even year-to-year basis what their product costs are. I remember a company that had originally estimated the cost of manufacturing its product to be about four cents per unit. Due to breakdowns in the machinery and difficulties in production methodology, however, the number of finished product rejects increased extraordinarily, necessitating hiring additional quality control people. These and other factors were never taken into consideration. The company never knew what its actual costs were. By the time the company found out that its unit cost was between 15 and 18 cents, it was too late. They ran out of money and failed.

To reiterate, product costs consist of both fixed and variable costs. The *fixed costs* includes office and administrative payroll, rent and utilities, facilities and service, etc. The *variable costs* include the costs (material and labor) incurred in manufacturing the product—in other words, the total cost of the product by the time it leaves the plant. Include shipping costs if you have to pay them.

Cost Plus Pricing

Cost plus pricing is used for nonstandard, nonproduction products, usually by companies either with no experience in making the product or by comanies whose product requires application engineering. The cost of building or installation can vary with each job.

When you utilize anybody's people, you have to pay for them. If a buyer uses your people, the buyer has to pay you for them. When a vendor supplies application engineering as part of the job, he is essentially guaranteeing the customer that when the job is finished, the customer is going to have something that works.

You charge the cost of the job plus a percentage add-on of usually 15 percent. This add-on is applied to any materials or products purchased for the client's project.

Markup Pricing

Markup pricing is generally used by retailers. With markup pricing, the purchase price of an item is used as a base, then a predetermined markup is added (usually related to the type of business). The percent of the markup is determined by the type of product, the retailer's overhead cost, and such factors as customer price expectations and customer demand. Pricing the product high or low, depending on customer demand, is rather tricky and must be monitored very closely. If there is little customer demand, the price is lowered. If the demand is high, price is also set higher. In either case, the product should never be sold below cost.

Pricing by Market

Another way of pricing is based on *market segments*—that is, set different prices for different markets, different prices for different channels of distribution, different prices for different designs of essentially the same product. For example, a manufacturer might sell one of its coffee pots through a retail outlet at one price, yet sell essentially the same coffee pot, with a slightly different design, at another price through a catalog.

Competitive Pricing

Competitive pricing can be used when short-term costs and profit returns are of secondary importance. Either you plan to establish a foothold in a certain market, and stay in that market, or you want to protect your share of an existing market that's being challenged by a competitor. Your market share is at stake, and you must maintain competitive prices. For example, the Crazy Eddie chain operates on the advertised basis that they will meet any price of any competitor as advertised. I once saved myself several hundred dollars by finding a competitive ad in the paper for the same item at a lower price. Competitive pricing can also be used to make inroads into a Competitor's territory.

In competitive pricing, lowering the price of the product is not the only means of gaining an edge, nor is it necessarily essential. The concept of competitive pricing takes into consideration offering the customer such things as more service, a greater advertising allowance, absorbing the shipping costs, delayed invoicing, etc. The ways of competitive pricing are as many as the imagination. But always remember . . . although you might not be lowering the price of the product itself, you are increasing your cost of the product by anything you offer. This cost was usually not considered when the price of the product was first established.

Transfer Pricing

Transfer pricing is the price you charge when you are selling a product from one division to another division in the same company. I know of instances when the division buying the product did not know that the product it was buying was made by another division in the same company. You can have different prices for two different customers in the same region as long as these customers are not competitive. Generally speaking, it is illegal to discriminate in setting prices. In other words, if you sell to General Electric at a certain price or discount structure, you must offer other companies the same price or discount structures.

SETTING PRICES

There are about as many ways to set a price on products to be sold as there are products. The most important consideration in establishing any price is to make sure that when you sell, you make a profit (see sidebar).

One of the most popular methods of setting prices is based on *determining the factory costs* (materials and direct labor) *and using a multiple*. The multiple varies from company to company, depending on the pricing objectives. The multiple can range from two to eight times factory costs. The difficulty is accurately establishing factory costs.

Another method is based on *determining total operating costs*, including factory, general and administrative, and any other costs that might occur. These total costs are then divided into the total number of units produced to yield a unit cost. Then a multiple is applied or a predetermined percentage is added onto the cost.

Add One Percent

I remember asking my father how he set prices. He responded, "It's very easy. I add one percent to anything I buy and that's the price."

"Pop," I said, "That's not very much. How can you make a living?"

"I make out okay, I'm not greedy. One percent is enough for me," he replied.

"It sure doesn't seem like much. How does it work?"

He looked at me with a slight smile and said, "Well, if I buy something for a dollar, I sell it for two . . . one percent!"

A third method is based on *determining the average or acceptable price* the competition is charging for the product in the marketplace and using that as a measure. When using this method, it is wise to determine your costs before you jump into the market. Many companies find out the hard way that costs are higher than anticipated.

Many companies deliberately set their multiple at a higher that usual level, even though this means that the consumer price might be higher that the prices presently acceptable. They will then use the difference to support a higher than usual advertising budget. This method sometimes lends itself to the introduction of a new product. After the product is established, the multiple is reduced and so is the advertising budget.

In order not to sell below cost, you must know your costs. Any kind of profit is better than no profit

It makes very little difference if you're setting a price for services, industrial products (including heavy machinery), research and development projects, products requiring application engineering, institutional products, consumer products, or anything else. The first requirement is to determine costs, either by actual costs per unit or actual time spent doing the job. When actual costs or time are not yet known, you can make an educated guess by reducing the job or product to its basic elements, then adding the costs for each element to determine the total cost of the product. It's a dangerous practice to set a price by pulling a figure out of the air.

When you set a price for a product or service that requires a substantial outlay of money prior to its completion, provide yourself with a safety net. Insist on receiving one-third of the price upon starting the job, one-third when the materials are delivered, and one-third upon completion. There are many variations of this method, but all have the same objective: if something goes wrong, you will at least recover your costs.

This overview of pricing discusses many of the areas pertaining to pricing, but there are many more. A smattering of knowledge can sometimes be disastrous. Before you set a price on your product or service, study the area thoroughly.

Chapter 12
The Pro Forma

THE PRO FORMA IS A SUMMARY DOCUMENT. EACH LINE IN THE PRO FORMA summarizes the work sheets used to calculate the data for the line. After the pro forma is completed, a summary sheet is prepared as the first page that lists each major area and the data pertinent to that area.

The *layout of the pro forma* is as follows: major subject areas are listed in the left column, subsidiary subject areas pertinent to minor areas are indented and listed beneath each major area. Each of the next columns represents one month, either by a number (1 to 12) or by the month's name. The last column has the total for the data in each row across the page. Data are added to a line only for those months in which activity occurs. (See samples of pro formas in appendix B).

I have also found it extremely helpful to construct *timing flowcharts* (see sample in appendix B). This chart lays out in calendar time (by weeks) the events that are expected and planned to take place during plant setup prior to real production. It lists in detail all the equipment that needs to be purchased, the expected arrival time of each piece, and the time required for installation. It also lists the time when plant personnel are expected to come aboard. The chart in appendix B is really a summarization of activity. Each area was listed and reviewed and then relisted until both the timing and items were as accurate as possible.

The pro forma and the business plan can cover a large number of subjects. This section will cover the following areas:

Administration	Contingency
Advertising and promotion	Consultants
Packaging design	Debt maintenance
Selling costs	Production personnel
Facilities and services	Variable costs
Accounting	Capital equipment
Legal costs	Sales
Maintenance services	Summary sheet
Miscellaneous	

These areas are not listed in order of importance nor are they all the subject areas that can be used. It is up to you to determine the subject headings pertinent to your needs and the business you are setting up. Remember, *the primary purpose of a pro forma is communication*, not only to yourself but also to potential investors. Use only those areas that are relevant to your business.

One of the major mistakes that entrepreneurs (particularly engineering and new product people) make when starting their own businesses is that they take on too many jobs themselves. They are not supermen; they are human beings with all the shortcomings of human beings. I firmly believe that if you plan your job properly, you should be able to do it successfully and still have a life beyond the business you are starting.

ADMINISTRATION

The first subject area in the pro forma is administration. Administration includes president, vice president of marketing, chief engineer, office manager, typist, and travel and entertainment. In addition, it includes any personnel that operate as part of the administrative function—secretary, bookkeeper, file clerk, a "go-fer" or assistant, plus other functions you consider necessary to administer your company. The most important person(s) in your office is your secretary/bookkeeper, not you. You have the ideas and the gumption to start the business, but the person who keeps detailed records and takes care of correspondence can be more important than the president of the company.

Although most start-up and small companies cannot afford to support a market research function, it too, belongs in this category as a subfunction. My recommendation is to add it the moment it's economically feasible. A good market researcher can, with a minimum of budget, provide you with invaluable operational information such as customer identification, sales analysis, and secondary data sources. When you get the money, a market researcher can oversee your primary research as it is carried out by an outside market research firm.

ADVERTISING AND PROMOTION

The advertising and promotion area includes trade shows, advertising production makeup (copy, pictures, TV programs, etc.), media (TV, radio, communications, publications, etc.), sell sheets, and promotion.

Communication is an extremely important factor in any business. The communication that flows back and forth between you and the marketplace, even if you are only a small business, is vital to your business. You must optimize your ability to keep track of what is going and your ability to react to it in time.

PACKAGING DESIGN

If you have a product line, you want a design that will identify your product or company and carry over to tie in all the products in the line. Whether the design is done by you or an industrial designer is something that you will have to decide. However, beware of conceit. You are probably not the best designer in the world; even if you think that your design is absolutely gorgeous, the design might not be acceptable to the consumer.

For example, my colleagues and I designed a product and a package that, when exhibited, could have won a prize in an art show. When we sold it and put it in a store for test marketing, we (its creators) walked around the store several times before we found it. Our beautiful package was in the right product area, but we just couldn't find it. It was lost, camouflaged by the other products. The product that caught our eye was the one with the most blatantly bad design. It had two colors—yellow and green. The package practically shouted, "Here I am! Buy me!" Ours was beautiful, but you couldn't detect it. We had to go back to the drawing board and start all over again—to design it so that people could see what we had to sell.

SELLING COSTS

Selling costs include shipping costs and commissions that have to be paid. As you work on a pro forma, you are going to go back and forth from line to line, transferring data from work sheets to pro forma, etc. You will be making corrections and changes for each line. You might also find it necessary to change your formulas and calculations for some lines. You can't enter sales commissions until you know how much you are going to sell. You can't enter shipping costs until you know where you're going to ship your product. The point is, as you gather information and find, through your research or by deductive reasoning, that you must refine your data, you alter the appropriate formulas, calculations, and lines to conform to the new information.

FACILITIES AND SERVICES

The facilities and services area lists rent, heat, power and light, and telephones each on a separate line of the pro forma. If you are using power for purposes other than heating, it is treated separately. It might be that the electric power is consumed by a large outdoor advertising sign; in which case, the cost of the power consumed by the sign should show up as part of your advertising budget. Or, for example, it might be part of your production needs.

For instance, in the manufacture of a certain product, I had to use continuous action microwave ovens, monster ovens that drew enormous amounts of power. The cost of power used by these machines came under the heading of "Variable Production Costs."

Add lines for office supplies and postage. If your office copier is leased or rented, list it on a separate line. Truck and truck maintenance costs also require separate lines as well as a subheading for fuel.

Add a line for insurance. Insurance might include general, liability, plate glass, and, most important of all, product liability insurance. It is almost impossible to run a company these days without product liability insurance. As of this writing, many insurance companies are either reluctant to or will no longer sell product liability insurance, particularly for a new product.

ACCOUNTING

If your company has investors, they will want to have a certified accounting of how the company spends the money. Every dime spent must be accounted for. If you work with investors, you must not only report to them how the operation generally is going, but you also must report the company's financial condition in great detail.

My method of operation is based on inclusion rather than exclusion. By taking investors into my confidence and seeking their advice, I have found that I am far better off than by postponing troublesome information.

LEGAL COSTS

Legal costs involve three subheadings: patent counsel, general counsel, and possibly licensing counsel.

MAINTENANCE SERVICES

Maintenance services includes costs of items required for the maintenance of the plant. These can include soap, mops, etc., as well as other cleaning and repair supplies.

MISCELLANEOUS

Miscellaneous is a heading for a catch-all area. It covers items that should be included in the pro forma but do not belong in the other lines.

CONTINGENCY

You can never be sure that the costs you estimated are going to be as predicted, particularly for a start-up situation. It is a good practice to leave yourself a safety margin for mistakes—a contingency line. For example, you might originally estimate that your telephone costs will be $75 per month; in actuality, they might come to $300 per month. This is not an unrealistic deviation because you might make an exceptional number of calls during setup. You also might find that your heat costs much more than you estimated because the building is not insulated properly.

On the other hand, sometimes you are lucky; the actual costs for some area might prove to be less than you estimated, and you have a surplus. Put that money immediately into a contingency fund as a reserve for future needs. I usually add 10 percent to 20 percent of a major area's expenses (depending on the particular area) as contingency. For example, for facilities and services, the total expenses might vary each month. Therefore, because the contingency portion is a fixed percentage of the total expense, it too will vary each month.

CONSULTANTS

Don't be ashamed to recognize your ignorance in certain areas. Seek help. When hiring a consultant of any kind, however, do not follow advice simply because you believe someone is an expert. Use your own judgment. Following advice blindly can be very costly if it is wrong, and many times experts are wrong. Your total overview of your situation enables you to better judge the value of the narrow view of an advisor.

Consultants cost from $200 per day to $2,500 per day. Some consulting firms hire out their juniors at $1,300 per day. Seniors, or partners or directors, generally charge $1,500 to $2,500 per day. Lawyers operate at up to $250 per hour.

This brings up a very touchy subject about consultants, lawyers, accountants, and anyone else you might hire. *Find out in advance exactly how much they will charge you.* You have a right to know (and certainly should inquire) how much time they put in on your job; what their per diem or hourly rate is; the time and hourly rate for any assistants, associates, or clerical help; and any expenses charged to you. In other words, demand a detailed breakdown of all charges to you and make sure to review them as they come in. Do not wait. *If you delay, the assumption is that the charges are acceptable.* Therefore, if necessary, question them immediately. List the consultants and type each on a separate line (mechanical, plastic, electronics, etc.).

When dealing with lawyers (even your own), one of the worst mistakes that you can possibly make is signing anything that he (or anyone else) gives you without reading it and understanding it completely. Know what you're committing yourself to.

This subject area also includes laboratory and testing, which reflects the cost of having your product tested by an independent laboratory. (These tests are sometimes necessary to convince potential investors, customers, insurance companies, or government agencies that your product functions as stated by you and is safe.)

DEBT MAINTENANCE

If you are successful in business, the odds are that you are going to owe a lot of money. When you borrow money, it must be repaid by the company within a specified period of time at a specific rate of interest. Each long-term or short-term loan takes a separate line. Fees and taxes are entered on separate lines.

Fees represent what a state might charge you to operate within its confines. For example, if you want to sell fertilizer within the state, you must be *licensed*, or have the approval of the Department of Agriculture of that particular state, in order to sell it. Florida used to require the seller to post a $1,000 bond and charge a fee of $250 in order to operate in that state. Nearly every state has some sort of fee structure. It's an important line, especially if you operate in various states.

License and *registration fees* are entered on separate lines under the Debt Maintenance heading.

Taxes on the pro forma are differentiated from fees and also are entered on a separate line.

Estimate *payroll taxes* after you decide how many people you are going to employ and how much you are going to pay them. Generally speaking, you can estimate that 15 percent to 20 percent of your payroll will go for payroll taxes. This estimated rate can be obtained from other businessmen in your product area.

Corporate taxes and other such taxes are entered on separate lines. Your accountant should provide these figures. You should be able to use his figures in your planning to estimate what the total corporate tax will be after all expenses are paid. The primary purpose is to have a guesstimate of how much of that income you can keep and how much of it you have to turn over to Uncle Sam.

PRODUCTION PERSONNEL

Under Production Personnel, list the plant manager and, on separate lines, the production personnel by function. Some of the people you hire might perform several functions. Production personnel will also include: (1) a quality control supervisor and quality control assistants, (2) shipping and receiving personnel, and (3) trouble shooters who are specially trained personnel who can help in areas that require additional assistance.

Review every function of production to determine who will do what, when it will be started, how long it is going to take, and how much it is going to cost for that particular individual on an annual, monthly, or weekly basis. The cost calculation will be done on a work sheet that indicates how you calculated the dollar or unit number that you put down as a monthly figure in the pro forma. If you have two quality control assistants and those assistants each earning $800 per month, the total amount of $1,600 is entered on the line for the months when both are working.

Consider for a moment, however, that you are starting up. You might first hire your quality control supervisor; then, when your production has increased, you hire a second person. When your production and sales have increased further, you hire a third person. All of these people are listed, but their cost (monthly salary) is listed on the pro forma during the month that each starts work. These categories will vary according to the particular needs of your company and your product.

VARIABLE COSTS

On your work sheet, list every material and ingredient that you will use in the manufacture of your product (even if it is aspirin for the boss). For the pro forma itself, unless the cost of each item is substantial, you will probably combine several items into either the line for materials or the line for ingredients. Certainly, as part of the backup information for the pro forma, you will list every single material and ingredient that goes into your product. The quantities of materials and ingredients and their dollar value listed in the pro forma reflect your requirements based on the sales production needs forecast.

Now, a caution. Sometimes in a start-up operation you might have proprietary information or ingredients in your particular product that you do not want people to know about. Under those circumstances, you do not submit the work sheets; you just include them under the heading of ingredients or materials.

It might be necessary to explain to the people to whom you are submitting the pro forma that it is proprietary information. The loss of proprietary information can lead to the loss of lead time. Essentially, all you have is lead time. Once you hit the market, there are companies capable of reproducing your product because they have your model to work with. By giving them the proprietary information, you substantially reduce the time it will take them to copy your product.

CAPITAL EQUIPMENT

Under Capital Equipment, list every piece of equipment that you need. Capital equipment is primarily, but not necessarily, your production equipment: desks, chairs, press, lathe, dies, plates, mixers, motors, controls, fittings, fixtures, tables, cabinets, and all the tools that must be purchased, down to the last screwdriver. Some of these items can be listed under perishable tools and parts because they are breakable or can be used up. List office furniture and equipment separately. List general equipment such as scales, compressors, and a forklift.

You might be renting a building. You start with an empty room with only four walls, and now you have to set up a plant. You might have to put up some walls and platforms; you might need electrical contracting, plumbing, carpentry. List each item like this separately under "Leasehold Improvements."

Inadequate attention to this area of the pro forma can cripple your chances of success. You are entering costs and prices for equipment that you have researched. These prices can change substantially, usually going higher by the time you are ready to start operating. For example, you might estimate $10,000 for a mixer, but by the time you get the money from your investors, six months have passed and the price has doubled.

Try to anticipate capital-equipment price increases. If it represents a substantial part of your capital needs, find out what the price history of the equipment has been in the last year or so—how frequently has the price gone up and what is the probability of future price increases? Consider the general economic environment, particularly how the area in which this industry operates will be affected. In estimating what the equipment will cost when you are ready to start, give yourself plenty of lead time because there is always slippage.

There has never been a single project that I was involved in where there wasn't slippage. There is always some factor that is not taken into consideration. Some vendor does not make delivery on the promised date, or an introduction to a potential investor does not take place. There is always slippage. Build in an allowance for slippage to protect yourself—in particular, for the prices you might have to pay. Don't forget your contingency line, but there is a limit to how much you can include in it.

SALES

Based on your forecast, list your sales in the pro forma by product, with a sublist of sales by salesmen, territory, manufacturer's representative, chains, house accounts, private label, etc. List the customers and the potential sales from each as well as the approximate date of the sale, then add slippage. Enter the anticipated time of payment for each listed customer.

It has been rumored that many department stores throughout the United States make it a practice not to pay their vendors for 30, 60, or 90 days after receipt of the goods. Some vendors believe (without any tangible proof) that there is a very deliberate policy on the part of the department stores and chains to place the withheld money due vendors in a money market account and thereby make money on the vendors' money. The dollar amounts can be very substantial because there are many vendors. This possibility, if it occurs, should be anticipated in entering the time of payment in the pro forma.

SUMMARY SHEET

The summary sheet becomes your profit-and-loss statement. The summary sheet lists each of the major headings and the dollars that apply to each: revenues (as income), expenses (fixed and variable). To obtain your profit-and-loss lines, deduct total expenditures from revenues. Enter capital expenditures as a separate line. To determine cash flow, deduct capital expenditures from your profit or add capital expenditures to your loss.

The most important line of the pro forma is your cumulative cash flow, which determines how much money you will need to survive.

To determine the cumulative cash flow:

1. For the first month, the total of your loss and capital expenditures equals your cash requirements for that month.
2. For the second month, add your loss to your capital expenditures (if any) to the cash requirements of the first month to obtain your cumulative cash flow for the second month.
2. For the third month, should there be a profit, deduct that profit from the previous months' cash flow to indicate the cumulative cash flow for the third month. (See example in appendix B.)

I recommend making up two pro formas, one for yourself and one for your investors. Now, I don't consider this suggestion unethical. It depends on where and how you get your money. For example, if you want to pick up a piece of equipment from a junkyard and spend your own time fixing it up and making it work, that's your prerogative. Investors do not like to take chances, however. They want to be assured that you are going to buy a piece of equipment that's going to do the job, preferably a new piece of equipment. Items like forklifts or trucks don't have to be new. You can indicate that you can save a lot of money by buying used equipment—if you have a guarantee that it works. But if you have to lay one finger on it to make it work or have to invent a production machine for your product, then put that item into "your" pro forma (and business plan), not the one you are going to show to an investor.

Begin the preparation of the pro forma. List all of the areas (the lines) that are pertinent to your business. If in doubt, put it in, don't leave it out. Fill in the units or dollars wherever possible. You don't have to fill in every line; you simply cannot do it in the beginning. Be prepared to justify any item or number that you enter.

Remember, this is a first draft. Use work sheets and estimates; they are acceptable, but don't enter estimates without some justification. On the work sheets, for every line include your upper and lower estimates in units or dollars for everything that is listed. Again, be prepared to justify your range and your numbers, if to no one else but yourself. When you've added all the categories by month in each major heading, record the total on the line of the major heading. It is much easier to read that way.

Begin your listing with yourself, say as president, under administration. Now, you cannot be everything—production manager, president, chief cook and bottle washer, porter—but you have to put yourself down for a salary somewhere. Put yourself down for salary only *once*. The trick in putting together a new company is to keep your salary as low as you possibly can. The reason for this is the higher your salary, the higher your employees' salary will be, and the more right they have to demand more money from you. But if you are getting a low salary, you can use this as justification for everybody else's salary. Your salary is entered for each month and totaled for the year in column 13.

Some people might start at the same time you do and their salaries are entered the same way. Others might not start until the third month; therefore, their salary will be entered then. Each subject area and item is treated the same way. It is entered onto the pro forma in the month it becomes functional.

The following summary lists some of the subject areas that might be included in a pro forma:

A. Administration
   President, vice president of marketing, chief engineers, office manager, file clerk, typist, secretary, bookkeeper, market researcher, customer service, technical service, etc., plus travel and entertainment
B. Advertising and Promotion
   Trade shows, advertising production makeup, media (TV, radio, publications), printing, sell sheets
C. Packaging Design
   Product 1, Product 2, etc.
D. Selling Costs
   Commission 10%, shipping 5% (of sales)
E. Facilities and Services
   Rent, heat/power/light, telephones, office supplies, postage, insurance, office copier, maintenance truck and fuel, accounting—legal/patent, general, maintenance supplies, contingency, and miscellaneous

F. Consultants

By type, mechanical, chemical, plastics Electronics, laboratory testing

G. Debt maintenance

Debt maintenance/long term/short term, license and registration fees, payroll taxes, corporate taxes, income taxes, etc.

H. Production Personnel

Plant manager, production personnel (each function listed where personnel required), quality control supervisor, quality control assistants, shipping/receiving, specially trained personnel that cost more than ordinary production personnel

I. Variable Costs

Materials and ingredients (each listed in terms of requirements based on sales forecast and production needs), ingredients, containers, cords, plastic sheet, display cases

J. Capital Equipment

List all production equipment required such as dies, plates, tanks, mixers, motors and controls, jugs, fittings, fixtures, tables, cabinets, etc. Machine shop—where necessary, list all tools that must be purchased down to the last hammer or screwdriver. Nails, screws, tool kits, etc. are listed as perishable tools and parts. General equipment—weighing and measuring, compressors, forklift, etc.

K. Sales

By product and sublist of sources, manufacturer reps, chains, house accounts, private label, etc.

L. Summary Sheet (Profit-and-Loss Statement)

Revenues as income, expenses fixed and variable, packaging design, total expenditures, profit or (loss), capital expenditures, cash flow, cumulative cash flow.

Chapter 13
The Business Plan

THE *BUSINESS PLAN* EXPLAINS YOUR BUSINESS AND WHAT YOU HOPE TO achieve. It explains every facet of your pro forma. It is a means of presenting your pro forma in an orderly manner, stressing those important factors that might not be immediately apparent. It helps you clarify and communicate to yourself and others your ideas and your needs. The business plan is a primary sales tool and a guide to running the company. You will refer to it constantly as the company grows, checking actual progress against planned progress. And if your projections are off, it will give you the opportunity to analyze your mistakes and enable your future planning to be more realistic.

Consider who the business plan is for. It is not only a sales document for potential investors, but also a guide for you and your company's managers. It should be realistic and truthful. This does not mean that it must be pessimistic. (I believe in radiating hope.)

Once the first draft of your business plan has been completed, put it aside. The first draft is rarely an even-tempered document. It is usually either too optimistic or too pessimistic, often leaves out important details and subjects, or explains uninteresting trivia in painful detail. You can use it, though, to construct a more readable and measured business plan, one based on everything going exactly as planned. Don't forget to include caveats, however. Sophisticated investors are skeptical; they will generally double your expenses and halve your revenues.

I do not know, at this point, how many people you can show such a document to before it violates Security Exchange Commission (SEC) rules and regulations regarding a public offering. (Check with your attorney or the SEC). You should carefully check the maximum number of people that you can show a document of this kind to without registration, particularly the number of people who are knowledgeable in business and investments. I personally wouldn't show the plan to unsophisticated investors.

PRESENTING YOUR BUSINESS PLAN

One purpose of your business plan is to convince potential investors that your project is worthy of investment. There is no point in showing it to probable noninvestors. You don't want people to think that you're "shopping" the project.

Try very hard to make the presentation of your plan in person, rather than by mail, either by yourself or with some of your key people. The personal presentation gives you and your key people a chance to prove that you know your stuff. If you don't know the answers to the questions they ask, don't lie, ever! Say you don't know or that you will find out. You can't build confidence with people if they catch you in a lie. First impressions are extremely important.

Normally, during the first meeting you don't want accountants, consultants, experts, or lawyers present. The only exception to this is the lawyer; if they have one present, so should you.

The time to bring in other people who can be helpful is when you are making a deal. Once during a set of tight negotiations, while I was trying to hammer out a deal, each side had their complement of lawyers, executives, experts, and assorted personnel. I brought in a friend who happened to be a president of a major corporation. His presence, prestige, and experience as a negotiator awed the opposing president, and that tilted the balance in my favor.

Before making any presentation, it's advisable to discuss strategies with your key management, your attorney, accountant, or any other professional in whom you have confidence. It is also a good idea to establish, in advance, who will say what and how. In addition, establish "interruption" signals so that anyone straying or being long-winded or on dangerous territory can be stopped. In other words, plan and, if necessary, rehearse your presentation before you make it.

Strive for understandability, comprehensibility, and accuracy. I do not believe in going to extraordinary expense to dress up the written plan. Clearly stated, a neatly presented business plan is more effective than a four-color brochure. From my point of view, overdone promotion detracts from the business plan. Spend whatever is reasonable to make sure that your plan is easy to read, understandable, and neat.

Keep in mind who your audience is when you are writing it. Is it tech to tech (technology to technology)? Is it technology on your part to "intelligent laymen"? Or is it to just plain folk who happen to have money? Just because people have money doesn't mean that they are dummies, nor does it necessarily mean that they are smarter than average. Don't talk down to them. Recognize that their areas of understanding might be different than yours. Use descriptions and vocabulary that they will understand; don't swamp them with buzzwords and technical nonsense. Don't exaggerate; it makes acceptance and the establishing of a level of confidence very difficult. Keep your facts straight.

Do your homework. After you have written the business plan, study it. You must understand every detail and be capable of explaining every aspect of the plan to the particular audience you are addressing. The very worst thing you can do in making such a presentation is being unsure of the information in your plan. Don't ever omit the technical information in a plan because you are presenting it to laymen. If your project is highly technical, explain it in terms a layperson can understand in the plan itself.

When I used to address my board of directors with a plan, my first objective was to make sure I was understood. Then, if one person disagreed with me, I would assume I was just as right as he was. If two people disagreed with me, I would begin to question what I was saying. If three people disagreed with me, I would keep quiet and rethink everything I was saying.

Keep your facts straight. Point out the places where you are making forecasts and what they are based on. If you are aware of problems, disclose them. Don't try to hide them, and don't let others find them for you. This doesn't mean that you have to dwell on problem areas, but it shows that you understand that some problems exist and are able to explain their relative importance.

MAJOR ELEMENTS OF A BUSINESS PLAN

The following are the basic areas that I consider to be the major elements of a business plan. If you find other areas that you consider pertinent to your business, by all means, include them if they contribute to clarity and understanding.

Every business plan will include:

- ☐ A disclaimer on its first page
- ☐ An executive summary
- ☐ A table of contents
- ☐ A company history and background (if it exists)
- ☐ How the money you wish to obtain will be used
- ☐ Product(s) or service(s)
- ☐ Future plans
- ☐ The potential market

☐ The immediate market (the one you can reach)
☐ How the product will be made and its production capabilities
☐ Management (key personnel)
☐ Problems
☐ Risks
☐ Present company ownership
☐ Present finances of the operation
☐ Your financial plan (the pro forma)
☐ Appendix (backup data, studies, or tables you have to describe your plan in detail.

The depth of detail devoted to each heading is directly related to the explanation required for each heading. In other words, explain each heading in as much detail as necessary to make it understandable to others. Do not go into too much detail. The primary purpose of the business plan is to communicate with others, in particular to convince your readers that:

1. You are competent.
2. You understand your product thoroughly.
3. What you are trying to do is worthwhile from a business point of view.
4. The venture can be profitable.

The bibliography in appendix A lists a number of books that discuss the subject of business plans. Use only the ideas that are relevant to your needs and ignore the rest. When you are debating whether you should include a certain area in your business plan, follow the rule: "When in doubt, leave it out."

Disclaimer

The *disclaimer* is a simple, carefully worded statement. Here are some sample clauses:

☐ The document is not a prospectus.
☐ The information is speculative.
☐ There are no guarantees that the forecast will occur.
☐ There are no guarantees that the product can be made.
☐ There are no guarantees that after the product is made it will work.

Before you use any disclaimer, make sure to check with an attorney to determine that it meets your needs. I suggest that you go to the library or a stockbroker's office and examine a number of what is known as "red herrings." A *red herring* is the slang financial term used to describe a prospectus that is issued by a company trying to raise money in the stock market. The first page is usually printed with red borders (hence "red herring"). Each of these includes a disclaimer. Take a look at several and note the clauses you might wish to adopt for your own business plan.

Executive Summary

The *executive summary* should be no longer than two pages. Most of the top executives in the United States operate on the basis of executive summaries. The executive summary is your opportunity to convince the executive or investor that what you are proposing is worthwhile and that he should read the full business plan to find out how viable your project is. Your executive summary, which highlights the main points of your business plan, is written after the rest of the plan is completed.

Table of Contents

Don't make the table of contents too detailed. The table of contents should enable the reader to locate the sections he is particularly interested in. One reader might want to look at the resumes of the key people before he reads the rest of the plan. Another might want to look at your production data. Another reader might skip from one subject to another. Make it easy for the reader to find the material he is looking for.

Company History and Background

The company history and background describes when and where the company was formed; whether it is a company, a corporation, an individual proprietorship, or a partnership; and who formed it and for what reason it was formed. List the key people and discuss your progress to date. Provide the reader with an overview of its potential for your industry (the one you will operate in) and of your customer's industry. Describe in general terms how you are going to use the money you are trying to raise. Be specific only where you have to be. Don't duplicate the section on "How the money you wish to obtain will be used." This section is usually called "Use of Funds." State your case in an anticipatory manner so that the reader is prepared for the details later on.

Products and Services

For the sake of brevity, I shall use "products" to cover both products and services. Describe your product, particularly its unique features. Highlight the features of your product that make it different from and superior to competing products. You want to be able to say, "Here is why my product is needed. Here is how my product solves this problem. Here is the market that is waiting eagerly for my product."

Describe whether you have a proprietary position—in the form of trade secrets, patent applications, trademarks, or copyrights. Provide a conservative estimate of how long you can make your product before competition can copy it. You must realize that there are people out there who can copy your product. They have the advantage of having your product from which to start working on a product similar to yours. If anybody wants to copy your product, he can do so in a much shorter time than you took to develop yours in the first place.

Include visuals, such as photographs, concept drawings, charts, and graphs, in a business plan only if they assist in communication. The inclusion of a prototype, whether it is a working model or a display model, is very questionable. Show three-dimensional drawings, models, and prototypes only during a personal presentation of the business plan. Use flip charts if appropriate.

Keep in mind that presentations should not be lengthy. Assume that people have a limited attention span. Also assume that if they are interested in your proposal, they will ask for further and detailed information. Don't be offended by interruptions and questions. If the answer to a question is covered later on, say so, but also be prepared to answer it immediately. Remember . . . what might seem to you to be a logical and sensible presentation that builds block by block, might be more easily understood by the listener if the blocks and sequence of presentation were rearranged.

When possible, verify not only that your product works, but under what conditions it works. If you have engineering studies from independent laboratories verifying the functions of your product, refer to them (see sidebar). Include portions of the study in the text or include the entire study in the appendix.

If you have to do any additional research and development to make your product viable for manufacture and sales, or if you are raising money in order to first develop the product, tell your readers. Tell them what you are working toward, how far you have advanced, and what additional problems might have to be overcome. Give them some idea of what it will take and how long it will take to successfully complete the project.

Future Plans

Discuss your future plans for existing products and the direction of your research for the development of new or improved products. Tell your readers where, when, how, and under what conditions you are going to expand your product line.

For example, with the automatic plant feeder, we knew when we started that we could change and manufacture complete lines of different types of

---

Testing by Independent Labs

I remember trying to produce a small automatic plant feeder for potted plants. The possibility existed that a child or a dog might pull it out of the pot and eat it. I needed product liability insurance, but in order to obtain it, the product had to be put through a "death test."

This was done by the Wisconsin Alumni Research Foundation Institute, a testing laboratory in Madison, Wisconsin. They fed the product to rats until the rats died. The rats consumed two to three times their body weight before they died. This was accepted as proof by the insurance company that the consumption of less than an ounce would not be harmful. The tests results were included in my business plan.

I, for one, never thought there was a problem. The material tasted so bitter and awful that the immediate reaction of anyone tasting the stuff was to gag, rinse, and find something to eat or drink to take the taste away. During production, high-pressure lines occasionally exploded and the material splattered all over the place. That's when I discovered that it tasted bitter. (The experience also taught me to keep my mouth shut—most of the time.)

---

fertilizers for different types of plants. We stated this in our plan. However, we kept the program in abeyance until we were able to secure a portion of the market for the existing product. In other words, rather than spend capital trying to expand the product line, we used it to concentrate on our existing product.

As you add new products, you have to modify your pro forma to reflect the costs and expenses required for the new product—even though the modification might be as minor as changing the color of the product. Whenever the packaging is changed, costs are involved. Product line expansion should not be done casually.

Before you introduce a new product, you must be sure that the product is complete and ready for the market. What are the problems, as they relate to production and marketing that must be solved to bring it to that point? What does it take in terms of time and money to solve the problems? These factors must be considered when you discuss your product. (There is a point relating to product introduction that should be stressed. There are some markets that demand a complete product line. A single product in these markets can be difficult to introduce. It is, therefore, prudent to determine the characteristics of your market before you jump.)

Potential Market

When discussing your potential market, you must demonstrate comprehensive knowledge of your customers and the industry your customers are in:

☐ Who they are
☐ Where they are (geographical location)
☐ How they operate
☐ How they evaluate competitive products
☐ How much of your product they are willing to buy

You want to discuss your major competition:

☐ Who they are
☐ Where they are
☐ How their product may be better than yours
☐ How your product is better than theirs

Discuss your sales strategy:

☐ Identify the major competition in your *targeted* market. Explain how you intend to deal with them.
☐ How is your product sold to your customers? By whom (your own salesman, manufacturers' representatives, distributors)?
☐ How do your competitors sell their products?
☐ How do the companies in your market do their purchasing? Do they have a central buying office? Do they buy seasonally? What terms do they include in their purchase orders? What quantities do they buy?

Essentially you should discuss the background history of the industry that buys your product and their purchasing methodology. Even if your product is new and there are no other products like it on the market, the same questions must be answered. In other words, how has your market grown over the years? Discuss the technological trends of your industry and your market—particularly if these trends affect your potential market.

Estimate the sales of your product in dollars and units, the share of the market you are aiming for, and how long it will take you to achieve that share. Take into account that your estimate is probably optimistic. You can be sure that any investor is not going to feel quite as optimistic as you do. Remember what I said about halving the income and doubling expenses. Be as realistic as you can.

Immediate Market

Define the location of your immediate market. There is a big difference between your potential market and your immediate market. Your *immediate market* is what you can reach. What you can't reach, don't count. Then define the location of your next market area, and so on. Estimate the time period for reaching each of these markets. In your pro forma, you have indicated how much you expect your company to grow from the time you start to the end of the year.

Explain how you intend to reach your customers, emphasizing sales (sales representatives or your own salesmen) and the sales support you intend to provide. If you are building a company for the long term, your company must earn a reputation for reliability and service. Describe how you propose to establish this reputation.

List by name each customer of importance, the size of the order he has given you, or an estimate of how much he will buy. If you consider the information appropriate, discuss the physical distribution of your product and shipping factors and costs, particularly whether you, your customer, or your vendor will be paying shipping costs.

Explain your price policies and discount structure. Price policies vary by product and industry. You might want to discuss how inevitable price fluctuations might affect company revenues.

Customer communications (advertising, promotion, public relations, one-to-one sales, trade shows, handouts, letters) inform your customers about your product. If appropriate, include an advertising budget or communications program. Indicate if it's tied into discount allowance. The objective is to let your reader know how you intend to communicate with your customers.

Production Capabilities

Describe your company's production capabilities: plant location; whether you intend to lease, build, or buy a building; setup costs; make or buy decisions. List the crucial material for your product. If you happen to have a single supplier situation, explain what methods of protection are available.

During the setup and production of one of my inventions, we found only one company that could supply the horticultural vermiculite we needed. Wary of being limited to a single supplier of a crucial material, we did a worldwide survey of vermiculite sources—and still found no other supplier of horticultural vermiculite. We knew from the very beginning that we were locked into one company as long as we made that particular product, and we revealed that fact in our business plan.

Describe the existing production facilities and how you intend to expand them if required (capacity and production rate, present or desired). Discuss machinery only if pertinent. For example, if you need some extraordinarily expensive machinery, indicate that these will use up a large portion of the monies that you are raising. If your operation requires special training for personnel, or if unions play an important role in your particular industry, your business plan must mention this factor. If government regulations will affect your particular operation, discuss them. Sometimes a lot of money gets tied up unnecessarily in inventory; therefore, you might want to explain why you might have an unusually large inventory of raw materials, parts, or finished products.

Management

In the management section of the business plan, include resumes of key management, especially when management has unique skills or experiences. You might want to put full resumes in an appendix; however, in the body of your statement, use a paragraph or so to describe each individual. The reader wants to know whether the company's management has the ability to run a successful company. It is not necessary to go into any more detail than required to demonstrate these abilities. The resumes should emphasize the skills needed for this company and persuade the reader to have confidence in its managers. Don't include too much detail, however. It's very easy to talk too much. Sometimes you can talk your way out of a deal.

Name the members of the board of directors. Provide brief resumes and explain how they will contribute to the welfare and planning of policies. If you are operating with your own money, you can have relatives, wives, children, etc., on the board of directors. It really doesn't matter what you do when it's your money. When you are operating with other people's money, however (and, I feel, even when you are operating with your own money), try to get people who are knowledgeable as members of the board of directors.

Try to get your investors to participate as members of your board. Other people's input can be very valuable. First, they don't live with the problems on a day-to-day basis like you do. Second, they are interested parties. Third, their objectivity can be very enlightening, even if it's just an informal critique of a policy. I believe in the principal of inclusion rather than exclusion. This does not mean that you won't occasionally have a real troublemaker on the board, but that troublemaker can do you more good, if you work it right, than any other member of the board.

Problems and Risks

If you consider it appropriate, you might want to include an organization chart in the business plan. Discuss the problems you expect to find and how you propose to solve them. Don't overemphasize them; include them to show your reader that you're honest and sincere, and that you have the problems under control. Unless you can make a statement of that sort, you should not present a business plan to potential investors.

Discuss the risks that your company might face with knockoffs by copycats, patent suits, or a competitive price war. Explain what action you propose to either reduce these risks or deal with them. (Include items only if you deem them appropriate to your situation). For instance, you might have to discuss the possibilities of patent suits from competition. Even though there might be no question of infringement, competition might sue you as a means of draining your capital. Unions can present problems if technology displaces labor.

Discuss risks that may occur, but don't discuss "created" problems just to show how brilliant your solutions are. Include problems only if they actually exist. You want to show that you're not trying to deceive anyone and that you have possible solutions.

Present Company Ownership

List the company's owners by percent of individual ownership. If any of the owners participate in management, describe the position (for example, on the executive committee of the board of directors), particularly if they are consultants. An investor might make his participation a condition of his investment: "Hire me as a consultant, and I'll be there whenever you need me." This practice is a red flag to other potential investors. They don't mind people participating in the business who work on a full-time basis, but they do mind people who work part time and draw money out of the business without making a substantial contribution. As previously stated, investors are not stupid. If anyone besides active management will receive compensation, indicate how much and what for.

Finances

A financial statement reflecting your present finances should be prepared by an accountant. In some cases, it might be necessary that this financial statement be certified or certifiable. If the statement includes qualifying clauses that might raise questions in the investor's mind, explain them.

The Pro Forma and Appendix

The pro forma is the final section of your business plan, followed by the appendix. The appendix contains pertinent backup information that assists the reader or explains in detail general statements made in the business plan or pro forma—engineering reports, laboratory tests, market research studies. You might include pictures of expensive equipment that you are going to purchase.

> *The purpose of the business plan is to communicate. If the information is pertinent, if it helps your reader decide to invest his money in your company—include it!*

A pro forma and a business plan are not idle documents. They're not the kind of things that you dash off in a few minutes, toss in front of somebody, and say, "Here, let me have a million bucks." What you must do is write it, read it, show it to people, rewrite it, and edit it. Make sure it's clear, concise, and understandable. Communication is an extraordinarily difficult thing to achieve. Quite frequently, the words that you use might not be understood or have the same meaning to the person you're communicating with.

When you're using a pro forma and a business plan to communicate, you're using a document. You cannot count on body language. You cannot count on saying, "Oh, this is what I meant." Make it clear and readable the first time you present it. Before you present it, bounce it off knowledgeable people to make sure that what you have to say is understandable. If someone should criticize it, don't take the criticism lightly. Your goal is to make sure that you've been able to get your objectives across to the reader. Your objective—to spark enthusiasm in your reader as well as confidence in you and your product or your business so that he will put money into your project.

Chapter 14

Marketing and Sales

To UNDERSTAND MARKETING AS IT IS PRESENTLY PRACTICED, YOU HAVE TO understand something about the history of production and marketing in the United States. Up until the 1920s, the total orientation of American Industry was toward production. At the conclusion of the Civil War, the North had in its possession an industrial machine that was capable of turning out products in enormous quantities. The industrial machine had to be fed and its products distributed and consumed by people who could use them. The insatiable giant needed both raw material sources and markets.

These needs were immediately available in two areas that were acceptable and accessible to the industrial North. One was the South. It had been totally devastated physically and economically. It was a ready market for goods and services that could be provided by the North. The other area was the West. A westward movement had just begun, and to support this movement, there was a wide open immigration policy. Newcomers were sought for the purpose of taking over the western lands before they might be contested by other countries.

Immigration was also used as a means of maintaining a hold on labor in the industrialized areas of the United States. The more people who immigrated, the more ready labor was available. There were always more people than available jobs and, therefore, always a means of keeping the workers in control. The promise of work and free land brought in people, and as people came in, the industrial empire grew and grew. The more people, the more goods were needed. Factories could hardly keep up with the demand.

In addition to the vast markets of the South and West, two other markets opened up: Europe and South America. Anything that was made, regardless of the quality, was consumed.

Soon, America found itself in need of protecting its growing industrial empire and interests. There was a need for a navy to guard outposts, also an army and marines. It was the birth of gunboat diplomacy. All were needed to protect our new commercial interests. These forces also became markets for the industrial machine.

The need for goods was so great that until the 1920s, the prevailing attitudes of industrialists were:

- ☐ If you could make it, you could sell it.
- ☐ The cheaper you made it, the faster you could make it, and the more you could sell.
- ☐ Even if the quality was poor, you could sell it because there was a demand for product.

> The attitude of 1920's industrialists was epitomized by Henry Ford who said: "You can have the car any color you want, as long as it's black."

There was a railroad tycoon who said that he would rather ride pigs to Chicago than people. It cost him less, and he made more profit. The fact is that people didn't count. Production counted, industry counted, the movement of production counted. Environment didn't count. If a forest was denuded, it made little difference as long as production could continue at full steam.

Then, around the 1920s things began to change. After World War I, American industry remained intact while the rest of the world's industry was devastated. As the industry in the rest of the world began to recover, the competition for these markets intensified, and industry suddenly found itself in a position where making it faster and in greater quantity no longer sufficed. This was a severe blow to most industry. The sudden rise of competition required a new form of product disposal. Because the consumer could now choose between products that were functionally the same, it was no longer acceptable to simply put one's product on the market and expect that it would be purchased.

Companies were now faced with the task of convincing the consumer that their product was better than the competition's. The result of this effort was the birth of marketing as we know it today.

Convincing the Customer to Buy

What is *marketing*? It is nothing more than a system of education used to persuade consumers to buy your product rather than the competition's. It is also a mechanism of distribution that enables the producer to transfer his product from production facility to the consumer.

This total explanation can be summarized in one word: *selling*. Companies quickly learned to use various methods of communication (advertising and publicity) to presell consumers on the superiority of their products.

Another factor began to strongly influence consumer purchasing behavior: *reliability* and *backup service*. Industry had to recognize that the mere function and competitive price of a product were insufficient. It found that purchasing behavior was now based on reliability, service, and then price.

BASIC MARKETS

Before an industry can sell to people, it must first find them, identify them, and ultimately persuade them. The first stage is identifying the basic markets that presently exist. The *basic markets* are industrial markets, institutional markets, stocking distributors, and retail markets.

The *industrial market* buys products used in manufacturing or as a component of another product.

Institutional markets include government agencies, hospitals, and non-profit organizations. All buy products primarily for use in their own operation. There is an exception, however: hospitals. For example, when hospitals buy aspirin, they do not give it away for free. They generally charge their patients for it. Government markets range from the local village up to the federal government.

Stocking distributors, generally known as *wholesalers*, are businesses that purchase products for resale to various other organizations such as retailers, government, industry, and institutions. A stocking distributor buys products in bulk, stores them in a warehouse, repackages the products into smaller units, and resells them.

Retail markets buy your products for the purpose of reselling them to individual consumers. Retail establishments can also be chain operations such as Caldor, K Mart or Sears.

Each of these markets can be divided into a multiplicity of subsegments. Each segment might require a different marketing approach. In most cases, buyers for different classes of products are different individuals within the same organization, each fiercely protective of his own area of activity.

For example, a manufacturer who sold appliances to department stores thought that he could also sell his metal kitchen cabinets to the same buyer who bought his dishwashers. He found, however, that kitchen cabinets were purchased by a different buyer within the same department store. The fact that he already had a track record with the appliance buyer did not mean that the cabinet buyer would give him the time of day.

Each segment requires a different selling approach to a different buyer within the same company. You need to establish a support system to foster buyer confidence in you and your product. These days, without buyer confidence, it is almost impossible to sell your product. Support systems build and reinforce a product image of reliability, service, and value. Support includes customer information and service before the sale, during the sale, and after the sale.

ANYONE CAN SELL

There is nothing very difficult or secretive about selling, but there are many myths that have grown up around selling. Some people, however, have a talent for inspiring confidence in others. Let me tell you a typical story about a super salesman.

A grocer had several dozen cartons of salt sitting in a corner of his shop. A friend of his noticed the stock and commented, "Gee, you must sell a lot of salt." The grocer shook his head and sighed, saying, "No, I don't sell a lot of salt. The guy who sells me salt . . . now, *he* sells a lot of salt!"

The meaning is that there are some people who have natural selling talent, but they are few and far between. Most people don't have that ability. In fact, most salesmen lack this capacity. Natural talent aside, selling is based on: (1) knowing your product, (2) knowing the customer's needs, and (3) knowing the competition.

A young man came to me for advice. He did not impress me as being the most ambitious person in the world. As a matter of fact, he seemed rather laid back, California style. He called me to say, "I just got a job as a salesman. What do I do now?" I said, "I will help you only if you listen and promise to do what I tell you to do."

As a result of my advice, he was salesman of the month for three months in a row and was named salesman of the year. This is what I told him:

1. Learn everything you can about your product.
2. Learn everything you can about your competitor's product.
3. Never knock your competitor's product.
4. Go where your potential customers are.
5. Maintain contact with old customers.

It's as simple as that, but let's look at it in more detail.

First, analyze your product. Learn everything you can about it.

Second, analyze and find out everything you can about your competitor's product.

Third, *never* knock your competitor's product. Use a positive approach by pointing out the benefits of your product over your competitor's product, but never knock it. Answer every question as directly as you possibly can. Don't misstate, exaggerate, or lie to your customers. If you don't know the answer, simply say, "I will find out." What you have going for you is your knowledge of your product and knowledge of your competition.

Fourth, to sell effectively, you must go where the potential customers are. Analyze your company's existing sales. Use a computer listing of every customer in your territory to break down the customer list by products purchased from your company, by industry, and by type of company. Try to match the company with the same kind of companies listed in the *Yellow Pages* of the telephone book. If you cannot match them up, go to the *Thomas Register* to locate the company and find out its size, what it makes, and what it sells. Sometimes, you can infer what it buys.

Once you have established the company's category, go back to the *Yellow Pages*. The industry categories in the *Yellow Pages* are very unique. In many ways they are better than the Standard Industrial Classification established by the government because their ads are written in more understandable English.

> *If you find a company that buys your product listed in the* Yellow Pages, *you can assume that all of the other companies listed in that category are potential customers that are ready, willing, and able to buy your product.*

Establish a priority list for these customers in relation to the types of products and the quantity they buy. By noting their location on a map, you can figure out how many people you can see per day so that your time and travel are as productive as possible.

Fifth, maintain contact with your old customers. Call on a certain number per day. Also, call on new customers at a constant daily rate. *Apportion your time* between old, new, and potential customers. That is what pays off. As you can see two things are being accomplished:

1. Calls are being made to customers who use the product and might need more
2. Calls are being made to noncustomers who are in need of the functions performed by the product.

By systematically calling on customers and potential customers, you will find that you don't have to be a super salesman. You need only present your product honestly and in its most favorable terms. That's selling. You are not lying, you're not cheating, you're not falsifying, exaggerating, or being a hustler. You're saying it straight. You have found and evaluated your customers. You've developed your approach in relation to their needs. You've studied so that you can make a proper presentation of your product. You've studied your competitor's product. And most important of all, you are able to make a favorable comparison between your product and your competitor's product.

THE SALES APPROACH

Before you approach a customer, find out exactly who you want to see, then call for an appointment. Avoid making "cold calls." Whenever possible, try to get referrals. Even if it's "Joe sent me because he thinks that you can use this product." Don't make a pitch over the phone, just try to get an appointment. Be polite, very patient, and don't prolong the conversation. Once you have an appointment, *stop.* Sell when you get there.

When you arrive for your appointment, be prepared to be patient. You might have to wait in a buyer's office long beyond the appointment time. You might think it is such an awful waste of time when you have so many things to do, and I agree. I find it difficult sitting around waiting for a buyer to give me a few minutes of his time. But that's why I am a poor salesman. There *are* people who are patient, and they are the ones who make good salesmen.

A Matter of Courtesy

When a situation occurs that makes it necessary to keep someone waiting beyond the appointment time, it is only reasonable and courteous to send your secretary or go yourself to apologize for the unanticipated delay. At the same time, indicate how long you might be. This gives the person waiting the choice of continuing to wait or rescheduling the appointment. To me, it's simply a matter of common courtesy.

Regardless of what you think about the buyer's personality, you must assume that he is reasonably knowledgeable about the product area he is responsible for. Most of the time he knows what is going on. When talking to a buyer, it is essential that you also listen attentively.

There was a recent study made about people who have been successful in any enterprise they entered, particularly in industry. They were able to do three things that were absolutely vital to success.

1. They were able to communicate directly and succinctly. They were able to tell other people what they were thinking in a manner that was fully understandable.
2. They were able to understand what the other person was saying, not just the words, but beyond the words to the body language— the facial expressions, hand and eye movements, whatever means of communication was being used. Because they could understand what the other person really meant, they knew better how to communicate their thoughts.

3. They were able to intuitively recognize the power source wherever it existed. The *power source* is the person who formulates decisions.

The president of an organization is not necessarily the person who runs it. You will frequently find somebody with an unimpressive job title, perhaps a clerk or a secretary, who is really responsible for the decisions. For instance, it is rare that a congressman runs his own office. If you want prompt action from a congressman's office, see his chief clerk, assistant, or secretary. That's where you get the action on a consistent basis, not from the congressman himself. Most of them don't have the time. When you are dealing with the government, you must find out who the decision maker is and who the power source is.

The same is true in any company or situation in which you might become involved. A friend of mine who was trying to sell locks to the city found that he was getting nowhere because he could not find the right person. It turned out that the person who specified the kind of locks to be purchased had some obscure title and had nothing whatever to do with the section that issued the purchase order for the locks. He specified, and the buying section bought them.

Prepare your sales "pitch" in advance. Tailor it to suit the person you are presenting it to. If appropriate, try to demonstrate your product. If your product can be handled, it is preferable to show the product rather than use pictures or words alone to describe it.

Know Your Bottom Line

When you are selling standard products or services, prices are usually fixed. When your product is new or unique, be prepared to negotiate. To negotiate, you must know the product's bottom line: how much you are willing to give up for the particular order you might get. Before you go in, you must know the bottom line so that you can negotiate from the top down. Fight for every inch you can get and trade for every inch you have to give up. It can be done with a great deal of aplomb.

You can negotiate factually and effectively as long as you know what you are doing. You must be thoroughly familiar with your company's current discount structure. Too many salesmen get clobbered because they did not realize that they were offering the buyer a larger discount or concession than the company wished to give up.

Although many deals are negotiable, never give away anything unless you must. But when you must, do not give it away with reluctance. Do it with seeming generosity. It doesn't make any difference if yours is a standard product. Sometimes you can negotiate a sale by offering discounts, advertising allowances, six units for five, extended service, etc. For whatever you give up, however, try to get something in return.

Closing the Sale

Closing the sale is the most difficult area of selling. One of the best techniques of closing a sale is to ask the buyer what specifications he requires. As he gives you details (quantities, color preference, sizes, etc.), write it up as an order, then when he is finished speaking, casually present it to him for his signature.

Closing in and of itself is a techniqe that can be learned. For the kinds of things you will be selling, you will learn to close only by talking to a number of buyers that are interested in your product. The odds are with you. The more buyers you talk to, the greater your chances are of closing, and the sharper your capability will become to close.

The most important advice that I can give anybody in selling is that, *once you've sold your product, keep quiet.* There are more sales lost by people talking too much than by talking too little, particularly after the sale has been made. The main thing to realize is simply not to talk yourself out of a sale once the sale has been accomplished.

Follow-Up

The next area is follow-up. After a sale is made, check back to make sure that your customer is satisfied with the product and its performance. Use this follow-up as an opportunity to find out if you can make an additional sale of either the same product or of another product that you are selling. In addition, use that time to make any adjustments or corrections and to solidify your position with the buyer. Convince him that you and your company are reliable. Be careful during the follow-up, however. You might find yourself with an experienced finagler who is going to use that follow-up time to get concessions out of you that were not in the original purchase order. Although you want to present yourself in the best light possible, you also want to be cautious. It's the kind of thing you learn the hard way.

YOUR SALES FORCE

Marketing and sales use various types of salespeople: application engineers, technical service people, telephone order takers, inside order takers (who serve behind a counter or desk), outside order takers (lower level salesmen who are not too familiar with the product and are sent to established customers for repeat orders.) Many salespeople are considered nothing more than order takers.

The sales force also includes the most important group in today's market—sales and service information people, prospectors or finders, and educators. Suppose you are selling something that is new and different. You cannot pinpoint your market as readily as you wish, but you know in general where your market is. You might first hire *prospectors* to talk about your product and find potential customers who are interested in it, then you can send a salesman around to talk to them. It is a less costly way of utilizing a highly experienced technical person who is far more expensive than a finder (prospector). For example, American Express has finders and service representatives. They pay a finder about $1.75 per store to go to retail establishments to place and check the supply of credit card application forms and to check with the retailer to see if everything is okay. If there is any problem, or if the store doesn't have American Express services and they are interested in them, a knowledgeable service representative will then call. The same might be true if you are selling machinery. After the prospector has done his job, an application engineer goes in to finish the sale by installing the equipment.

Quotas

Quotas can take various forms. They are minimums that you establish as goals for your sales force. They can be based on:

1. Product mix (number of units of individual products in a product line or sales dollars for those products)
2. Profitability
3. Territory (number of customers, size, type)
4. Sales calls per period (you can demand that the salesman make X number of calls per day in the territory)
5. Sales per period or per territory
6. New products per period or per territory

I'm not sure that setting quotas is effective. I think that operating on the basis of averages and curves for sales, new calls, sales expenses, etc. is more practical because it then takes into consideration the nature of the company image and the product being sold.

Compensation

Salespeople are compensated in various ways: straight salary, commission only, salary and commission, draw against commission, salary and expenses, commission with expenses, and combinations of the these, plus *perks*. A perk can be a car you provide for a salesman to use, ostensibly for business purposes. The fact that he uses it over weekends and at night to take his girlfriend out is a perk. You are paying for the gas and the upkeep of the car, but he has the use of the car. He might also have an expense account that gives him the ability to take customers out to lunch or dinner, but if he takes his girlfriend out, that's a perk. Contests, prizes, or other incentives offer another form of compensation to salesmen.

Each form of compensation has advantages and disadvantages. *Straight salaries* are preferable when developing new territories because you are dealing with the need to find customers and with educational and nonselling activity. Without a salary as a backup, there isn't much reason for a salesman to prospect. The advantages are that you have more control over your salespeople because you have provided them with financial security, and more importantly, all your sales costs are predictable. The disadvantages are that there are no built-in incentives for the salespeople, and your sales costs are not always proportionate to the sales. In other words, your sales costs can be much higher than the number of sales that you will eventually get. In addition, it requires very tight control over your sales force.

The *commission-only basis* can be used when salesman control is very limited, and there are few nonselling tasks to be performed by the salesman. He doesn't do any prospecting. He knows approximately what the customer list is and is generally familiar with the industry. It requires a self-starter, hustler type of personality who generally works very hard, but at his own pace. When paying commissions, your selling costs are always proportionate to your sales. The disadvantage is that you have little control over your salespeople, and they concentrate their sales effort on popular items. In other words, they're going to devote their efforts to selling those items that are easiest to sell. You might have some items that you are anxious to sell because they are more profitable than other items in your product line, although they might not be as popular. These items are lost without additional incentives to the salesmen. There is no financial security for the salesmen unless territory, customers, and commissions are protected.

Another type of compensation is *draw against commission*. When a territory is partially developed (territory requires some nonsales activity and prospecting as well as some salesman control), a draw against commission might be the best form of compensation. Because you advance the salespeople's pay, you have a degree of control over their activities. The advantages of this combination are that the incentive factor is built-in, there is some degree of security for the salespeople, and the sales costs are more closely related to sales. The disadvantages are that it requires an alert and active control because the incentives are limited, and prospecting is mostly by "push." Even though the salespeople are getting a commission, the sales manager still has to exert constant pressure in order to get the salespeople to do any nonselling activity such as prospecting.

SALES PROMOTION TECHNIQUES

Various types of sales promotion techniques are used for consumer products:

- ☐ Retail coupons (cents off on the package)
- ☐ Demonstrations
- ☐ Trading stamps
- ☐ Point of purchase displays and materials

☐ Free samples
☐ Money refunds
☐ Premiums
☐ Cents off without stamps
☐ Consumer contests

Sales promotion to the trade (distributors, chains, and large volume outlets) include:

☐ Buying allowances
☐ Temporary price reductions
☐ Buy-back allowances
☐ Free merchandise
☐ Merchandise allowances
☐ Cooperative advertising
☐ Dealer listing (advertising)
☐ Premiums
☐ Push money for salesman
☐ Sales contests

The business end of marketing and sales essentially consists of finding the customer and convincing him to buy your product. That is what sales and marketing is all about. In order to inform a customer about your product, you might require a national or local advertising and promotion campaign. Whatever happens, you want to get your customer's attention. It makes little difference how you do it. The point is you must communicate with the end user of your product to let him know that your product is available for him to buy. Market research, motivation research, secondary source research, advertising, public relations, and promotion are all aimed at nothing more than locating your customers, educating your customers, and selling your customers.

The trick today is no longer the ability to make the product. What counts today is the ability to sell the product. If you can control the market, you can control the product (business).

Many markets are there. Many markets can be established. Many markets take a great deal of work to establish because they are new markets, new to you as a seller or to a new product. The ability to expand in today's industry is based primarily on being able to find what additional products your buyer will buy. To expand your business, if you find out what else your one buyer is additionally capable of buying, then you have an opportunity to add new products to your line. It costs you no more than a fraction to present that same buyer with several products than it does to present him with a single product. Essentially, that is marketing and selling.

Chapter 15

Prodution and Facilities Setup

I T SEEMS REASONABLE TO ASSUME THAT IF YOU'RE INTENT ON STARTING A business, you're going to require a place from which to conduct the business, even if it's just your basement or garage. As a preliminary stage, there's nothing wrong with any of these places. They are simple and relatively easy to manipulate, cost little, require very little planning, and provide you with an opportunity to test product accceptance. The major problem is that the operation is limited. It's difficult to take it seriously, not only for others, but mostly for you. Until it moves to it's own "house" it's difficult to consider it a "real" business.

Once you're ready to take the next giant step into "proper" facilities, however, you'd better stop fantasizing about a plant the size of a square block with your company name on the security gate. Begin to do some hard thinking based on your business plan, forecasts, up-to-date customer experiences. Needless to say, you'll also need some good old common sense . . . particularly on how much you can afford.

In all probability, once you know the type and size of your space requirements, you'll work with a real estate agent to help you find a place. The more information you are capable of giving him about your needs, the better he will be able to help you. Be cautious, however. There are some real estate agents that seem to live in their own fantasy world. All they're interested in is quickly culminating a deal, whether it's to your benefit or not. Decide on your specifications and stick to them. Change them only if you're sure it's helpful. These agents always seem to show you places that are higher in price than you specified as your top. They've nothing to loose. If you take the higher priced place, they earn more commission.

PROPER FACILITIES REQUIRE PLANNING

There's nothing mysterious about facilities planning. Most of the time, the end result is dictated by deductive reasoning. A few things to remember:

1. The amount of space required is the sum total of the square footage of all the components and functions needed for immediate operation plus, where appropriate, room for expansion and growth.
2. The type and location of the space is dictated by custom and customer expectations in relation to your industry's accepted practices. In other words, if you never expect to see any customers at your plant, you can locate it in the boondocks. But, if you are a garment manufacturer, for example, rather than having buyers come to your plant, set up a showroom in a fashionable and convenient area.
3. Structural configuration of the space is dictated by the functions to be performed in specific areas within the space; i.e., office vs. plant.
4. As a rule, it is much less expensive in the long run to pay more for space that is close to the physical configuration you require than to restructure the facility to meet your needs.

Suppress the inventors desire to remake things in his own image. It takes precious time and money to restructure. I can vouch for how tempting it is to walk into a facility with nothing but four clean walls starring back at you begging to be partitioned. By the same token, however, don't be put off if you can turn bargain space around to meet your needs. Just remember one very important thing. Unless the place belongs to you or your company, you're improving someone else's property. In addition, you might be required to remove any changes and restore the place to its original condition when you move.

For purposes of discussion and illustration, assume that you will occupy whatever place you rent, lease, or buy for a minimum period of one year. To keep things simple, also assume that all you need is office and factory facilities. With this as a premise, you can now begin to calculate requirements and plan. For both office and plant you look at the pro forma for the basic information.

OFFICE FACILITIES

Based on the pro forma, you know how many people will work for the company in the administrative work area by the end of one year. You also know their rank, function, and privacy needs. These dictate the type of space required for each individual. Private offices or space is called for where confidentially of work or conversation is necessary as part of the function to be performed by the employee. The remaining administrative employees can function effectively in a large open area.

Don't go overboard in providing private offices to personnel. Do so only if it's absolutely necessary. Private offices cost money. There's no reason why key personnel shouldn't share an office. Indeed, in some cases it is highly desirable for key people and functions to be close to each other and overlap.

Office Functional Requirements

Break down your administrative space needs into the required functional areas. (Not all the example areas listed might be appropriate for your needs.) Functional areas to consider might be:

- ☐ Administration
- ☐ Secretarial
- ☐ Bookkeeping (and computer records)
- ☐ Clerical
- ☐ Stationary storage
- ☐ File and record cabinets
- ☐ Sales (internal)
- ☐ Meeting room(s)
- ☐ Show rooms
- ☐ Waiting room
- ☐ Drafting and design (with or without computers)
- ☐ Coffee and water (kitchen)

The trick is to keep it simple and, where appropriate, keep it tight. As previously stated, functional areas can and sometimes should overlap.

In arranging the functional area, however, pay strict attention to factors of personnel accessibility and confidentially as related to functions and records. You certainly don't want confidential information openly exposed to either uncleared personnel or strangers who, because of your setup, are exposed to the information as they pass by. Keep those areas out of normal pathways so that unauthorized personnel and visitors do not inadvertently wander into them.

The strictness of barrier setup breaks down to the type of people you want to let into particular areas and those that you want to keep out. For example, the waiting room area should normally be sealed off from both the office and plant, with admission to either by permission only. It simply is not a good idea to have nonemployees wandering around the premises, if for no other reason than insurance risk. By the same token, it is a good idea to have a neutral corridor leading to both executive offices and conference rooms. This keeps both strangers and nonauthorized employees away from sensitive areas. The same type of corridor might be necessary if an entrance to the plant requires nonoffice personnel to pass through or near the office area. Arrange the corridor (by counter or desk manipulation) so that these people cannot wander into the office area either out of curiosity or a desire to chat with one of the secretaries.

Phones and Keys

Regardless of how open and trusting you are of the people you work with, you must recognize that, at times, certain telephone conversations and records must be kept secret. Therefore, you must take certain precautions.

To ensure privacy on the telephone, install one private incoming telephone line connected to a separate single-line telephone in your office. Do not have the private incoming line hooked into a multiline push-button telephone. The phone is meant primarily for confidential calls, so keep the number private and release it on a need-to-know basis only.

To ensure the privacy of your records, make sure that confidential files are kept under lock and key and that access to the keys are carefully controlled. Keep a record of who has these keys on a signed out basis.

Now that use of computers have become common, protect your access codes and guard the storage of your computer disks. Some companies maintain several levels of access codes and also change the codes periodically.

Those private records that are kept either in your office or your secretary's office must be secured. Make sure that only both of you have keys and that these files are locked when both of you are not in the immediate vicinity. Curiosity has led to the common practice of some employees staying late strictly for the purpose of wandering through private files. As a matter of convenience, many secretaries keep these keys in their top center desk drawer, then forget to lock it at the end of the day. It isn't hard to deal with this problem, but it must be dealt with.

Furniture and Office Equipment

The next step is to allocate office furniture and equipment to each functional area and individual. All desks, chairs, files, cabinets, bookcases, office machines, etc., need not be alike in appearance or cost. (Remember to be stingy . . . but not so stingy that the place isn't pleasant to work in.) Once this allocation is made, it is time to begin measurement and layout.

There are no set patterns or methods to accomplish the best layout and subsequent determination of space requirements. However, the use of scale model cutouts of each partition, piece of furniture, equipment, etc., will enable you to manipulate the layout in terms of the priority and placement of functional areas and corridors. You will get a chance to do this later. For now, get an idea of what the administrative area will look like and how many square feet of office space you require.

Do not be intimidated by the amount of space that you think you need. Nothing is carved in stone. Review each function, piece of equipment, number of personnel, and each person's space allocation. See what can be shared or eliminated altogether. Particularly review your and your executives offices. It is sometimes appropriate to shift some functions into the plant and thereby reduce the amount of office space.

PLANT FACILITIES

Unlike the office arrangement that is based primarily on function, efficient plant design is based almost entirely on flow, both process flow and materials flow. The two must mesh in order to achieve the most economical use of space and manufacturing time—from the storage and movement of incoming raw materials and parts to the storage and shipment of finished goods.

Return to the analysis of the product that was made during it's initial construction. Now you will carry it a step further.

This step requires utmost concentration. If you do it yourself, see to it that you're undisturbed. Mistakes at this point can be very costly. After you're finished, review the plan with some knowledgeable person. Better still, try to have a compatible knowledgeable person work on it with you.

If you can, take the product completely apart. This means every screw, nut, washer, etc. Lay them out on a table to achieve an exploded view. Now, either using your old lists or making new ones, list separately in two columns each and every part that you will manufacturer and each and every part that you will purchase.

Process Flow Analysis

First consider the list of parts that you will manufacture in your plant. Examine each part separately to determine its precise manufacturing sequence from raw material to finished part to assembly. List these operations for each part. Leave nothing out. If a part must be turned in the milling machine in order to work on a different side, list it and describe the operation. If more than one hole is to be drilled, list them sequentially, particularly if the holes are of different sizes. List the size and the fact that the drill bit has to be changed. List any setup or jig as they relate to individual operations. Of utmost importance, describe and show the parts movement between machines and operations. Again, leave nothing out.

This examination and listing must be made for every single part *you make* that goes into the final product. Once this list is completed you should know precisely what kind of machines and equipment your plant requires.

Next, using your list, construct a flowchart showing the movement and activity of all the parts. This is best done by drawing a series of boxes representing the machines. Then, using thin-colored adhesive graph tape, with each color representing a different part, connect the appropriate boxes. Number the boxes (machines), in the same color as the tape for that part, to indicate the flow on a step-by-step basis.

Some machines will be used for more than one part. Because of this, it is sometimes easier to construct a flowchart for each part using its own set of boxes, then constructing a master flowchart where all the parts are included. Another suggestion is that you work big for the preliminary drafts. In other words, buy the largest drawing pad you can find and a box of crayons. You'd be amazed how much easier it is on the psyche if you make a mistake working with kid's stuff.

This method will enable you to confirm how many machines of each kind you will need. It will also help you schedule production in an economic manner that makes maximum use of the equipment you have. *Do not*, as yet, finalize the position and location of each manufacturing machine, assembly table, quality control inspection table, packaging, finished goods inventory storage, and shipping areas.

Materials and Purchased Parts Flow Analysis

Next, analyze in exactly the same way any and all materials and purchased parts that will be included in the finished product. Make sure to include an area for receiving and storage in the flow.

When this step is completed, all you should have is a series of colored tape connected boxes (or crayon drawings) showing the manufacturing movement of process and the movement of material and purchased parts. You should have a very precise idea as to where any materials and parts are needed during any phase of the movement and transfer in the manufacturing process.

Next, construct a master flowchart to combine process flow and materials and parts flow. If the operation is complex, you can add a second step in the flowchart drawings to make it easier. I transfer the crayon drawing to acetate overlays and then to my final layout using the colored adhesive tape.

LAYOUTS

This is the fun part. Using your flowcharts as a guide, make a "scale" cutout of every piece of equipment you've indicated as needed during the manufacturing and assembly process. This should include any furniture tables, chairs, benches, large cabinets, etc., that are also required to complete the product. The next step is to arrange your first layout of the cutouts so that your machinery placement and installation relates to the flowcharts. Now is also the time to determine some of the areas that require partition. (Again, use scale cutouts in the layout.) You'd be amazed at how much time, effort, money, and aggravation this type of planning saves. Your layout should include the following:

Work Areas. Position each piece of manufacturing machinery to its related work areas. Include any furniture belonging to that function (assembly, quality control, packaging, etc.).

Storage. Set aside areas to store raw material and purchased parts (incoming) inventory as well as semifinished and finished goods (outgoing) inventory.

Receiving and Shipping. Layout a secure area for receiving and shipping. This area should also contain provisions for "records control" of anything and everything that comes in or leaves the plant. It should *not* be an area that is used as an entrance or exit by employees.

Pathways. In developing a layout, make pathways wide enough for safe and easy movement throughout the plant.

Restricted Areas. Mark off any areas of limited accessibility. In every plant there are areas that *must* be kept under strict control. This is particularly true of materials or work areas that are hazardous. The fewer people around these areas, the safer and less costly a mishap will be.

There is another reason for tight control—security. It's nice to trust employees; however, somehow or other tools, parts, and product disappears. I recommend simple precautionary measures. Fence in the areas containing any kind of inventory . . . particularly parts and tools. Maintain limited control of the keys to these areas.

Eating Facilities. Depending on your location, it might be necessary to maintain a area that can be used by employees as a lunchroom. The criteria for establishing a lunchroom is based on the nearness and availability of food vendors. The space need not be elaborate, and if there is a real problem with space availability, you can schedule its use in shifts. Whether or not to install a kitchen is more a matter of available funds and employee pressures than need because most employees brown bag it. You will need coffee, soft drink, and snack vending machines, however. Depending on the number of employees, there are many vending companies that would be delighted to install, maintain, and restock the machines; or you can buy your own vending machines and stock them. Much depends on the accessibility of outside food places.

Service Lines. Once you have settled on a general layout that seems reasonable (remember you're just moving around paper cutouts so things can be changed at will), you can begin to include and position the electric, gas, and water lines that might be required for the machinery. At this point, if it is a necessary part of your operation, plan your waste disposal. Don't take shortcuts with waste disposal. Too many manufacturers have had slipshod or inadequate waste disposal operations come back to haunt them. It just isn't worth it, particularly if part of your waste is toxic.

Safety and Comfort. The next area to consider is safety and creature comfort. Perhaps my attitude toward these items are out of step with general cost-conscious thinking, but I believe that you end up with greater safety, fewer accidents, more productivity, less absenteeism, and a much happier shop when a little more time and effort is put into planning these factors. For example, lots of light and color-coded pathways make it easier to see and move. Do what you can to keep the noise level down, possibly partitioning off excessively noisy areas. It's amazing how noise contributes to fatigue, and how fatigue contributes to accidents. Sometimes, music can be advantageously piped in. More important, if it is possible, include air conditioning. It works wonders for productivity during long hot summer days. And last but not least, washrooms and toilets. Make arrangements to keep them clean, even if you have to do it yourself. There is nothing so debilitating or depressing than dirty facilities. I believe that dirty and filthy toilets and washrooms create conscious and unconscious resentments that show up in the work.

Time Clocks and Supervision. Place punch-in time clocks in a supervised area. You might be tempted to place it near an entrance and exit, but don't. Place it where it can be seen by security, a receptionist, or supervisor.

As to supervision. This doesn't refer to the foreman or boss. It refers to layout. If possible, try to adjust the layout so that as much can be seen and taken in with a glance as possible. For example, if you have an enclosed tool bin, arrange the tools in a manner that let you to tell at a glance what tools have been signed out or are missing. It not only helps you, but it provides incentive for the employee responsible to fill the empty spaces.

A well-done layout is an asset. When your plan and layout is completed, you can use it to verify the capital equipment, space, and facilities costs you estimated in your pro forma.

Chapter 16

Handling Money, Inventory, and People

WHEN YOU SPEND COMPANY MONEY, BE STINGY. DON'T PUT FUNDS THAT you do not immediately need (within a week) in your checking account. Keep the money in a liquid assets or money market fund where you can quickly withdraw it when needed but where it earns interest when idle. The important thing is that the money be productive; at very least, it should earn interest for you. Every major company operates in this manner. When you have excess capital, estimate your needs for approximately the amount of time it takes to easily transfer money from the fund back into your active checking account. Carrying a large balance in your checking account really doesn't do you very much good.

BORROWING MONEY

If you want to borrow money after start-up, you can turn to several sources. Banks and insurance companies lend money on the basis of company assets (inventory, machinery, receivables, etc.). Many vendors, as part of their method of operation, will lease you machinery and equipment. Many lenders also will advance funds to you for the purchase of machinery. They lend you money using the machinery as collateral. They might also lend you money on your inventory or other assets. Various types of financial institutions will make loans that are *collateralized*, or backed up by something they can sell to recoup their money if you default on the loan.

157

Factors operate by lending you money on your receivables. They discount a percentage of your receivables then lend you money on the remainder (anywhere from several points above prime to who-knows-what). Their lending policies fluctuate in relation to the availability of money and the degree of risk. In essence, they lend you money on money that is due you. For example, suppose you have money due you from a particular store and you can't wait until you're paid. Factors will give you a percentage of the money that is due you on the bill immediately. Then when the bill is paid, the full amount goes directly to them. They deduct their charges and you get the remainder.

Factor charges vary. But, one thing is certain . . . they are high. The problem with dealing with factors is that once you get into their clutches, it is difficult to work your way out. The factor is taking an appreciable part of your profits with him when he takes his percentage. Unless you can build that "factoring" cost into your pricing structure, it becomes difficult to free yourself from the factor.

There are private sources of capital: individuals or small groups with money to lend. Many of them are legitimate, but some are sharks. I have yet to come across a private source of funding for business that you don't have to watch very, very carefully. Make sure that you read and understand whatever you sign. Consult your attorney. Private sources can be very dangerous. Be careful: know what the consequences will be if you do not meet your payments on time.

BUYING AND PAYING

Buy only what you need in the smallest economical order quantity (EOQ). Again, be stingy. Let your distributor or your vendor store your raw material or parts inventory. Find out how long it takes to get his product from him and how reliable he is. Don't keep more product on hand longer than the time it takes between an order on your part and delivery on his part. (Sometimes, you might want to buy a small emergency supply of an item, depending on its importance to your operation.) Don't tie money up unnecessarily in inventory that you don't need immediately. Sometimes you can get a bargain when you buy in quantity, but in most instances, it is better to have the cash than the material.

Bargain when you can. Don't accept prices on a face value basis. See what you can do about negotiating its price. Bargaining is as American as pumpkin pie. The point is that your survival and your future is at stake. To grow and prosper, you must bargain.

Pay as late as you can without injuring your credit. If you feel compelled to pay for work or materials immediately, consult a shrink. Keep the money for yourself as long as you can; earn as much as you can on that money or keep it in reserve to take care of an emergency. *Use money as a tool*; don't use it as a means of ego satisfaction.

Make-or-Buy Decisions

When your company gets into production, you are going to have to make many make-or-buy decisions. If it is more profitable to buy a product than to make it, buy it. Make-or-buy decisions should be based on whether or not you can make it cheaper, better, different—in whatever manner that enables you to end up with the maximum profit. There are times when the cost of capital equipment dictates "buy" rather than a "make" decision.

In costing for a make-or-buy decision, consider questions like these. How much inventory must you maintain of the product? What machinery will you require in order to make the product? How many additional people will you need and how much will they cost? Do they need special skills? etc. Base your decision on relative costs for make or buy. Sometimes the decision is not clear cut; it lies in a grey area. When in doubt, my feeling is buy the product rather than add another step in your process of manufacture. You might even save yourself a lot of aggravation, time, and money.

However, if there is a reasonable possibility that you can make a profit by making it yourself, then you should seriously consider doing so. The final decision should be based on the profit you make on the ultimate product—not on the money you save by making a particular component.

Quality Control

Quality control is without question one of the most important aspects of running a business. I do not care what you make, how you make it, where you make it—before you ship it out the door, you must make absolutely sure that it is a good product. Bad products come back to haunt you. It takes a long time to overcome the bad taste of faulty products resulting from poor quality control.

There is nothing more stupid than sending out a product that is bad. The cost to your company, and to the customer, is so high that it is well worth the extra time, effort, and cost to review the product very carefully before it goes out the door.

It is less expensive to maintain an operation in tip-top condition than it is to rebuild it or buy new equipment. It is also a lot safer when you keep the plant clean, and setup so that people can see what they are doing. When the noise level is kept down and the work environment is pleasant, productivity goes up.

Inventory Control

I have discussed inventory control before. It is not difficult to keep your inventory in line with your forecast. Do not maintain a sizable finished product inventory unless necessary. Think of all those idle dollars that are tied up. Having a backlog of orders for finished goods can be very comforting. If delivery takes a couple of weeks, people will wait for a good product. You are not going to lose many sales by having a backlog; as a matter of fact, it creates quite a good impression. Don't keep any large inventory of either raw materials or finished goods than is absolutely essential. Think money. Think survival. The only time a large inventory can be valuable is if somewhere along the line the cost of material in inventory is going to shoot up. The only other time you might want a finished goods inventory greater than what you actually need is when you anticipate a strike or some sort of interruption of your work process. A strike might not only shut down production, it might also shut you down completely—in which case you've got a lot of reserve capital tied up in immovable inventory.

If I were to give one piece of advice to anyone going into business, I would say, *"Think and anticipate."*

COLLECTING

I have found collecting money due me to be extraordinarily difficult. It must be done with a reasonable degree of politeness, patience, and charm—characteristics I happen to have in short supply.

A secretary or bookkeeper who has the special capability of asking a customer for money on the phone does a lot better than someone threatening the customer with all sorts of nasty things. I have found letters (either nice or nasty) ineffective. The point is that you want to collect your money. If you can do so easily, great! You might even end up keeping a customer. You might reach a point, however, where you must say to a customer that you can't ship him any more unless he pays up for the last delivery. You might lose a customer, but on the other hand, if he isn't paying you, you are just giving your product away.

Some companies impose penalties if payment is late. Some companies add on 0.5% to 1.5% per month to any unpaid balance. Take a look at credit card operations and you will immediately see that they extract penalties for late payment. Imposing penalties depends on how strong a company is. To put it another way—how important are you to your customers, and how important are they to you?

EMPLOYEE RELATIONS

In the area of employee relations, my advice is, "Be friendly, but don't be a father to your employees." Never be intimate, and I mean *never* be intimate. If you have troubles, tell them to a shrink or to your wife or to a friend—*never* tell them to your employees because it scares them.

Be fair and reasonable. Employees are not your family; and they don't own part of the business. Your personal policies must be related to your capabilities as a start-up operation. People understand that you have very limited resources and that you are going to be working just as hard as they are if not harder.

As a start-up company you are limited in the amount that you can pay to your employees. You can make it clear that after the company becomes better established, you will be very willing to increase people's salaries and benefits. Think carefully before you make any promises.

Don't get involved in your employees' troubles. You are not a psychiatrist or psychologist, and the probability is that you can't help them. They might talk to you about their problems simply because you are an authority figure. Maybe you do know more than they do, but the chances are you don't, so don't get involved. It is their situation. If their personal problems affect their work, then you must take proper action. Do not let any employee difficulties interfere with business. And certainly not your personal life.

Again, be friendly. Be nice. But don't try to be a father to them all.

Chapter 17
Where to Look
For Money

BEFORE YOU START LOOKING FOR MONEY, DETERMINE EXACTLY WHAT YOU are willing to give up for it—how much of your company and how much of your life.

The first time around some people (and, I suspect, many venture capitalists and banks) will deliberately give you just enough money *to fail*. Your first projections—your evaluation of your abilities, markets, etc.—are usually on the optimistic side. Because you want the money, you might underestimate your actual needs. These people will pressure you into reducing the requirements, as projected in your pro forma, to the bone. And you end up saying, "Okay" because you're so anxious to start the business. Inevitably you will need more money. You haven't failed, but you need more money.

How much you give up to get that money is always negotiable. It depends on how much the investors want in and on how well you've been able to sell the product. It also depends on how succesful you are at the time you're looking for money. Give up as little as you can. Remember you're going to make mistakes, so try to get enough money to survive them.

Most investors are not interested in money for contingency purposes. Some will even refuse to consider it. I believe that ignoring contingency funding can lead to disaster. The smart inventor will include contingency funds somewhere in the pro forma, even if he has to hide them. Remember, *survival is the key*.

The first time around you might make a reasonable deal: the percentage

162

you give up is not bad . . . not the greatest percentage, but not bad. The second time you go for funds, you need the money to keep the business going so it won't fold. Your investors know that you are in a precarious position; they know that you are tied into them; therefore, the second time around, your give-up is going to be pretty hefty. At that point you either get enough to succeed or you fail because, the third time around, you have practically lost it all—then you are working for them.

The moral of the story is try to get what you need the first time. Work the deal so that as additional capital is required, the dilution of your percent ownership is limited.

COMPANY CONTROL

If you don't get as much money as you want the first time around, and you have to go back a second or even a third time (with dilution taking place each time), you have not necessarily lost control of the company. The percentage of ownership in the company does not always dictate who controls it. Actual control is exercised by the person who is capable of running the company and does it effectively. People who put up money might think they are capable of running the company, but they generally are not. Thus, if they throw you out, they will have to find somebody to bring in and run the operation. Of course, some investors might line someone up to run the company before they throw you out. (And they can throw you out because, after all, they are on the board of directors and vote their shares of stock). Many entrepreneurs, specify in advance that the board of directors vote on the basis of one man, one vote—not on the basis of number of shares each director owns. This is one possible method of keeping control.

Another way to keep control is to create a board consisting of people you know you can rely on. This method is very tricky. If you have to go back for money, the people who have the money are the ones who are in control. They are the ones who can dictate who you go to for the money, where you go for the money, and under what conditions you are to take the money. To repeat:

1. Try to get all the money you will need in the beginning.
2. Try to negotiate the deal so that you are still in control every time additional funding is procured by protecting yourself against excessive dilution, regardless of the number of times that additional capital is invested.
3. Qualify any promises or forecasts that are in your business plan or pro forma. You want them to be as accurate and truthful as you can possibly make them. To protect yourself, however, include as many caveats and as many disclaimers as are necessary, preferably in the beginning of the pro forma and at the time you're negotiating the deal. Take care not to make yourself vulnerable to a

lawsuit by anyone later claiming, "Well, this is what you said; this is what you promised could be done."

THE MONEY PEOPLE

Remember, it is not necessary to know an investor personally. I think it's important to stress this point. Too often I've heard the plaintive cry from people that they couldn't find backing because the didn't know who to approach. Just keep in mind that money people are looking for good deals just as hard as you are looking for money people. You don't have to know them personally to call them or write to them. However, if you know them personally (and they are not family or friends), as people who have money to invest, you can approach them. They might also know others who might be interested in investing. If your deal is attractive to them, the chances are that they will circulate it among their friends and associates.

In dealing with money people, make sure that they are legitimate; I say that with all due respect for the word "legitimate." Too many people get taken very quickly and very easily. Let me caution you:

If you ever you go to somebody for money and they ask you to put up money, run! Get away from them as fast as you can because it is a scam.

A legitimate investor is not going to ask you to put up anything out of your pocket, or pay for anything other than what you have already invested in your invention. If it is a good deal, he's the one who is going to be putting up the money. If any investor comes along and says, "I'd love to back you, but I want to be sure that you're going to work very hard. Therefore, to protect my investment, I'd like you to put your house or your property up as collateral for the money I put into the your project, and I'll just take a second mortgage on your house." Run like crazy! Legitimate people don't act like that. Legitimate people want you to be secure; they want you to be able to concentrate on business. If you are going to have to work under the pressure of having your home under the gun, you are not going to do the best work that you can. You will be too anxiety-ridden to work effectively.

At times, the amount of money that you are looking for might not seem to have much relation to the type of business that you are involved in. You just have to justify the amount you need and make the project sound exciting to potential investors. It has always seemed to me, however, that it is just as hard to raise $50,000 as it is to raise $500,000. It might even be easier to raise $5,000,000 than it is to raise $500,000. The same amount of work, if not more, goes into raising the $50,000 or $500,000 as for $5,000,000, it just costs more.

It might sound silly, but that is approximately the way it is. People seem to be more willing to listen to bigger numbers. The main factors appear to be "newness," return on investment, and degree of safety. The bigger the potential return, the better your chances.

AVOID FAMILY AND FRIENDS

In looking for money, if at all possible, avoid family and friends. If your money comes from family members, resentment and acrimony are bound to result. If you fail, you will never live it down. If you succeed, it will be because they provided you with the funds. When you get money from family, their underlying feeling is that they're taking a chance on you only because you're a relative and that you're essentially gambling with their money. This feeling creates the basis for difficulty down the line. If you fail, they might resent your using any money (yours or theirs) to live on. If you take a vacation, they'll say, "Why aren't you paying back the money?" You might be working very hard, but if you are not working hard enough (in their judgment), they will grumble. If you make money, they might resent your living high on the hog because they might not be making as much on their investment as they thought they would.

The list of potential difficulties can go on and on. The best policy is that, if at all possible, never go to the family for money.

The same holds true for friends. If you possibly can, never ask a friend for money.

Whether you succeed or fail, money from friends also leads to resentment. It is enough to say that family and friends always have unrealistic expectations, and misunderstandings ensue. More important is the way it might make you feel having to go to them for funds. If it makes you feel like "the family failure," for goodness sake don't do it. You need all the self-confidence and strengrth you can muster to make the business succeed without carrying that on your back.

The place to look for money is where money is available: professional sources.

PRIVATE INVESTORS

When dealing with private investors, you are dealing with individuals who have access to money. These people usually act as if this has made them brighter, smarter, and certainly an expert in every field. Although very few possess all of these characteristics, to quote a famous maxim, "With the rich and mighty, one must be patient."

BANKERS, LAWYERS, AND ACCOUNTANTS

Your best bet is probably to take your plan to a bank. Ask the bankers if they have any investors who are looking for new business ventures. Many banks have such a service for their accounts. People come to banks looking for investment opportunities.

Law firms, another source, frequently have clients who are always looking for investments. The firms will circulate a proposal so that the partners and people working within the firm can inform their clients about opportunities of interest.

Accounting firms and accountants operate in the same way. Although brokerage houses rarely get into start-up situations, you might give them a try.

VENTURE CAPITALISTS

Another source is venture capitalists (VC), people who have formed companies that include specialists in management and risk money investment. Most big money people—managers of foundations, pension funds ,and others, such as very rich individuals who allocate a percentage of their investment protfolio to "risk" ventures—no longer look to the banks, accountants, or legal firms for opoprtunities to invest for them or are solicited by the firms for individual deals.

As a professional grouping, venture capitalists are ready and able to put up the money needed to get a venture going. There are several places you can find venture capitalists, but the best source is a massive directory that lists 800 companies in the United States and Canada. It is published by Venture Economics, Inc., 1640 Laurel Avenue, Wellesley Hills, MA 02181. The directory is called *Pratt's Guide to Venture Capital Sources*. There are also VC magazines and a VC association that provides a directory of members.

The directory lists the VC companies and names the person to contact. It tells you what kind of money they are willing to put up, whether they are willing to put up seed money or get into R & D operations, second stage financing, etc., and what kind of businesses they prefer. It lists it all. About one-third of the beginning of the book describes how to work with venture capitalists. Each yearly edition has new articles aimed at keeping the reader informed of new trends and directions.

Working with Venture Capitalists

You must get to the right VC firm, a firm that specializes or deals with your kind of product. Once in the right firm, you want to reach the right person, the one who knows something about what you are trying to do. VC firms employ industry specialists (people who are expert in various areas such as electronics, computers, biomedicine, communications) as well as generalists (high tech, low tech, and no tech).

Venture capitalists consider many deals; some say between fifty and a hundred deals come into their office each month. They distribute these to the appropriate people in the firm.

How much time does a venture capitalist have to look at each new deal that comes in over the transom? Not much. For example, a VC account executive might have a portfolio of six or more companies. He is on the board of directors of each of these companies; he has to maintain contact with the presidents and executives of these companies and make sure things are working right to protect the money that his firm has invested. That doesn't leave him much time to examine pro formas, business plans, and proposals that come to him. Of the hundred that the firm might receive in one month, only one of five might be of final interest. To consider your proposal, he must take precious time away from the operations for which he is responsible. He has companies that are doing well, and companies that are doing badly. (He is probably spending of a lot more time with the companies that are doing badly.)

When you send your proposal to a venture capitalist, remember how busy he is. Don't feel hurt or discouraged if he doesn't call you immediately. Keep calling the man until you get an answer from him. Keep in mind that he is not ignoring you personally, and you should recognize this. You have to persist and persuade him to take the time to consider what you offer. Sometimes you are lucky. What you offer might stimulate him sufficiently to cause him to take a good, hard look at your proposal right away and possibly go with it. Some VC account executives even give you good grades for the degree of persistence you show in trying to reach them.

Venture capitalists are often considered arrogant. But, consider their position. They have responsibility for the money they invest, and they have to account for it to the people that have given them the money in the first place. Last but not least, their own income comes from successful operations, not losing ones.

If they invest in too many losing ventures, their judgment will be questioned, and their ability to get additional money to invest diminishes. They work under extreme pressure and are much too busy to be nice—and that's why they often get a reputation for being extraordinarily arrogant in personal relationships. (I believe that they would have fewer losses and be less pressured if they set up proper operating management support systems—but this is wishful thinking.)

VC firms probably know little about how a business operation should be run. But (and this is a big but from my point of view) they often know quite a bit about their own operations. You might not agree with it, but they will demand you justify the particular actions that you are taking. I feel that this can be the most productive aspects of running a company—demanding that the key people justify their actions.

Working with venture capitalists is probably the fastest path because they are prepared to put up risk capital. I have never worked with them, however; I have always worked with private investors. Working with venture capitalists presents problems. Most venture capitalists that I have met expect too much from the inventor. They expect you to be a full-fledged business-man, finance man, production man, marketing man, operations man, and administrator—all at the same time. If I could be reasonably competent in one area, I would be satisfied. You can have a smattering of knowledge in several areas of business, and that smattering can sometimes carry you through, but it certainly does not make you an expert in every area. It makes you capable of hiring people who can provide expertise in those areas in which you lack experience. Venture capitalists expect you to be competent in all these areas. It is impossible, absolutely impossible.

Venture capitalists are also chary of working with inventors because they consider the inventor to be a pain. The inventor might not know many of the areas that are required in running a business, and the VC expects him to run the business. They want his enthusiasm and his capability, but they refuse to recognize that he does not have the competence to do everything they expect from him.

Another reason VCs find inventors difficult to work with is that they won't stop improving things. They are constantly improving the methods of production of the product or anything that suits their fancy. The one thing that an inventor must learn in putting together a successful operation is: when you get it working, stop!

This compulsion to constantly work on an invention tends to drain the resources of the company. Not only does it create problems in the utilization of capital, it impedes production capability and delays the receipt of income. In addition, it's usually a waste of time and effort. It endangers the success of the company. Any inventor who does that must be stopped. If you perceive this to be a concern on the investor's part, do whatever is necessary to reassure him that what you have is what you're going with.

What Venture Capitalists Expect

What do venture capitalists really expect from you? What do they want to know about the business that they are backing? They would like a 10-to-1 return on investment in a period of three years. In other words, if they put up $10, in three years they want that $10 to be worth $100. That is great because if their investment has grown so well, yours has too. How do they make that money back? They make it by taking the company public, at which point, if the offering is successful, everybody makes out very well indeed. Their preference is not to sell the company to another company because that does not give them the return on investment that they can get through the public offering. That is how they really make their money. It is not by the growth of the company alone and the dividend payback over a long period of time. They make it on the basis that the company value has gone up sufficiently so that other people are willing to buy into it.

Buying and Selling Stocks

In nearly all cases (except for the corporate raider), when ordinary people buy stock in the Stock Market all they are buying is speculative paper, nothing more. Even in new issues when a company first goes public, the money raised through the offering doesn't always go to the company for working capital. The money might very well go to the owner who has decided to go public to get some of his accumulated assets or his money out of the company.

In the old days, when somebody found a gold mine, he made more money by selling certificates of stock in his mine than he did by mining the gold. If the value of the mine was estimated at a $100,000, he would sell gold certificates worth $1,000,000. Again, all that the people were buying was a speculative piece of paper, true a part ownership in a mine, but paper bought in the hope that someone else would pay more for it than they did.

The same principle is true in the stock market today. There are companies listed on the stock market whose stock value is maybe four to ten times more than the company is worth. If you sold all the assets of those companies, the return would be much less than the money invested in the stock of the company.

But there is another side of the story. The so-called "wolves of Wall Street" are people who look for companies that are undervalued. Although the outstanding stock of one of these companies might be worth $5,000,000, the actual value or assets of the company make it worth $10,000,000. So the wolves swoop in and buy up enough of the company stock to take control, then they sell the assets of the company for a handsome profit. For example, a multinational manufacturing corporation once carried a skyscraper located in the heart of the New York City financial district on it's books for $10,000. It was, of course, worth several million dollars. This situation was a perfect target for an attack by wolves.

The main thing to remember when you're buying stock is that you are dealing with paper—the buying and selling of a piece of paper. Paper that represents an idea. Paper that others will wish to acquire and thereby increase the value of the paper for others to follow and do the same until the trading in the paper is similar to kids trading in baseball cards. After a while, it has no direct bearing on or benefit to the company, just as the popularity of the cards have no bearing on how well the player will do on the field. The paper has value only to the people who want the paper. Venture capitalists use this situation to make money for themselves as well as make money for you.

Majority Interest

Venture capitalists want majority interest in the company almost immediately. They might demand up to 80 percent of any company that they put money into. Get the most you can get up front. You're going to have to give up more and more as you go back to the well. These are sharp operators who are, most of the time, very good businessmen. They are betting on your being successful just as much as you are.

Venture capitalists operate with the monies of wealthy individuals, pension funds, foreign investors, and independent investors. Pension funds are probably a major source of the funds with which venture capitalists operate.

When a VC company goes into a deal, the investors get 80 percent of the income that the VC company receives and the partners of the VC firm get the remaining 20 percent. Those percentages will vary depending on the kind of deal that has been made by the VC company with its investors. In most cases, however, the money that the VC company is using is money that is not theirs.

The people who run a VC operation do so on an incentive basis. The VC business can be considered a funds management business. VC operations vary a great deal in methodology. They may start with seed money and go all the way to leveraged buyouts. They run the entire gamut of funding. As an industry, VC companies provide less than one-half percent of the monies invested in public markets (bond and stock markets, money management funds, etc.). Even so, they control about tens of billions of dollars a year. Each of the companies is very competitive in it's search for areas in which to invest. But don't let that competition fool you. Venture capitalists are also very cooperative and often do a good number of joint deals.

What venture capitalists look for is not just a quick return but a growing return. If you brought them the hula-hoop, they might fund it, but what they are really looking for is the building of a business. Their objective is to build a continuing operation that grows, makes money, and develops into industry. When going for a deal, consider the innate prejudices of the venture capitalist company and their individual representatives. They and their company might prefer to work in particular industries; they look for areas in which they have experience, areas in which they feel they are going to make the most money.

In any new venture, venture capitalists focus on the marketing operation: Is it capable of paying the bills? Regardless of how well you start an operation, it is customers who pay the bills by buying the product. What the VC people are looking for is *sustainable competitive advantage*. They are looking at your proposition in the hope of finding *both* a great product and a great market. They would at least settle for a great market rather than a great product. The product might be the best in the world, but if it doesn't do well in the marketplace, it is not going to do anybody much good.

Venture capitalists like companies with the following: a strong independent distribution system or a working relationship with other companies that are going to buy, market, and sell their product. Unless they know that there are customers out there willing to buy the product, the venture capitalist won't give your invention top consideration. To him, the market and its size indicates the degree of success that might be forthcoming.

R & D Partnerships

Venture capitalists also get into an area known as Research and Development Partnerships. Some firms think very highly of R & D partnerships, and they do offer advantages to inventors. For every dollar that an investor puts into the development of a new invention, he gets a dollar for dollar write off on his income tax. Every dollar he gets back, he treats as capital gains. For example, an R & D partnership is put together, investors put up $100,000, and each investor writes off his contribution on his income tax immediately. When the inventor successfully completes an invention, the partnership licenses it to someone else and makes $500,000. The $500,000 that comes into the R & D partnership is treated by each individual in the partnership as capital gains income. That's pretty good. There are some drawbacks in setting up an R & D partnership, but there are many benefits too. If it seems to be appropriate to what you are doing, you might look for a venture capital firm that specializes in R & D partnerships.

Investing in People

Venture capitalists claim that what they are investing in is people. If the people fail, then they have to step in and take over. My feeling is that if this were true, they'd provide management backup as a standard practice rather than their usual overseer participation. They certainly replace any number of executives that get in their way. It might be necessary for you to impress a venture capitalist about how competent you are, but in the end, it is the deal itself that makes or breaks your relationship with the venture capitalist.

If you can get venture capitalists to sit on your board of directors, they can provide valuable criticism, contributing to the building and sustaining of a good company. Some VCs look for a good management team. They want persons who know their limitations, recognize when they need help, and ask for the help. They want people who will be dedicated to the job of creating and building up the company. The team that they look for is competent in five disciplines.

1. They want a president or chief executive officer, to run the show.
2. They want a marketing person to sell the product.

3. They want a financial officer to handle the finances of the company.
4. They want a production person who knows how to get the product made and get it made well.
5. They want the inventor . . . the technical wiz who puts the product together, who makes the next generation, who makes changes where necessary, and who does the R & D.

This makes up a good team—good to have whether the venture capitalist wants to be involved or not.

Your Business Plan

In addition to the management team, the VC will examine your business plan. He will examine the whole plan, probably stopping at particular areas for a closer examination. One area he will concentrate on is forecasting—not only the forecasts themselves, but how you intend to reach your sales and income target, whether this operation is seasonal, the number of customers in the market, the type of customers, the sales cycle, how frequently you might have to sell, how many sales calls are needed to sell each item, and what support services you require. *He evaluates the assumptions that you have made* for sales and revenues. If you have no history of sales or income, then the only thing he can judge is your assumptions.

Even companies with a long history of sales have great difficulty in making accurate sales forecasts. As I mentioned in chapter 12, the best way to put together a sales forecast is on a customer-to-customer basis. If you use market research as the basis, people will often say yes just to please you or get rid of you. (I am sure that you have already taken that into consideration and discounted a good deal of it before you put your sales figures down.) Venture capitalists are not dummies. They will look closely at your assumptions—how you reached your figures for the total market and the share of the market that you think you can capture.

Remember: if you can't reach it, don't count it.

The most important factor in attracting the interest of venture capitalists is to have a product market—a product that has a sustainable advantage. Hit him hard with proof that your product solves a problem or provides a convenience or an economy that the user cannot get elsewhere. This sustainable advantage is a key element in selling a venture capitalist on your project. Any proof you can supply enhances your position.

Even though venture capitalists are competitive, they go into deals with other VC firms. Consider this point when shopping your deal around. If you have seen several venture capitalists, they might be aware that you have seen others besides themselves. You might or might not want to disclose that you have presented your propositions to other VCs. I have no recommendations in this area. You must decide for yourself what you disclose to each VC

Funds From VCs

Generally, an individual VC account executive will be able to put up seed money; the amount depends on what his firm will permit him to do. The amount can range from $10,000 to $100,000. He might do this on his own authority if he is convinced you can do the job, but he is accountable to other people.

Depending on the policies of the VC company and the rank of the individual within the company, he might also be authorized to fund first-stage operations, which can range from $500,000 to $1,000,000. When it comes to big money, the VC wants partners. Most venture capitalists like deals between $3,000,000 and $5,000,000; some of the deals that they get into run to a $100,000,000 or more. When they get to that level, they look for some sort of insurance, similar to the way Lloyds of London operates. They bring in as many partners (other VC companies) as possible to take on as much of the deal as they want to sell to these additional partners. These people are not frivolous; they don't give money away. They might distribute your business plan to other venture capitalists if they feel the need for the insurance of wider participation. They might bring you along to help sell the deal to other VCs. as a joint venture. Venture capitalists will check your references and finances and those of all your key people. They will check everyone's history of dedication and commitment to the jobs that they have had, and their commitment to your particular enterprise. They might even check your customers, if you claim that you have customers. They might go to the marketplace and say, "Here is a product that I am thinking of investing in. What do you think about it?" They will do their own research if they feel they should. They want to know how well your product will sell, how you are going to sell it, under what conditions you are going to sell it, whether you are going to do it alone or are going to have to make a deal with someone else to sell it, or if it is best for you to hire your own salesman. The smart ones will check everything they can.

OTHER SOURCES

Substantial capital can be obtained from *private sources* in the form of grants. There is an enormous amount of grant money out there that is available from a large number of foundations. The *Foundations Directory* lists these foundations, describing what each of these foundations does, and what kind of money they have available.

All foundations operate under charters, which define how they must distribute their money. One cannot establish a foundation just for the purpose of accumulating funds and avoiding taxes. The entire purpose of the foundation is to be able to give money away. Each foundation has rules and conditions under which they must operate. These rules are available to the public under certain prescribed conditions. You can use the *Foundations Directory* to find them and determine their rules. If you are going to do something that might benefit mankind, you might be able to get your seed money from a foundation to get started—and then go on from there to get regular investment money.

Pension funds and *insurance companies* are permitted, under prescribed conditions to use a small percentage of their funds for "risk ventures." These can be another source for you.

Government agencies are a possible source of funds. I have never found any individual who has ever received money from them, however, and certainly not start-up funds. I have known government agencies that provide money for research to small businesses, but the federal government considers a small business one that has up to 500 employees. As a rule, if the average revenue per employee is $20,000, then a company with 500 employees would have an income of $10,000,000. Not many people would consider this a "small" company.

I personally wouldn't bother with government agencies (federal, state, county, etc.) unless I was absolutely forced to because the chances of getting anything are so slim. The various governments put on a big show of trying to establish new industry, new business, new jobs, but when you ask them for money, the standoff begins. By the time you go from one step to the next, you have exhausted yourself and wasted months of time. You end up with nothing.

If you insist on trying to get funds from a government agency, however, one of the best references was published by Capital Publishing Corporation in 1982 (now known as Venture Economics). The publication is out of print but should be available in libraries. It's called *"Source Guide to Government, Technology, and Financial Assistance*, edited by Harry P. Greenwald. It indicates all the areas of government, technology, and financial assistance and provides information on how best to work with government agencies.

Of course, in all of this there has to be an exception, and there is. It is the *Small Business Innovation Research Program*, simply known as the SBIR, which I discussed in chapter 2.

> *The major objective of the SBIR program is the commercial application of funded projects.*

The SBIR act was set up to stimulate technological innovation, encourage small innovative firms to participate in government research, and provide incentive for the conversion of research results into commercial applications. Eleven federal agencies participate in the SBIR program and publish quarterly solicitation announcements (see list in chapter 2). These announcements are specifications of devices, new products, inventions, and research and development programs required by the agency.

The program has established a process for taking a needed idea through the stages of research, development, and demonstration to commercial application. There are three phases to the SBIR program:

- □ *Phase I*—Provides up to $50,000 to support the effort in order to demonstrate the scientific and technical merit and feasibility of the innovation. Its primary purpose is *only* to show that the innovator's *concept* for the solution to the presented problem will work.
- □ *Phase II*—Funds successfully completed Phase I projects with awards of up to $500,000 to further develop the innovation. It is in this phase that a prototype of the innovation is built.
- □ *Phase III*—Requires private sector investment to support a project to commercialization. The Department of Defense, NASA, or the soliciting agency usually provide a ready-market for successful innovations they fund in the first two phases. Because the ready-market for the innovation is usually built into the project, it is generally easy to raise the necessary funds for the last phase.

A number of countries, particularly Japan, foster new ideas and new enterprises with low-interest loans and other financial and management assistance. Indeed, they will support a start-up operation for many years to permit it to develop and thrive. Their gains in terms of new industry has far outweighed any losses sustained through failures. Their programs are not phony. They are really interested in starting and supporting new ideas and new businesses.

GOING PUBLIC

Last but not least is the great adventure of raising needed money via a public stock offering. Although great amounts of money can be raised, the major problem with raising money in this fashion is that it is very risky. The cost is enormous. It can range from $150,000 up depending on what you're trying to do. There is an out to these costs, however; that is, finding a broker who has attorneys and accountants in tow and is willing to forgo his fees for a piece of the action. But, I'm getting ahead of myself.

The business plan and pro forma that you have prepared can be used as a basis for interesting a stock brokerage house in your project. This is primarily and particularly true if what you're involved with is on the leading edge of any area of high tech. Nevertheless, brokerage houses have been known to take on low and no tech projects if the situation seems promising to them.

If you think of stockbrokers as selling and buying agents, it will help clarify what they do. If you wish to buy or sell stock, they will do it for you for a commission. In addition to dealing with stocks that are already on the market, they will (with the help of attorneys, accountants, and printers) prepare and create a stock for offering to the public—after a stock has met all the regulation requirements, they will offer it for sale to their customers and other brokerage houses. It sometimes seems to me that, as salesmen, what stockbrokers really look for is "sizzle." Don't be misled by this. Brokerage houses and the stock market is probably the most regulated and patrolled business sector there is. True, brokers want something to sell, something to talk about and convince clients to buy, but they also demand substance.

Part of the risk in a public offering is that the sale of new issue is usually done on a "best efforts" basis. In other words, if they don't sell the minimum offered, the entire deal can fall apart.

Another factor to consider is that once you go public, you must adhere to a series of very stringent regulations dictated by law and administered by the Securities Exchange Commission (SEC). You can no longer just go ahead and do anything you want to do with the company or its stock, you must make sure that you're within the law. If not, you can be very heavily fined and sent to jail. All your books (financial records) and reports much be certified by a Certified Public Accountant (CPA).

With all of the problems inherent in going public, it is my feeling that if my product lent itself to such an offering, I'd try a brokerage house before I took the project to a venture capitalist. Who knows you might hit pay dirt. I see no reason why the public should not be offered the same opportunity in terms of risk and reward as venture capitalists. As long as it's honestly presented, you have nothing to lose.

There are several types of brokerage houses. The very staid firms deal only in listed stocks and will only consider a public offering if the company has been in business many years, has a track record, and has earnings of "X" millions of dollars. Other brokers specialize in unlisted *penny stocks* that are sold in the over-the-counter market.

My suggestion is that if this area is of interest to you, that you hasten to the library and look up over-the-counter houses specializing in new issues and pursue them. Some of the publications are newsletters that even list the types of new issues sold by the various firms. Before I pursued anybody, however, I'd do everything I could to learn about this highly complicated area of financing. There are simply too many pitfalls if you do not know what you're doing or getting into.

Chapter 18

Legalities:
An Overview of
Courts, Lawyers,
and Patent Protection

I HATE TO BE CHEATED, YET AS AN INVENTOR, I KNOW THAT THE CARDS ARE stacked against me. I know this, yet I continue to invent because I must.

I sometimes believe that the cheaters know this and therefore continue to take advantage of me regardless of the precautions I take. I believe that as time goes on, I have become less paranoid and take fewer precautions. I've begun to believe that the only way not to be cheated is to make a deal based on being personally needed in addition to the invention. Unless the deal is, and continues to be, mutually beneficial and reasonably successful, you can be cheated. I say "reasonably successful" with deliberation. If it's too successful, the resentment of paying you "all that money" in royalties builds to a point where plans begin to hatch about how to cheat you out of what's due you.

The trouble is that it's easy, very easy, to do. The law of the land is against you. The courts are generally both ignorant and against you. The lawyers love you like Dracula loves his victims. The odds are very much against you. And, most important, you as an individual generally don't have the ability or the finances to fight back.

With all this said:

1. The right to patent is one of the only three property rights granted by the United States Constitution.
2. The average cost of fighting a patent validity suit is $250,000.

3. If someone smokes on a bus, he will usually get in more trouble than if he stole my invention, even if it's patented. If someone steals my inventions, and make bundles of money on it, he'll probably get away with it.
4. Most patents are worthless.

Despite all this, the Patent Office is, as far as I know, the only branch of the American government that has never had a scandal associated with it. Never! It is the most honest agency that we have in our government. The people there are very conscientious and hard working. The fact that the courts have been so one-sided with patents is because industry wants the patent system to be weak in the sense that it takes money to protect patents.

It is terrifying to know that 80 percent of all patents brought before the courts are overturned or held invalid.

Nothing happens in this great country of ours unless some power group wants it to happen. When there's to be a change in the way the Patent Office operates, you can be sure that some lobby has its hands in the game and influences the decisions made by the federal courts hearing patent cases.

There are many reasons why I consider the patents issued by the United States Patent Office as worthless. It seems to me that the reason patents are worthless unless backed by large corporate legal bankrolls is that industry wants it that way. Most of the original and worthwhile inventions that occur in our country come from independent inventors. Keep the patent weak and the legal costs high, and industry can take anything it wants from anyone weaker. (Don't tell me about giants suing each other over patent rights. That happens because some executive has made a mistake or because the market is so large that a company has much to gain and relatively little to lose. And don't naively believe that corporations worry about such things as bad publicity relating to patent suits by independent inventors.)

Not too long ago, the Patent Office ruled that inventors must pay periodic fees to keep their constitutional right of monopoly. Do you really think that the Patent Office needs these fees to help its operating budget? I'll bet that the fees it gets from independent inventors don't appreciably affect its operating costs, but the fees sure impose a financial burden on individual inventors. As patents are abandoned because individuals can't afford to pay the fees, industry picks up the patents—for free.

It is a tragedy to me that America so little values its most productive people—the people who contribute so much to the good life, the people who until recently have kept America in the forefront of world industry; that is, before the giants of American industry began giving away our birthrights to other countries. I'm convinced that most multinational companies don't care about America or its people. It is these companies, through their support of a well-known lobbying group in Washington, that influence patent regulations and set the tone for the way industry and government treat the independent inventor.

I want American patents to protect the inventors. The Patent Office should issue valid patents or none at all. The Patent Office should protect (in court, if necessary) the validity of any patent it issues, or it should be abolished. The patents it issues are worthless unless the funds are provided to protect them.

Patents represent an additional means of helping you sell an invention. Probably less than $\frac{1}{100}$ of 1 percent of all of the people in the world (excluding patent attorneys) understand what a patent is. An invention has never really become an inventor's invention in the United States unless some judge has declared that it is a valid invention and that it belongs to you. Never has an invention belonged to an inventor until that point—never in the entire history of invention in the United States.

When you have a patent, anybody in the United States (or for that matter, in the world) can sue you, challenging the validity of a patent or the "obviousness" of the invention, or for a hundred other reasons. The reason I get patents is not that I consider them valuable in themselves, but valuable as a point that I can make when I talk to people who believe that the patent is going to protect the invention.

Major companies, as a rule, do not sue each other. It is rare that a major company will sue another major company for patent infringement. They apply for patents on everything they can—not because they feel that the patent provides protection, but because they want to scare people off. They recognize that the patent gives them a legal device whereby they can go after anybody who comes close to infringing, if they want to go after them. And they have the money to do it. That's the primary reason for patent operations within the company. Major companies rely on their money and marketing strength to protect themselves.

Most major companies, if one is infringing on another and the market is big, will make a deal—licensing or cross-licensing. They won't waste money suing each other unless they're jockeying for a position in the market.

The problem with American patents is not the Patent Office. The problem with American patents is our judicial system. The judges who must make important final decisions are ignorant about innovation, about mechanics, about electronics, and about most areas of creativity and invention. They probably know nothing at all about your invention; the theory and methodology are explained to them. As the judge sits on the bench, he is being educated by patent attorneys who often are just a little less ignorant of the functions and capability of the invention. I feel it's the rare judge who understands the invention in question, yet judges have the responsibility for deciding whether or not there is obviousness, prior art, or infringement in very technical areas. They can and often have invalidated patents simply because the invention has not been explained to them in terms the judge can understand. The most telling remark I ever heard, attributed to a federal judge, about an invention in an important patent case was, "Someone would have thought of it (the invention) sooner or later." This was the reason he gave for dismissing the inventor's suit against a major corporation.

I am convinced that those lawyers who present the court with the largest volume of paper wins. I frankly don't believe that much of the material presented to the court is ever read either by the judge or his clerks. Maybe it's scanned, but I'd be very surprised if it's ever studied. Go sit in federal court and watch the action. See the volume of cases before the court and take careful note of the quantity of paper presented to the court in each case. And remember, it's the judge who has to make the decision. It challenges the imagination to think that the judge can read, understand, and digest all that complex patent information. I cannot believe his clerks can do any better. In addition, if they do manage to read the briefs and pass the information on to the judge; all he gets is a summary at best and an unseasoned opinion that has even less understanding of the nuances of the case at worst. For the independent inventor with limited financial clout, it's a disaster, an absolute disaster.

If you think about how inadequately the American inventor is protected, you wonder how we ever became world leaders in industry. As a matter of fact, there seems to be a growing movement by individuals to offer their inventions to foreign countries because they not only are more receptive, but also provide greater protection to the inventor.

Consider the following. The Patent Office hires only highly trained personnel who are expert in various fields of innovation. As they work at their jobs, they become even more expert. In addition, over the years the Patent Office has established a system of patent presentation that clearly, if archaically, describes the invention and its usefulness, and establishes (via the claims) what is new about the invention. A patent application is difficult for the inventor and the patent examiner. Nothing is taken for granted; every detail of a patent application is meticulously reviewed. It generally takes up to two years for the process to be completed. Only after you've satisfied the diligent patent examiner, do you then get a patent.

> A cartoon in my office shows a cave man who has just hacked a wheel out of a square stone. He says to another cave man, "Making it was easy. Now comes the hard part—filling out the patent application."

In contrast to the Patent office, consider the lawyers and the judges, whose training in the same areas are questionable at the very least. Never do they consult the Patent Office. It is almost as if the Patent Office and its experts never existed. Like a businessman's attitude toward inventors, they all know better.

In New York, inventors have formed the New York Society of Professional Inventors. It is through this organization and others like it around the country that independent professional inventors stand a chance of being heard and changing the imbalance against them.

Once a patent has been granted, it should be protected by the attorney general against all comers. There is no reason, other than greed, practiced by major business interests, supported by avaricious lawyers, and condoned by ignorant judges that the same viable system of patent protection can't be instituted in America. The sham must stop. It is going to take a lot of hard work, but somehow it must be done if America is to recapture its industrial lead in the world.

Because of horrible legal experiences, I will never waste a dime protecting an invention again. If anybody steals an invention of mine, he is welcome to it. I am going to walk away from it. I don't care how much it is worth. I will never again apply for a patent unless there is someone very, very interested in making a deal. I have 26 patents, and about 50 inventions. I have too many things that I can be working on that are different and interesting to me. I'd rather work on them than take years out of my life being totally frustrated by patent lawsuits. My relations with my family and friends is endangered by anger at the people who are trying to steal my invention. It is easy to lose all sense of proportion in such a battle. Not only did I have to fight in two separate states, in two separate courts, with four different sets of attorneys (each collecting fees of $110 to $250 an hour), but I stopped being productive. I was "busy" 24 hours a day with planning, interrogatories, maneuvers, lawyers, courtrooms, searching old records. Busy, busy, busy, and not one new thing being worked on. It took two years before I woke up, fought for a settlement (not a very good one, but a settlement), and went back to doing productive work rather than being a paralegal.

Not too many years ago, the Supreme Court in essence ruled that if no invention existed, the licensee or manufacturer need not pay royalties for an invention. Unscrupulous manufacturers have since had a field day. When they want to cheat an inventor, they sue him, charging fraud in that he sold them a device that was in *public domain.* Therefore, the patent (if there was one) should be held invalid, and they not only want any monies paid to the inventor returned, but they also want the agreement rescinded (as if it never existed).

When sued in this manner, you have no choice but to fight back to protect yourself. If you don't, the opposition wins by default. What it comes down to is a matter of economics. If you have the money, you can fight back; if not you lose. (Don't start a lawsuit unless you can go through to the end. Your lawyer will drop you the moment you can't pay his bill any more.)

At one time, patents might have been an inducement for inventors to invent. Today they are traps for the ignorant.

Face reality: without financial muscle, you have no protection for an invention. A patent is nothing more than a license to sue.

Now, back to the world of make believe, where patents are considered important . . .

The time to sell an invention is long before it is patented. If you sell an invention after it is patented, you have lost a lot of your leverage. If you sell before it is patented, while the application is in process or pending (which means that the application is in the Patent Office), you give the purchaser or the licensee the right and capability to go for foreign patents. When the patent is issued, you are no longer permitted (by law) to apply for foreign patents in most important foreign countries. In addition, it is during the period of application that your claims are secret. Nobody in this world can get any information about your patent claims or coverage from the Patent Office. Once the patent issues, your claims are public knowledge, and your customers competitive edge might be reduced.

At this point, it is appropriate to talk about records and notebooks. Keep them carefully, follow the guidelines in keeping proper records (usually described in the introduction of good inventor notebooks). Keep accurate, dated records of every purchase and everything you do. Take pictures wherever possible and date them. Where possible, get objective witnesses, not your wife or kids but people recognized as independent and knowledgeable. Keep the records in decent order. You can never tell when you might need them to protect yourself.

Chapter 19
Now About Lawyers . . .

THERE ARE MANY STORIES TOLD ABOUT LAWYERS. MY FAVORITE IS THE ONE in the sidebar, which typifies the way I view several that I've met.

I have learned a hard lesson about dealing with lawyers, legalities, agreements, and sales or purchases: to minimize and avoid future difficulties, *confirm everything in writing.* Whether this confirmation is made at the time of the agreement or whether it is made in notes or a letter, it must be set down in writing (and dated) as soon as possible after it is made.

Equally important, if you ever have a complaint against anyone (a vendor, a lawyer, anyone), put it in writing. Send them a letter. Specify what you're not happy about; get it on the record.

I have lost a lot of money simply because what should have been in writing was not. Asking people on the phone, "What is going on?" is not a substitute for putting the question and answer in writing. You can call and write if it pleases you, but always put your complaint in writing.

For example, one of the areas that you should put in writing is purchasing. On the back of most purchase agreements there is usually a *boilerplate* that absolves the vendor from practically any liability for the product that was sold to you. If you read the boilerplate very carefully, you will find that you have almost no rights under normal circumstances. When buying from vendors I recommend that you cross out the boilerplate before signing the purchase order. Or if you accept the product, send him a letter saying that you do not accept the boilerplate. Better still, if you receive the product

183

Lawyers

A group of men were out fishing when their boat hit a log and sank. Fortunately, they were able to swim over to the log and hold on to it while waiting to be rescued. Everything went reasonably well under the circumstances. The weather was fair, it was a clear day, and they knew that sooner or later a boat would happen along. They sang and told jokes to keep up their spirits, and waited.

Then, suddenly, disaster struck. Sharks. First one, then another, until the entire area seemed to be filled with sharks. The sharks attacked the men and ate every single one of them except one. They never attacked or threatened this last survivor. In fact, they seemed to form a protective circle around him as they swam.

Eventually, a Coast Guard boat came along, spotted the lone man in the water, and headed toward him. As the boat approached, the sharks parted to permit the boat access to the man. They did not swim away until the man was safely on board.

Everyone on board was absolutely amazed at the sharks' behavior, particularly when they heard about the fate of the other men from the lone survivor. They pondered and pondered until the Captain, in talking to the survivor, asked him his profession. The man replied that he was a lawyer.

"Ah!" said the Captain. "That explains why the sharks didn't attack you. Professional courtesy."

---

and have not as yet paid for it, send the letter rejecting the boilerplate along with the payment. But do not go ahead and pay for the product and assume that you can clear up any discrepancy later. There are several ways to handle the boilerplate. Find the one that suits the situation best and use it—even if it means consulting a lawyer.

If a lawyer tells you something that you don't understand, make him explain it. Never, never let a lawyer take a position of superiority with you. If he does, or if he objects to explaining to you, get another lawyer. And make sure to get a copy of everything he has received or sends out on your behalf so that if you fire him, you have a complete record of the case.

Don't take anything for granted!

Ask when the fees begin and make sure you understand the *fee structure.* When a lawyer sends you a bill, make sure you understand it. Read it in detail, analyze it, do the arithmetic, calculate the hours times the hourly rate; question the amount of time taken for any particular item if you think it excessive. Under no circumstances pay a bill that does not explain in detail all of the services rendered and the expenses incurred. Never accept a bill if all it says is "for services rendered." Put in writing anything you disagree with. Remember, once you pay a bill without a written disclaimer on your part, it is legally assumed that you've accepted the charges and their conditions.

Several times recently, I've come across situations where the lawyer happens to be a friend of the family. Because of the friendship, the family is nearly always embarrassed to question him about anything. The expectation is that the lawyer, because of the friendship, is going to provide extra care, service and diligence to the family needs. In addition, it is somehow automatically taken for granted that he is competent in the area of legal need.

A word to the wise: more often than not, it isn't necessarily so. Put friendship aside and deal at arms length.

If the lawyer demands that you sign a *retainer agreement*, make sure you understand every single word of it before you sign. Take it home, discuss it with a knowledgeable person, then sign only if you really do understand its meaning. If there is to be an up-front retainer payment, make sure you understand how and when it is to be made, and how much and when it will be applied to your bill. Confirm it in writing. Remember, not all lawyers are as honest as Abraham Lincoln. As a matter of fact, few come reasonably close.

Don't be afraid to sound ignorant. Where is it written that you're expected to know everything? Isn't it enough that you're creative and have made an invention? Don't be greedy. Don't let anyone manipulate your ego so that you do something stupid. Like it or not, inventors must deal with lawyers.

If you have a decent lawyer, there are times when you're going to want him practically sitting in your lap—for example, when you're meeting a potential buyer again after the preliminary negotiations are completed, or when the opposition brings in one of their lawyers, or when the opposition is a lawyer. During these meetings, legal or procedural points come up that are over and above the sales or licensing agreement. There will also be particular points that your lawyer will bring up and want to discuss privately with you: "We want to look this over, we want to think about it."

Listen to his signals. The most important thing a lawyer can do in one of these meetings is to stop you from talking too much, a problem with too many inventors. A lawyer can stop you. The second most important thing a lawyer can do is to keep you on track. The third most important thing he can do is "interpret" what you mean;, if you say something stupid, he can say, "Well, he didn't really mean that; this is what he meant."

PROTECT YOURSELF

In this section, when I talk about "protecting yourself," I mean protecting yourself from your own lawyer. Now that might sound strange. Your relationship with your lawyer should certainly be based on trust. After all, he is supposed to be out there defending you in every way possible. You expect him to look after your interests and, theoretically, see to it that you never get taken advantage of in any kind of deal.

The sad news is that this might not be true. My experience with lawyers has been disastrous. For example, in one important patent suit, I not only had to protect myself against my own lawyer, but I had to bring suit against him because he was doing me more damage than the opposition was.

You must protect yourself against them. If a lawyer gives you anything to sign that affects your relationship with the lawyer (for example, a retainer agreement), be sure to read it carefully. You might even want to take it to another lawyer to make sure that your lawyer isn't taking advantage of you. Before concluding your agreement with him, know what the fee structure is going to be—exactly how much per hour he is going to charge you, not only for himself, but also for anyone he employs to work for you, such as office personnel, associates, or consultants. Make sure that the agreement, whether it be oral or written, states that the agreed upon fee structure will not change without prior knowledge and approval on your part. I've had lawyers initially come in with a low fee structure and then, in the middle of the case, suddenly hike the fees substantially without letting me know. The only way I was able to pick it up was by a detailed analysis of the bill.

You must keep a constant check on exactly what your lawyer is doing, how many hours he is spending on your job, and that his preparation for a forthcoming event is adequate. I have heard rumors that lawyers are human beings, but they do have a tendency to be arrogant in terms of doing something first and then telling you about it later. Insist on knowing everything that he does for you *before* he does it. He is your employee and you are paying his fees. As a businessman, keep close track of the lawyer.

Everytime anything takes place between you and your lawyer, have him put it in a memo, or write the memo yourself and put it in your file. If you can, have somebody witness it. You might want to record your legal transaction in a diary just as you use a diary to keep track of your work as an inventor. Do not rely on lawyers to be the most honest, upright citizens in the world. Rely on yourself to protect your own interests.

Lawyers can be extraordinarily helpful in planning strategies under particular conditions. In the final analysis, however, strategy is up to you. You know what you want. Discuss it with other businessmen, with your lawyer, and with anybody else you have confidence in. Get everybody's input that you consider potentially useful, if it is appropriate for you to get that kind of input. But under no conditions should you leave the planning of the strategy up to someone else. You are the one whose product, whose ambitions, whose future is on the line; therefore, it is up to you to make the final decisions. If you can't plan a competent strategy, then sell your invention or turn it over to somebody else. Don't do anything with it yourself. Get a manager.

Do not leave it up to your lawyer alone to plan your strategy. You can ask him what his thoughts are about a particular situation, just as you would other people. A terrific networking operation exists throughout the United States in the various inventors' societies. You can contact experienced people who can help you plan your strategies in particular situations.

KNOW YOUR OPTIONS

Keep complete control and list what your options are in relation to strategies, where you want to go, pro's and con's of one company versus another, or one potential customer versus another. All is not lost if you lose one customer, there are others. If one person out there has been interested in what you have, certainly you can find another customer. Under no circumstances should you give up your options simply because you are momentarily discouraged or uncertain about your own capabilities. Keep control of your total operation. And certainly, when you are dealing with a lawyer, demand to know everything that is going on.

One of the worst things you can have is a lazy lawyer. Lazy lawyers might come on brilliantly and make terrific presentations. They are going to protect you, they are going to do this for you, they are going to do that for you, and everything in between. But when it comes to putting things together, they have to be goaded because they have other things that they feel like doing (fishing, playing golf, whatever). Generally, they put in too few hours on your behalf (that doesn't mean they charge for too few hours). They operate on a very weird basis, somewhat like students who cram for exams. They feel that all they have to do is put in a couple of hours of cramming, or glance at something for a few minutes before the information is needed, and then they will be able to charge ahead, and you or the court or the opposition lawyer will never know the difference.

The truth of the matter is that everyone knows the difference. Their work is not "A" work; their work is usually "C" and all too often "F." Had they put in the necessary time and effort, the result would be a good piece of work—with nothing left out and everything covered properly. A lazy lawyer can be very, very damaging and dangerous. If you find that you have a lazy lawyer, get rid of him quickly.

The "too busy" lawyer has so any clients and so many things going at the same time that he does not tend to your needs. He is always running here and there; he has briefs and papers to write and committee meetings to attend. The end result is exactly the same as with the lazy lawyer: he short changes you. He doesn't give you the kind of thinking that is necessary to solve the kind of problems you have. I want a lawyer who is going to give me every bit of his capability and give me his best effort—not on an off-handed basis or a fast shuffle. I want a lawyer who will give me conscientious, concentrated professional competence.

I cannot stress too strongly that lazy lawyers and "too busy" lawyers are dangerous lawyers: they can do you much damage. At crucial times, they are unable to answer important questions. If they hadn't been too lazy or too busy to exert the effort that was necessary for your situation, they would have had the answers.

I remember standing before the judge in a court room with my lawyer. My lawyer did not know the answer to a particular question that the judge asked. He had not done his homework. We lost that motion (a very serious blow to our side.)

In another case, I had a brilliant lawyer who was quick witted, charming, well dressed, and made a great appearance. The opposition lawyer was exactly the opposite—short, stubby, without humor, exceedingly serious, and very dull. When we got to court it was like watching the "Tortoise and the Hare." My lawyer was nowhere near as well prepared and we lost. We shouldn't have, but we did.

Chapter 20

Disclosure and Confidentiality Agreements

$\mathbf{M}$Y FIRST REACTION TO CONFIDENTIALITY AGREEMENTS AND COMPANY DIS-closure agreements is: who is kidding whom? Theoretically, they give protection, but whose? The inventor's? Or the company's?

CONFIDENTIALITY AGREEMENT

A *confidentiality agreement* states that people will keep in strictest confidence anything that the inventor shows or passes on to them. The theory goes that it is really to the inventor's benefit that he have a confidentiality agreement signed by an official representative of the potential buyer, such as an officer of the company.

Absolute nonsense! The agreements aren't worth a dime. There is no way in the world that you can protect yourself with confidentiality agreements— regardless of how they are written. The person looking at your invention can say, "Gee, I've seen something similar to that somewhere else." Even if he hasn't seen anything.

The agreement doesn't protect you because there is always the faulty memory syndrome. Six months after he has rejected your solution to the problem, one of his engineers working on a similar problem is stymied. He says, "Gee, why don't you try it this way?" All of a sudden you have lost your invention.

If he feels like telling someone else about your invention, how will you know that he has violated the agreement? "Here's the way it works." he might say, adding that his company isn't interested but his friend or in-law or someone else along the line is interested.

There is no way in the world that you can be sure that a confidentiality agreement protects you. I don't even consider using them except under certain circumstances, such as with people who don't know the value of such an agreement. More often than not, it is the type of information disclosed that will determine whether it is kept secret—particularly if the company is interested in it. Someone once said to me that such an agreement has a psychological impact on the signers. I have yet to find it.

COMPANY DISCLOSURE AGREEMENTS

Never in the history of invention has there been anything more disastrous to an inventor than *company disclosure agreements*. There is nothing worse—absolutely nothing—for the inventor than a company disclosure agreement. Before you ever sign one, make sure you understand what you're signing—what you have or have not given away.

Most disclosure agreements are written to take advantage of the inventor. They simply state that once you have shown your invention to the company, the company can take your invention from you if they wish, regardless of what you say or do. You have no recourse. The inventor is helpless when he signs one of these disclosure agreements. The company will talk about the David and Goliath myth and how they don't want to be sued. After all, it would be bad for their reputation to be sued.

Absolute nonsense! In most cases, once you've signed, the company can take your invention with impunity.

Most disclosure agreements are based on patent claims—issued, pending, or applied for. If you have only the patent rights to protect you, and as discussed in chapter 18, patents aren't worth a dime in the United States, what is your protection in a disclosure agreement? Theoretically, a disclosure agreement protects both you and the company. Actually all it protects is the company's right to take your invention from you at any time they want.

If you took a sampling of disclosure agreements from various companies around the United States and reviewed them even on the basis most favorable to you, you will find that under no conditions are you reasonably protected. Many of these disclosure agreements insist that they are based on an issued patent and the rights of your claims within that patent.

Consider for a moment the impact of the condition. If any deal is to be made on an issued patent, unless you yourself have incurred the great expense of applying for foreign patents, you have lost not only your priority dates but all your rights to foreign patents. Once an American patent is issued, you are automatically precluded from obtaining most foreign patents. It is a short-sighted view for a company to insist that the agreement must be based on an issued patent. All of the foreign markets for your invention are lost. Any foreigner can take your invention; he need not apply for a patent in his country, but he can start making your invention and selling it wherever he wants to. And there is nothing you can do about it. So both you and the company lose out if the agreement is based on an issued patent.

THE PROBABILITY PHILOSOPHY

I do not know who to trust. Trusting people becomes a matter of judgment and personal philosophy. I have adopted what I call the *probability philosophy*. It has risks, but inventions on a shelf don't make money.

If you are showing a new invention to a company that does not know you, you face the problem of disclosure and disclosure agreements. Even if you show your invention to a company that you've investigated and find reliable, whether you sign or don't sign a disclosure agreement makes little difference. If they decide to go ahead with your invention, the probability is they will make a deal with you, and there isn't too much risk that they will steal from you.

Some companies, and they are difficult to recognize, actually are thieves: they pride themselves for not paying inventors for their work. My philosophy is based on the premise that it's to the company's benefit to deal with me rather than steal from me because the deal I propose is reasonable—not exorbitant. The deal will cost them less than having their own R & D department try to develop the product. However, I'm not so trusting that I will reveal any more about an invention than I have to. I will describe in detail what it does, but not how it does it. Most of my inventions require a great deal of effort, even when a successful prototype has been completed.

I have established a small company known as a *subchapter "S" company*, which means that the expenses of creating inventions can be deducted from your personal income tax. I use this company for two purposes: to purchase material and to sell my product. When I need to buy materials, I get more attention from suppliers if I call as a company customer than I would as an individual customer. The same principle holds true when I sell my invention. If I call up as a company to inform potential buyers about a new product that I have developed as part of my research and development operation, I have better access to the people I want to contact. A company-to-company operation is different from an individual-to-company operation. A company carries more clout than an individual.

When it comes down to the nitty-gritty—that is, a company is interested in my device and wants to license or buy it—then I have the contracts drawn up to me as an individual. I do that only because of the capital gains benefits.

Let me state for the record: yes, the probability philosophy has risks. It does not eliminate the possibility that you will be cheated. I have lost some good things by practicing the probability philosophy, but it's a lot better to take a chance than to see good inventions gathering dust on your shop shelves.

Chapter 21

Licensing Agreement

PRESUMABLY YOU HAVE ALREADY MADE SOME CONTACT WITH THE POTENTIAL customer and discussed with him the benefits of your invention. He is interested in it, and you've negotiated the essence of the deal. Before anything is ever put on paper by your attorney, you must have negotiated the gist of the deal. Remember: attorneys are for writing and not for negotiating. They can help, but the final responsibility is yours. If you know someone who is really very good at negotiating, hire him to help you. It's a tricky business.

WHAT GOES INTO A LICENSING AGREEMENT

The boilerplate can sometimes make or break a licensing agreement. A *boilerplate* is the standard legal paragraphs that are incorporated into agreements. The boilerplate is decided by the two attorneys and the two principals (the buyer and the seller). Very often a deal will fall through because one of the attorneys will object to some of the conditions in the boilerplate. If cool heads don't prevail at crucial moments, people might walk out of the room mad as hell, and the deal is lost.

For example, one of the conditions that the seller (the inventor) might want to include in the boilerplate is that any legal disagreement be settled in the state of the residence of the inventor. If the condition is not incorporated in the boilerplate and the buyer resides in a different state, he will take the seller to court in his state. The seller, an alien in the buyer's locale, now has all sorts of problems, such as having to hire a stranger (an attorney), to represent him in that state. If conditions like this are left out of the boilerplate, the seller might be vulnerable. His attorney might omit such conditions because he wants to make the deal go through as smoothly as possible and not make any waves. Details like this can have major repercussions in negotiating boilerplate.

The same conditions hold true for arbitration. Most people consider it very wise to include an *arbitration clause* in any agreement. Arbitration is a means of settling disagreements without the formalities and generally high costs of going to court.

Except for the boilerplate, licensing agreements are nothing more than a series of statements describing what the seller wants, what the buyer wants, the conditions under which the seller wants it, the conditions under which the buyer wants it, conditions relating to the royalties, conditions of possible guaranteed royalties, conditions relating to up-front payment. Licensing agreements should never be based on patents; they should be based on know how and the selling of an exclusive right to a licensee.

When the seller knows all of the details he wants the agreement to incorporate, his attorney will put them into legal language—language that will protect the seller effectively.

I personally have never come across a single agreement where it was not necessary for me to tell my attorney specifically what I wanted, what I would settle for, and what I would not accept.

In my opinion, no licensing agreement should be submitted to the buyer until the seller (that's you) has very, very carefully read every sentence, every word, every comma and period to make sure that what he wants is in that agreement. He should ask questions and more questions until he understands the meaning of every word. He should not be afraid to appear dumb; his future as well as his profits are on the line. The seller must make sure that the attorney has included all aspects of the deal that have been negotiated.

Now the licensing agreement must be reviewed, step by step, with the buyer and his attorney, and all the details in the agreement worked out. This stage is one of the most difficult in making a deal, and the most anxiety provoking.

CASE STUDY: LICENSING AN INVENTION

As an example, let's look at an agreement that was consummated. It stated that I would turn over to the licensee a complete product, that I would build a pilot plant for the licensee, and that I would manufacture the product for him on a cost plus basis. After I finished manufacturing this product for him, and he had introduced it into the market, I would then turn over the plant (lock, stock, and barrel) to him. From that point on, I would collect a royalty. I would turn over the know-how, teach his people how to make the product, and do everything that was essential for him to manufacture it.

Two basic protections were built into the agreement in relation to what was being done.

1. *Up-front money*, which would cover costs and possibly make a profit on the initial development of the invention.
2. A *minimum guaranteed royalty*, vital to the agreement, would be received.

When a product is licensed to a manufacturer, a minimum guaranteed royalty is vital. That's your only insurance that the manufacturer will do something with the invention; otherwise, he can sit on it forever. Or you can stipulate that if he doesn't do something in a year or two, you can get it back. But that means little because two years from now the invention might not be worth what it is worth now, or it could be worth more. The point is your investment has been sitting in limbo. Time has been invested as well as money, effort, and creative ability. You are entitled to a return on your investment.

I cannot stress too strongly to always try to get a guaranteed royalty, regardless of the amount, in every licensing agreement that you make. It is one of the most important incentives you have going for you.

In this particular agreement, the prepayment or up-front money was $500,000. The up-front money that I immediately received was $210,000 plus all the costs necessary to put up a pilot plant and get the product back to them—about $150,000.

In addition, the guarantees were as follows: $35,000 for the first year. It was anticipated that the first year would be devoted to setting up the manufacturing facilities, the selling operation, and the marketing operation. Working out the details of the transition from the laboratory to the plant was going to be difficult. Never dream that you are ever going to be able to do a complicated project on schedule. There has always been slippage on any project that I have worked on or heard about. In the first year, I would be paid $35,000 no matter what. If there were sales in the first year, that $35,000 would be deducted from any royalties that were due me (over and above the cost plus factor for the product and the plant).

The second year's guarantee was $100,000. This meant that regardless of what was sold in the second year, I was guaranteed a payment of $100,000.

When the period of guaranteed royalties was over, the manufacturer had the right to cancel the entire contract by a carefully specified procedure. He had to inform me in writing, ninety days before the end of the agreement year, that the contract was going to be cancelled. If he did not inform me within that period of time, if he was even one hour late, he would owe me another $100,000 for the next year, regardless of whether he went ahead with the project or not.

The agreement also stated that the licensor (the seller) would pay for the patent applications, and the licensee (the buyer) would pay for the prosecution of the patent. The buyer would pay my attorney (not his) to prosecute the patent. This is your assurance that the patent will be prosecuted properly. It works for him too; it assures him that you can't come back at him claiming that the prosecution was faulty.

It is usually up to the licensee to decide whether or not he wishes to pursue foreign patents and which countries he wants to pursue them in. As far as I am concerned, this point is open to negotiation because the licensee might be interested only in the domestic market or perhaps only a limited number of foreign countries (whereas the inventor might recognize the potential in additional countries for patent protection and markets).

ESTABLISHING ROYALTIES

The question of royalties often presents difficulties in licensing agreements. If you put the problem in proportion, however, it becomes less difficult. If the invention is going to be successful, you are going to make money on it; if it isn't successful, it really doesn't make any difference what your royalty agreement is because you're not going to make money. Through the up-front money you've retrieved out-of-pocket investment. You both have taken a gamble. You haven't made as much money as you had hoped for, and the manufacturer hasn't made as much he hoped for. If the invention is successful, you both make money.

I establish a royalty arrangement as follows. I have never had an argument with any licensee about royalty arrangements because I try to make my demands reasonable. Some people demand 10 or 15 percent, or whatever they think they can grab. They are trying to make a big killing, and it works against them. I want to make sure that I can make a deal and that I can make money out of it, so I propose a deal that looks good to the manufacturer.

I spread the royalties over eight years. The first year it will be 6½ percent. Each year after, it will work its way down by ½ percent until it reaches 3 percent in the eighth year. It stays at 3 percent for the remainder of the agreement. Thus, the royalty percentage goes from 6½, to 6, to 5½, to 5, to 4½ to 4, to 3½, to 3.

I have never had any difficulty with the manufacturer about a royalty agreement on this basis. I think it is very fair. He recognizes, of course, that in the first few years the 6½ percent or 6 percent isn't significant because it isn't until the second or third year that the product is really getting out in quantity. He is still going to pay the guaranteed royalty, but it is down to 5 percent when the product reaches a substantial market, and the figure will go down from that each year. As a matter of fact, it's easier to argue for a guaranteed royalty if your basic royalty demands are reasonable. And quite frankly, I'd rather get the up-front money and a decent guaranteed royalty than a high general royalty.

Royalties are generally based on the manufacturer's selling price, but there are exceptions and factors pertaining to the net sales price. I suggest that you review each of the agreements that are submitted as part of appendix B to understand how royalties are calculated. The area should be defined very carefully in any licensing agreement.

CASE STUDY: LICENSING A CONCEPT

The second kind of licensing agreement applies to situations where no product existed to start with; the invention was just in the idea stage. The licensing agreement was based on the development of a concept. The essence of the agreement was as follows:

1. I was not obliged to reveal to them any factors relating to how the device worked.
2. We agreed to the exact specifications of the device in terms of:
   - ☐ What it would do (a long detailed list)
   - ☐ Its size
   - ☐ Its approximate cost
   - ☐ The state of the prototype (just working, not pretty)
3. I received $15,000 nonrefundable "sincerity" money.
4. I had six months to complete the project. At the end of the six months, they could decide to go on with the project if I failed to make it work, or they could drop it.
5. If they succeeded where I failed, the deal would still remain in force.
6. I would build the device at my expense.
7. I would test the device at my expense.
8. The test organization was to be mutually acceptable and approved by them.
9. After the testing organization certified that the device met the stated specifications, the licensing agreement automatically went into effect.
10. In accordance with the agreement, I immediately received payment of $100,000.
11. The minimum guaranteed royalty portion went into effect from the same date.
12. A patent application was made and paid for by me.
13. They were to pay for prosecution of United States and foreign patents using my attorney.

All that remained was the boilerplate, which was similar to that in the previous agreement.

OTHER LICENSING FACTORS

In addition to the areas already covered, there is a lot more that goes into a licensing agreement. I will discuss a few briefly, but it would be to your benefit to review each area more thoroughly with an attorney to make sure that you understand their implications to you as the licensor.

Tax Laws. Check the tax laws that apply to any deal that you make. Although new laws have recently taken effect, there are sometimes quirks in the law as it applies to selling or licensing an invention. In certain situations in the past, if you sold or licensed an invention to a single company (rather than to more than one company), and it was an exclusive arrangement, you were able to claim capital gains for any income you received for that invention. If it was a nonexclusive agreement, however, the benefits changed. Keep accurate records of the costs you incur in developing your invention because these costs can be deducted.

Option Periods. You might want to consider various option periods Consider how these option periods are related to different tests that the licensee might wish to conduct. He might want to do a series of market tests, and you might agree to give him an option to do it for a specified period of time.

Patent Searches. Another area might be patent searches. They might be included in the licensing or sales arrangement because you might want to conduct a more thorough patent search—particularly if no invention exists at the time of the licensing arrangement. If an invention does exist or a patent application is in the works, the licensee might want to conduct a series of patent searches to make sure that if and when a patent is issued, he knows its approximate strength. Why it is to be conducted, who conducts it, and who pays for it—these factors are all negotiable. If the licensee wants to conduct a patent search, he can do it and pay for it by himself—unless, of course, you want to keep everything secret until you have to present your invention. The decision depends very much on the situation.

Ownership. The inventor's invention might be assigned or licensed to other people. The patent application and the patent must be in the name of the inventor. If you assign the invention to a company, it essentially becomes the property of the company that you have assigned it to. If you license the invention to a company, you still own the invention. You simply are permitting them to use it.

Slippage. The next area to consider is slippage, whether it be on their part or yours. If it is on their part, you are protected through the guaranteed royalties. If they are showing due diligence, you might permit them to go further without penalties. If the slippage is on your part, ask for more time (in writing, if possible) so that the project can proceed.

Product Specifications. One word of caution in establishing product specifications: try to keep the specifications as loose as you possibly can. Even though you believe that you can make the invention with tight specifications, try very hard to make them as loose as acceptable. If you bring the invention in with tighter specifications than promised, you are a hero.

Sincerity Money. If a company is interested in what you doing, and you are going to be developing it for them at your expense, the sincerity money will probably cover the legal, travel, and other out-of-pocket expenses. If you can make more than that on sincerity money, that is great. If they are sincere, they won't mind putting up the sincerity money. After all, you're the one taking the gamble and laying out the development costs. If they are not sincere, then you have some ground to question whether or not they are going to go through with the deal, even after it is completed. I would try and argue very strongly for up-front sincerity money that is nonrefundable.

Failure to Deliver. What happens if you fail to deliver a working invention? I suggest that you study one of the licensing agreements in the appendix to learn what happens when you fail to deliver. After working on the invention for some time, you might have been unable to solve a particular problem, and you can't make it work. Suppose you are required to turn your invention over to someone else. He simply turns a knob, switches a switch, puts something else in, or makes a minor adjustment . . . and low and behold, the invention works! Should you be left out in the cold? I don't think so. I think that you should try to include, in any agreement, conditions that protect you in situations like that.

Testing. To avoid disagreement about whether your invention works or doesn't work, it should be tested by a third party. Once the invention proves itself, then the agreement should automatically go into effect. The anniversary date of the agreement is not the day that you started working on the invention, but the day that you actually deliver whatever you promised to deliver. The anniversary date, therefore, is the date that the third party has indicated that your product works.

Recordkeeping. In the development of your invention, keep *accurate records* not only of your expenditures but of your development procedures. You can refer to them if any questions arise about concept dates, development procedures, and costs. Review these records continually as development takes place.

Verifying the Books. As the licensor, you have the right to examine the books and records of the licensee as they pertain to your invention royalties. Your agreement should state very clearly how frequently and under what conditions—who on the licensee side will certify the records and who on your side will examine them. You might want your own people to examine the records, or you might hire a certified public accountant. I would establish this review as a precedent after a reasonable period once they start selling your product. Until they start selling the product, you should be receiving your guaranteed royalty payments quarterly.

Infringement. Who pays for any court suits? Review the existing agreements that are in the appendix. Also, review the termination conditions; how can the agreement be terminated—when, by whom, and why. These complex areas deserve careful attention. You might want to know that there are a number of ways to terminate an agreement. The agreements in the appendix are examples. The one you adopt has to suit your particular situation.

Notices. I strongly suggest that all notices be put in writing and sent by either certified or registered mail to ensure that the addressee has received the notice.

Assignability. Another factor that is included in a licensing agreement is the assignability of the license by the licensee to a third party. This factor is negotiable. You might want to deny it or permit it, depending on the situation. If it is going to be assigned to a third party, you certainly want to benefit from the assignment and always maintain control over your licensing agreement.

Sublicensing. If there is to be sublicensing by the licensee, include it in the agreement so that you will benefit from the sublicensing. Make sure that the sublicensing does not deprive you of any of the benefits of your own invention.

A New Company. What happens if the company that you licensed your invention to is sold? What happens to your assignment agreement? Your agreement should include a provision that the new company must accept the terms of the licensing and assignment agreement accepted by the original company.

Bankruptcy. What happens if the company that you have licensed goes bankrupt? Your licensing agreement should specify that if the licencee goes bankrupt or goes out of business, your invention is your property: you own it. The patents, the benefits, and everything pertaining to your invention reverts to you. Your invention does not become a part of the assets of the bankrupt corporation.

Forced Acquisitions. There are innumerable "what if" factors that can bring disaster to a particular operation. You can't protect yourself against all contingencies, but consider some of them (like bankruptcy). The chances of a major corporation going bankrupt are pretty slim. In this era of forced acquisitions, however, you must make sure that whatever happens to the companies you are dealing with, you're protected by your licensing agreement.

Invention Improvement. I believe that you (the inventor) should benefit from any improvements made on your invention—whether you make them or the licensee makes them. The original concept is yours; the original invention is yours. If any improvements are made, they should be made in your name and benefit you. I am convinced that this condition must be included in any agreement you reach. The agreements in the appendix include examples.

Know-How Transmission. In the area of know-how, you or key people associated with you transmit to the licensee information pertaining to the invention—technique or information that enable him to produce your invention more efficiently. Your agreement should specify the conditions of know-how transmission: who is going transmit it, for how long, and when. The conditions might provide a fee for this transmission of know-how to the licensee. Under some conditions, the up-front money covers this area; under other conditions, you are going to benefit from the royalties when the licensee begins to utilize your invention.

ABSOLUTE MUSTS ABOUT LICENSING AGREEMENTS

1. All legal disputes must be decided in your home state. I have already stated, as emphatically as I could, why this is vital.
2. Any legal dispute must go to binding arbitration. "They" have more money than you, and they can use their money as a weapon to take away all the benefits of your invention. Arbitration is to your benefit; you want to be able to settle a disagreement or any dispute as quickly as possible, and in your favor. The longer a disagreement takes to settle, the more money it takes (and you know who has more money).
3. Never base the validity of an agreement on obtaining a patent. You can never outguess a patent office. In the United States, you must remember, more than 80 percent of all the patents that go to court are held invalid for obviousness. Until patent laws change, basing your agreement on patents of any kind is hazardous. Base your agreement on know-how that you can transmit.
4. Insist on paying for the patent application yourself. Then you know it's done right. The buyer should pay your attorney for the patent prosecution (your primary protection).
5. Make sure you are included in the product liability policies of the company you are licensing your invention to. When liability suits are filed, everybody in creation is named as a defendant, including the inventor of the product. Therefore, in your licensing agreement or sales agreement, it is essential that you be covered by the company's product liability policies.
6. The agreement must state clearly what the conditions of invention recovery are. How do you get your invention back and under what conditions if disaster strikes a company?
7. Licensing agreements are not worth much if you're dealing with a crook. Any kind of agreement is nothing more than a piece of paper, no matter how well written it is. You have to avoid dealing with a crook. That's why it's so important to do the research and find out as much as you can about who you are dealing with.
8. You now have a deal with a manufacturer for your invention, a deal that is satisfactory to all parties concerned. Now what? As

the inventor, you should keep in constant touch with the buyer. For your own sake, you must know what is happening. Do not hesitate to phone or write a letter to find out how things are going. When you keep in touch, you can make it clear to the buyer that you will be glad to help him.

9. Try to get a consulting fee for help you offer. Try to get paid for whatever contribution you make over and above the fact that you are the inventor.

10. Keep a careful check of any design or mechanical changes that might be made in your product. Know exactly what the basis for the change was, who made the change, and how the change might affect the product. Later, you suddenly realize that a series of changes has been made and the buyer says, "Why should we have to deal with you? You didn't contribute to this."

11. Attend the trade shows where the buyer exhibits. Review everything. Be casual, be polite, but don't be cut off from contact with your buyer and your invention. Don't take up too much time, and don't get in the way. Try to be available but without being a pain in the neck.

12. Never talk to the buyer's competitors about what you sold or licensed to the buyer. Not only is this wrong, but it can be very damaging to you. You might be letting the cat out of the bag. Your buyer might have marketing plans and new product introduction plans that can be damaged if competition gets wind of them. Competition might even try to knock off your product.

13. Keep records of the things you do in writing. Whether it is a casual conversation with the buyer, with one of his representatives, or with your lawyer . . . write it down. If anything important has changed, write a letter to the people concerned informing them about the changes.

14. It is very difficult sometimes to stay friendly with the buyer. Quite frequently, once the deal is made, he no longer wants to talk to you. All you can do is keep in touch, be helpful, and remember that not everything has to be done your way.

Chapter 22
How and Where
To Find Information

IN THE UNITED STATES, THERE IS A VAST ACCUMULATION OF INFORMATION. Name any subject, and there is more data available than you will probably ever need. There are hundreds of places to get information. The major problem is getting only pertinent information without being sidetracked. It is very easy to be sidetracked or lost in the wealth of primary and secondary source information that is out there.

In my opinion, there is probably no such thing as an industrial secret. As an employee of a management consulting firm, I was asked to review a company's activities to see what could be done to improve their marketing program, which was based on mailing lists of various church choirs; elementary, junior, and senior high schools; colleges; even nursery schools. They rented and sold caps and gowns to the graduating classes of these institutions.

They guarded their mailing lists with absolute secrecy. Only a few of the top executives were permitted entry into the room where they stored files and cross-files. These files contained the names of personnel in these institutions throughout the United States that they considered potential customers.

To find out what their marketing program was, it was necessary for me to look at their lists, but I ran into a stone wall. I was an outsider and they were not going to trust their customer lists to anyone, even someone who had been called in as a consultant to assist them. I wanted to know where their markets were, who they were, the breakdown of their primary and secondary markets, how they approached them, which ones were more profitable, etc.

Amused by the refusal of the company to give me access to their precious lists, I told them that I was sure I could not only duplicate their lists but add to them—and in a short period of time. They laughed at me. My assistant researched various secondary sources, and within a week, we had directories for each of their primary market areas. We not only duplicated their lists but doubled them. As a matter of fact, our lists were more accurate and complete than theirs because our sources were updated regularly and more closely reflected the potential market. The moral: industrial secrets are really very rare.

You must determine what information you really need, or you will fall into a twofold trap:

1. Getting caught up in *curiosity information*. This is fascinating but irrelevant information that is particularly dangerous to inventors, who are curious to start with.
2. The sheer *volume of information* available. The amount can camouflage or smother the particular information you are looking for.

Research is a tool. As with any new tool you bring into your shop, you have to learn how to use it. It can be used with precision or casually; in either case, if you know what you're doing, there is more likelihood that you will achieve your objectives.

FINDING MATERIALS, PARTS, AND TECHNICAL INFORMATION

There are many sources where you can find information about materials, parts, or technical data. One of the best places is the *Yellow Pages* of the telephone book. The breakdown of companies by industry category makes it simple and easy to use. The following list is simply a guide to reference sources and places where you can find materials, parts, and technical data.

☐ Materials Selector issue of *Materials in Design Engineering*
☐ Business-to-business directories
☐ *Thomas Register* (probably the most used industrial directory by buyers and sellers)
☐ Supply houses: steel, aluminum, brass, hardware, plastics, bearings, motors, gears, etc.
☐ Junkyards: scrap metal, auto, machinery
☐ Catalogs from company and supplier: parts sections, instructional sections
☐ Technical service departments of companies
☐ Technical and science section of libraries: general, specialized, associations
☐ Technical and how-to handbooks
☐ Trade association directories

To supplement the above, check the reference section of your library. In addition to the general secondary sources, you might find people during your search who are knowledgeable about the area you're researching or about other sources of information. Sometimes it is even necessary to search out these people. Take every opportunity to talk to them.

Asking questions. Finding the right person to ask is important. Ask the questions as specifically as you can so that you don't waste people's time. List your questions before you make the contact. Review the questions before you ask them to make sure the answer will provide the information you're looking for. Don't hesitate to ask the person you're talking to whether he knows anyone else who might give you further information.

If all else fails . . . read the directions. I am continually surprised at the number of people who are desperately looking for information—and fail to read directions and instructions in directories, manuals, handbooks, parts catalogs, software, etc. An amazing amount of information can be derived from a directory simply by reading how it was put together and what are its objectives. Many people fail to get the information they're looking for because they do not understand how the data was compiled. This is particularly true when you're looking for extrapolation information. You must then apply deductive reasoning.

TECHNIQUES OF RESEARCH

First and foremost, you must define what you are looking for. This is really the most difficult part of any research project. The rest—finding the data—is relatively easy by comparison. The same research techniques are used to find materials, parts, customers, or the identity of key people.

There are two very distinct parts to defining your research objectives.

1. List the type or kind of information you need. Under each category, if possible, detail your specific data requirements. In other words, list what you're looking for in the greatest detail you can.
2. Next to each item on your list, explain why you need the information, and how you intend to use the information.

By using this method, you will be able to clearly define your information needs and, as a result, substantially reduce the amount of time and cost of the data gathering process. Mostly, it will enable you to keep a sharp eye on your primary objectives and not get lost in peripheral or curiosity information.

Six major steps are used in obtaining information:

1. Identify the source of your information and determine how to get it. Review various directories and list the sources of information that might be available to you.

2. Locate the source of information. This might sometimes require extensive research. There will be times when you find the right person to talk to immediately. Other times, you will go from person to person to person and still not find your information. Keep trying. You'll either get your information or decide that it probably is not available.

3. Determine the methods of obtaining information from sources—how to get it from them. Sometimes the sources of information are not libraries or associations, but people. This needs thinking out. Must you travel to them? Can you phone or write? Will they respond? Is the information considered confidential?

4. Evaluate the information for reliability and accuracy. How good is it? Don't be surprised if you sometimes obtain misleading data. This happens with groups who have one set of data for their members and another for the government and public. *Don't look for more data and more precision than is necessary to meet your objectives.* Review general information carefully to make sure it gives reliable answers to the questions you have asked.

5. Analyze the data to determine exactly what it means. Don't lock yourself into a conclusion until you have analyzed the data completely.

6. Use the information. Integrate the information to fit your needs. If you get misleading or wrong information, you might have to work back and forth as you analyze it until you are satisfied that the information answers your needs.

You must accept and understand one extremely important factor about the accumulation of information: that there are probably thousands of variables related to each step in the accumulation of information. Keep your eye on what you are looking for so that you don't get lost. It can cost a great deal to pick up an enormous amount of curiosity information that is really of no value to you. The main thought to always remember is: what are you going to do with the information once you have it? If you can't use it, don't even bother going for it. It might be something that is nice from a curiosity point of view, but from a very practical point of view, it takes up a lot of time and effort and gets you nowhere fast.

SIC NUMBERS

In order to maintain some uniformity of data, states, counties, cities, and private sector directories and publications have adopted the United States's method of identifying industry by using *SIC numbers.* These Standard Industrial Classification numbers identify companies by industry category. They range from two-digit numbers to eight-digit numbers. The two-digit numbers are used to designate basic industries such as mining, chemicals, agriculture, etc. As the number of digits progress, so does the detail of identification. The eight-digit numbers and the NEC (Not Elsewhere Classified) sections specifically list product categories. Many local governmental and private sector directories will vary the number of identifying digits. A company might have one or more SIC numbers, depending on the number of different industrial areas in which it operates.

You can use SIC numbers to identify similar industries and similar companies. The Department of Commerce and Bureau of the Census publish handbooks explaining the SIC numbers and how to use them. They are usually available in public libraries.

SOME MAJOR SOURCES OF INFORMATION

When dealing with an unknown but potential source, always ask if there is any central agency or source for the data. Many major companies, particularly service companies, publish technical service papers for their clients and as a means of promotion.

Government Materials

- [ ] Federal statistical services—every agency
- [ ] *Standard Industrial Classification Manual*
- [ ] *Monthly Catalogue of Government Publications*
- [ ] Specialized reference lists
  - *Marketing Information Guide*
  - *Statistical Abstract of the United States*
  - *Lists of specialized publications of each agency—i.e., Bureau of Labor Statistics*

Trade Publications

- [ ] Identify publications dealing with specific industries
  - *Standard Rate and Data Service*
  - *Industrial Marketing Guide*
  - *Applied Science and Technology Index*
  - Business Periodicals Index
- [ ] *Encyclopedia of Associations* (read the directions)

Company or Industry Information

- [ ] Dunn and Bradstreet directories. Lists address, names of officers, and number of employees; uses SIC numbers; million dollar, ½ Million Dollar; big book; also specific and individual company reports; issued by subscription

☐ *Fortune Service 500.* Compilation of important statistical information; ranking according to sales.

☐ *Fortune.* Magazine article index

☐ *Moody's* (several publications). Provides operational information about company or community status; address of main office and plants; names management, product lines, and products, sales, profits, and other vital statistics (Industrials, transportation, public utilities, international).

☐ *Thomas Register.* Probably the most comprehensive product listing anywhere. Lists companies by product category, geography, address, size, etc.

☐ *Standard & Poor's Register.* This organization publishes many directories and reports about industry and the stock market that are incredibly detailed and informative. They provide current information on companies, their management, finances, sales, forecasts, directors, products, and much more.
  • Industry surveys
  • Corporation records
  • Register of corporations, directors, and executives
  • Stock reports (all exchanges)

☐ *Directory of Corporate Affiliations.* Lists major corporations and their divisions, subsidiaries, and affiliations

Newspaper Subject Index

Some major newspapers also maintain computer data banks that are available by subscription.

☐ *Wall Street Journal*
☐ The *New York Times*
☐ The *New York Daily News*
☐ Most major newspapers

Other Sources

☐ Telephone books. Do not underrate this marvelous source of information. The *Yellow Pages* lists companies by industrial categories.
☐ Educational institutions
☐ Specialized libraries
☐ Databases
☐ Knowledgeable individuals

Economic Information

☐ Department of Commerce—Office of Economic Analysis Bureau of the Census, *U.S. Industrial Outlook*

☐ Department of Labor—Bureau of Labor Statistics
☐ Department of Agriculture—Economic Research Service
☐ Federal Reserve System—Board of Governors
☐ Department of Treasury—Bureau of Internal Revenue Service, Tariff Commission
☐ Executive Office of the President—Council of Economic Advisors
☐ Legislative Branch—Congressional hearings and reports
☐ Sales—Survey of Buying Power, Survey of Industrial Activity
☐ Bank publications
☐ National Industrial Conference Board
☐ American Management Association
☐ *Dodge Reports* (construction)
☐ *New York Times*

Industry and Product Information

To fully understand the volume of information available to the researcher, you can simply scan any of the census studies listed below. Each is specific in its own way, and each can be combined with other data to provide specifics undreamt of in any other country. In fact, were you to try to obtain some of this data in some other countries, you would probably be shot as a spy. One can only admire the diligence of those hard-working government employees who have painstakingly accumulated the data.

☐ Census studies—Census of Manufacturers, Census of Business, Census of Wholesale Trade, Census of Retail Trade, Census of Service Industries, Census of Population, Census of Housing, Current Industrial Reports, Office of Technical Service, Show Exhibit
☐ Annual statistical supplements of selected trade publications—*Encyclopedia of Packaging*, buyer's guides, Shows,
☐ Investment services—Standard and Poor's *Industry Survey*, Dunn & Bradstreet
☐ Trade association reports
☐ Dunn & Bradstreet's *Operation Ratios*
☐ American Management Association Series
☐ Private newsletters, market studies, and surveys for special markets by companies such as Starch, Arbitron, Nielsen, etc.
☐ Technical product bulletins

Appendix A
Additional Reading

THE FOLLOWING PUBLICATIONS CAN PROVIDE ADDITIONAL INFORMATION IN some of the various areas covered in this book. Most of the titles are self explanatory.

I urge you to review the reference manuals and directories that make up the last part of the list. At minimum just read the directions or the methodology of accumulation and scan the rest. Although you might not require the information immediately, just knowing where to look can be extremely helpful when you are in a jam.

Amabile, Teresa M. "The Social Psychology of Creativity." *Science* (August 31, 1984).

Boorstin, Daniel J. *The Discoverers*. New York: Random House, 1983.

Comiskey, James C. *How to Start, Expand & Sell a Business*. San Jose, Calif.: Venture Perspectives Press, 1985.

De Camp, L. Sprague. *The Heroic Age of American Invention*. Garden City, N.Y.: Doubleday, 1961.

Drucker, Peter F. *Innovation and Entrepreneurship*. New York: Harper & Row, 1985.

Farrel, Kevin. "A Federal Program For Entrepreneurs." *Venture*. May, 1984.

Gardener, Howard. "Science Grapples With The Creative Puzzle." *New York Times* (May 31, 1984).

Greene, Gardiner G. *How To Start and Manage Your Own Business.* New York: New American Library, 1983.

Greenwald, Harry P. *Source Guide of Government Technology and Financial Capital.* Wellesley, Mass.: Capital Publishing Corp., 1982.

Gwynne, Peter. "R & D Funding." *Research And Development* (August 1985).

Heller, Robert. *The Common Millionaire.* London: Weidenfeld and Nicolson, 1974.

Henderson, Carter F. *Winners: The Successful Strategies Entrepreneurs Use To Build New Businesses.* New York: Holt, Rinehart and Winston, 1985.

Heyn, Ernest V. *Fire of Genius.* Garden City, N.Y.: Doubleday, 1976.

Jessup, Claudia, and Genie Chipps. *The Woman's Guide To Starting a Business.* New York: Holt, Rinehart and Winston, 1979.

Jewkes, John, David Sawers, and Richard Stillerman. *The Sources Of Invention.* New York: Norton, 1969.

Johnson, Clifton. *The Rise of the American Inventor.* Garden City, N.Y.: Doubleday, 1935.

Kishel, Gregory F., Patricia G. Kishel. *How To Start, Run & Stay in Business.* New York: Wiley, 1981.

Kivenson, Gilbert. *The Art and Science of Inventing.* New York: Van Nostrand Reinhold, 1982.

Lesko, Matthew, and Sharon Zaroszny. *Information U.S.A.* New York: Viking Penguin Books, 1986.

Lowry, Albert J. *How To Become Financially Successful by Owning Your Own Business.* New York: Simon and Schuster, 1981.

McCracken, Calvin D. *Handbook for Inventors.* New York: Scribners, 1983.

Mancuso, Joseph R. *How To Start, Finance, and Manage Your Own Small Business.* Englewood Cliffs, N.J.: Prentice Hall, 1984.

Mancuso, Joseph R. *The Small Business Survival Guide.* Englewood Cliffs, N.J., 1980.

Moore, Arthur D. *Invention, Discovery and Creativity.* Garden City, N.Y.: Doubleday, 1969.

Mucciolo, Louis, ed. *Small Business: Look Before You Leap.* New York: Arco, 1981.

Nevins, Allan, and Henry Steele Commager, *A Pocket History of the United States.* 7th ed. New York: Washington Square Press, 1981.

Pratt, Stanley E. ed. *Guide to Venture Capital Sources.* 7th ed. Wellesley Hills, Mass.: Capital Publishing Corp., 1983.

Pride, William M. *Marketing: Basic Concepts and Decisions.* 4th ed. Boston: Houghton Mifflin, 1985.

Rice, Berkley. "Imagination To Go." *Psychology Today* (May 1984).

Stevens, Mark. *Thirty-Six Small Business Mistakes & How To Avoid Them.* Englewood Cliffs, N.J.: Prentice Hall, 1982.

Stewart, Doug. "Teachers Aim At Turning Loose The Mind's Eyes." *Smithsonian* (August 1985).

Sun, Marjorie. "Weigh The Social Costs Of Invention." *Science* (March 19, 1984).

Tetreault, Wilfred F., and Robert W. Clements. *Starting Right in Your New Business*. Reading, Mass.: Addison-Wesley, 1982.

Welsh, John A. *The Entrepreneur's Master Planning Guide*. Englewood Cliffs, N.J.: Prentice-Hall, 1983.

White, Richard M., Jr. *The Entrepreneur's Manual*. Radnor, Pa.: Chilton, 1977.

Wilson, John W. *The New Venturers*. Reading, Mass.: Addison-Wesley, 1985.

NO AUTHOR

Agency Sales with Agents & Representatives. Los Angeles, Calif.: Manufacturers' Agents National Association, January 1974. (Magazine—Special Issue).

Smithsonian Book of Invention. Washington, D.C.: Smithsonian Books, 1978.

REFERENCES

Doing Business with the Federal Government
   General Services Administration
   U.S. Department of Commerce
   U.S. Bureau of Census
   U.S. Census of Manufacturers
Dunn & Bradstreet   *Million Dollar Directory*
Dunn & Bradstreet   *Half-Million Dollar Directory*
Dunn & Bradstreet   *Reference Book*
Encyclopedia of Associations
The Foundation Directory
Gale Directory of Publications
MacRae's Industrial Directory   New York State
Moody's Industrial Manual
New York Telephone Company
   Yellow Page Directories
   Materials Selectors Guide
Standard & Poor's Corporation Records
Standard & Poor's Register of Corporations, Directors and Executives
Thomas Register of American Manufacturers

Appendix B

Sample Infomation

212

PROPOSAL

Dear Mr.

I have developed a product that is capable of dispensing into a stream of water various types of liquids at precise PPM rates regardless of changes in water pressure.

The product consists of a dispenser and disposable cartridge. The cartridge is prepackaged at a filling plant.

The product can be used as a dispenser of prepackaged insecticides, herbicides, etc. In fact, it can be used to dispense any liquid in very very exact and specific quantities into a stream of water.

The product can also be attached to a brush for washing cars. In this use it would dispense a specific premeasured and prepackaged quantity of liquid soap or detergent into a stream of water.

A prototype of the product has been built and tested. In addition, the product has been tested by Battelle.

Patent has been allowed. A continuation in part is in process.

The following is a list of product data and specifications:

1) Liquid dispenser and cartridge to accurately mix with flowing water, any liquid in terms of PPM.

2) PPM may vary with type of liquid to be dispensed but same dispenser will be used and accuracy in PPM will be maintained.

For Example:

- Liquid "A" must be dispensed at 150 PPM

- Liquid "B" must be dispensed at 550 PPM

- Liquid "C" must be dispensed at 1500 PPM

- The number and types of liquid and
  cartridges can be many and varied

- Each cartridge may vary in liquid volume

- Each cartridge is acceptable by and can be
  used with the dispenser

- The PPM required by each liquid will be
  accurately dispensed over the life of
  the cartridge using the same dispenser

- The PPM required for each liquid is
  predetermined and accurately dispensed

- The user cannot vary the PPM

3) Dispensing is unaffected by variations in
water pressure, even if water pressure changes
during operation of the dispenser.

4) Dispenser may be used with hand-held nozzle or
hooked up to a sprinkler system. For central
watering systems for commercial use, it may be
necessary to increase the size of dispenser.

5) Prototype is made to be used by a hand-held
nozzle or sprinkler. It has male and female
hose connections.

6) Dispenser mechanism can (if necessary) include
a check valve and anti-siphon (vacuum breaker)
device.

7) Not included in the present prototype is a
method of stopping the flow of liquid from the
cartridge while water is running through the
dispenser. This function can be added if it is
deemed desirable. It seems that its
usefulness would be appropriate for washing
only. It might be considered counterproductive
if incorporated into the dispensing of
insecticides etc.

8) Size of dispenser as related to maximum
quantity of material to be dispensed will be a
marketing decision. The prototype will
dispense up to 1/2 pint of liquid.

9) Dispenser is reusable and should, with care,
have a reasonable life of several years.

10) Dispenser can be made of either metal or
plastic and can probably be sold retail at
between $15 and $25, profitably. The prototype

is made of metal and plastic.

11) The cartridge is disposable.

12) The cartridge is recapable so that if only part of the liquid is used, the remainder can be stored for later use.

13) At no time does the user come in contact with the liquid to be dispensed (unless, of course, he gets in the way of the nozzle or sprinkler)

14) The cartridge is prepackaged at filling plant.

15) The amount or quantity of liquid in the cartridge is a marketing decision. Quantity of liquid in cartridge can vary according to the type of liquid to be dispensed. Cartridge size (volume) can vary in same dispenser. Prototype will accommodate cartridge and volume up to 1/2 pint.

16) PPM to be dispensed will remain the same throughout the life of the cartridge.

17) Cost of cartridge will vary according to the cost of ingredients. The container portion of the cartridge may be in the vicinity of $.10 to $.30 for material.

18) The prototype has been developed for the purpose of demonstrating the principle by which the dispenser and the cartridge work and therefore, only two cartridges will be submitted, one at a low PPM dispensing rate and another at a high PPM dispensing rate. The rates can be mutually specified. In either case, the dispensing rate will be specific and can be replicated.

For purposes of the acceptance of the prototype, accuracy of the dispensing rate in PPM is to be defined as plus or minus 15%.

The liquid to be used for determining rate being dispensed during any test for acceptance will be salt solutions except of course, in the case of liquid soap or detergent where it is assumed that predetermined quantity is important.

19) It is assumed that once the principle is demonstrated and working, your company will be able to make the various adjustments required

for the dispensing of as many different
liquids as you desire.

20) It is also assumed that your company will have
the dispenser and cartridge redesigned in
terms of aesthetics for consumer acceptance.

If you are interested in manufacturing and selling such a
product I would be happy to discuss a license arrangement
with your company. We can of course negotiate the terms of
the licensing agreement.

However, in order to maintain a competitive edge and not
prematurely reveal the operational aspects of the
product it would be necessary to enter into an agreement
prior to having the product revealed to you.

For our mutual benefit we can work in the following
manner:

1. a. We would review the specifications of the
product and keep or alter them as desired.

   b. If any of the specifications are altered time
   would be required to incorporate the changes
   into the prototype.

2. We would negotiate the terms of a mutually
acceptable licensing agreement.

3. The product could be tested by any
mutually acceptable independent testing
organization for verification that the
product has met the specifications.

4. If the product specifications are verified
the previously negotiated licensing agreement
automatically goes into effect.

I would be happy to hear from you.

Sincerely,

LICENSING AGREEMENT:
. . . INVENTOR TO COMPANY

AGREEMENT

THIS AGREEMENT made and entered into as of the _____ day of _____, 19____, by and between _____ of _____ (hereinafter referred to as "LICENSOR"), and _____ INC., of _____ _____ (hereinafter referred to as "LICENSEE");

WHEREAS, LICENSOR warrants that he has devised and is the owner of the entire right, title and interest in and to a product in the nature of a dispenser for various types of liquid such as insecticides, herbicides, fungicides, and the like, consisting of a prepackaged disposable cartridge containing insecticide or other liquid, and a reusable dispenser unit into which the cartridge is to be removably and replaceably inserted, with the dispenser unit adapted to be connected to a garden hose, and the dispenser unit and cartridge being operable in combination to micro-feed the contained liquid into a stream of flowing water at a constant rate thereby enabling the user to treat plants or foliage (hereinafter referred to as "PRODUCT");

WHEREAS, LICENSOR has the capability of constructing an operative prototype of the PRODUCT which will dispense liquids in accordance with the specifications hereinafter set forth (hereinafter referred to as "AN OPERATIVE PROTOTYPE");

WHEREAS, LICENSEE desires to obtain and LICENSOR warrants that he has the sole right and capability of conferring, for the United States of America and all foreign countries, the exclusive right and license to manufacture, use, sell and have made the product and to sub-license others to manufacture, use, sell and have made the same, after LICENSOR has produced AN OPERATIVE PROTOTYPE and submitted the same to LICENSEE;

WHEREAS, LICENSOR is willing to grant such licenses to LICENSEE; and

WHEREAS, LICENSOR intends to timely file application for patent on said PRODUCT in the United States Patent and Trademark Office after the same is fully developed and AN OPERATIVE PROTOTYPE submitted to LICENSEE;

NOW, THEREFORE, in consideration of the promises and mutual covenants herein contained, the parties herein agree as follows:

1. Upon execution of this agreement, LICENSEE agrees to pay to LICENSOR the sum of Fifteen Thousand Dollars ($15,000.00), the receipt of which is acknowledged by LICENSOR. This sum shall constitute partial reimbursement for LICENSOR'S expenses in developing and testing the PRODUCT and the preparation of an application for letters patent on the PRODUCT, and said sum shall be non-returnable by LICENSOR.

2. Upon execution of this agreement and the payment of the sum specified in paragraph 1 hereof, LICENSOR agrees to commence development of the PRODUCT promptly. LICENSOR shall have a period of six months from the date of execution of this agreement in which to construct and submit AN OPERATIVE PROTOTYPE of the PRODUCT to LICENSEE. If no such OPERATIVE PROTOTYPE is submitted to LICENSEE within said six month period, this agreement shall automatically terminate unless LICENSOR is notified in writing within thirty (30) days after the expiration of said six months period that LICENSEE desires to continue development of the PRODUCT. Upon receipt of such written notification. LICENSOR agrees to make available to LICENSEE all information (including but not limited to, all technical information and data, all drawings and other documents of whatever nature, all prototypes and components thereof, all tooling and all other physical devices) in the possession, custody or control of LICENSOR relating to the PRODUCT and to assist, on a voluntary basis, LICENSEE with the continued development of the PRODUCT. Upon such written notification, this agreement shall remain in full force and effect until such time as LICENSEE determines and notifies LICENSOR in writing that the PRODUCT is no longer feasible, at which time this agreement shall automatically terminate.

3. LICENSOR agrees to use his best efforts to construct AN OPERATIVE PROTOTYPE of the product and submit the same to LICENSEE within said six month period, and also agrees to obtain independent laboratory tests confirming the dispensing rate of the prototype, by a laboratory approved by LICENSEE.

4. LICENSOR warrants that the prototype of the PRODUCT submitted to LICENSEE shall conform to the following specifications:

a. The dispenser unit and cartridge shall be capable of accurately mixing with flowing water, any liquid at a ratio of parts per million (PPM).

b. The reusable dispenser unit shall be capable of dispensing liquids accurately at different PPM ratios, for example one liquid at a ratio of 200 PPM, and another liquid at the rate of 4000 PPM.

c. The dispenser shall be capable of receiving cartridges of different size and content volume, with each cartridge adapted to dispense liquid accurately at a predetermined PPM ratio over the life of the cartridge and using the same dispenser unit, and with the construction of the cartridge being such that the user cannot adjust the PPM.

d. The dispenser will feed liquid at the predetermined PPM ratio regardless of variations in the water pressure employed and regardless of water pressure changes during operation of the dispenser.

e. The dispenser may be used either with a handheld nozzle or attached to a sprinkler system. For commercial central watering systems, a dispenser of increased size may be necessary.

f. The dispenser mechanism is adapted to include a check valve and an anti-siphon (vacuum breaker) device, if desired.

g. The dispenser prototype will be capable of dispensing up to one pint of liquid and as little as one ounce of liquid.

h. The reusable dispenser unit can be made either of plastic or metal, or a combination of both such materials and should be able to be retailed profitably at a price between $15.00 and $25.00.

i. The cartridge will be disposable, but will be capable of being re-capped after partial use, so that it may be stored and re-used subsequently.

j. The dispenser parts are capable of being handled and assembled without the user contacting the liquid stored in the cartridge. The cartridge is prepackaged at the filling plant.

k. The dispenser will be capable of feeding liquid at the same PPM ratio throughout the life of the cartridge. For purposes of this agreement and acceptance of the prototype, accuracy of the dispensing ratio in PPM is defined as plus or minus 15%.

5. The parties agree that the prototype will be constructed and submitted by LICENSOR to LICENSEE for the purpose of demonstrating the principle upon which the dispenser unit and cartridge operate. For this purpose, LICENSOR shall submit as part of the prototype two cartridges, one of which dispenses at a low PPM ratio (under 200 PPM), and the other of which dispenses at a high PPM ratio (over 4000 PPM). LICENSOR will also supply LICENSEE with such information as to the operating principle of the PRODUCT as to enable LICENSEE to manufacture cartridges capable of dispensing liquids at intermediate PPM ratios.

6. When LICENSOR submits to LICENSEE or LICENSEE develops AN OPERATIVE PROTOTYPE of the PRODUCT conforming to the specifications set forth in paragraph 4 herein and to the terms of paragraph 5, herein, LICENSEE shall pay to LICENSOR within thirty days after said submission, the sum of One Hundred Thousand Dollars ($100,000.00), said sum constituting full payment for the development and the building and testing of the OPERATIVE PROTOTYPE of the PRODUCT. LICENSOR warrants that the OPERATIVE PROTOTYPE of the PRODUCT shall not infringe any unexpired United States patent.

7. Upon payment of said $100,000.00 by LICENSEE in accordance with the terms of paragraph 6 hereof, LICENSOR shall and by these presents does grant to LICENSEE during the life of this agreement the exclusive right and license to make, have made, use and sell, and to license others to make, have made, use and sell said PRODUCT, and the inventions disclosed and claimed in any patents and patent applications coming under paragraph 12 hereof, throughout the United States of America, its territories and possessions and all foreign countries.

8. After the sum of $100,000.00 has been paid to LICENSOR in accordance with the provisions of paragraph 6 hereof, LICENSEE shall thereafter pay to LICENSOR royalties as follows:

For each dispenser unit and/or cartridge constituting the components of the PRODUCT, or combination thereof, made in accordance with the OPERATIVE PROTOTYPE submitted by LICENSOR, or developed from said prototype and incorporating the principle of operation thereof, the following percentages of the net sales price of said components shipped by LICENSEE during the following years subsequent to the payment of said sum:

First year	6.5%
Second year	6.0%
Third year	5.5%
Fourth year	5.0%
Fifth year	4.5%
Sixth year	4.0%
Seventh year	3.5%
Eighth year	3.0%
Each following year in which the PRODUCT is sold by LICENSEE	3.0%

9. During the period in which royalties in accordance with paragraph 8 shall be payable, LICENSEE agrees to make written reports to LICENSOR quarterly within thirty (30) days after the last day of each quarter during the life of this Agreement and, as of such dates, to state in each such report the number of cartridges and/or dispenser units of the PRODUCT sold or otherwise disposed of during such quarter. The reports shall be certified to by an officer of LICENSEE and the first such report shall include all of said articles sold or otherwise disposed of between the date of this Agreement and the date of such report.

Concurrently with the making of the foregoing reports, LICENSEE agrees to pay to LICENSOR the total payments due in accordance with paragraph 8 hereof for said cartridges and/or dispenser units included in said reports.

10. LICENSEE agrees to pay LICENSOR a minimum royalty under paragraph 8 hereof at a rate of $35,000.00 for each of the first and second years designated in paragraph 8, hereof, and $50,000.00 for each year thereafter during the life of this Agreement. The minimum royalties for the first three (3) years shall be guaranteed and shall be payable regardless of whether the royalties actually payable during such three years, under the schedule designated in paragraph 8, are less than the minimum royalties for those years. In the event that royalties payable by LICENSEE during the fourth year or any year thereafter are less than the minimum royalty specified above, LICENSEE shall have the right to pay to LICENSOR an amount equal to the difference between the minimum amount specified and the amount of royalties actually paid to LICENSOR in accordance with the quarterly statements submitted for that year, in order to maintain this agreement and the license granted herein. In the event that such additional amount is not paid to LICENSOR within thirty (30) days from the submission of the last quarterly statement for the aforesaid year, either LICENSOR

or LICENSEE may terminate this Agreement and the license granted herein, by the sending of written notice to the other party.

11. LICENSEE agrees to keep accurate records showing the sale of said PRODUCT, including the cartridge and the dispenser unit, under the Agreement herein, in sufficient detail to enable the payments payable hereunder by LICENSEE to be determined, and further agrees to permit its books and records to be examined from time to time to the extent deemed necessary by LICENSOR to verify the reports provided for in paragraph 9 hereof, such examinations not to exceed two per year and such examinations to be made at the expense of LICENSOR by an auditor appointed by LICENSOR who shall be acceptable to LICENSEE, or by a certified public accountant appointed by LICENSOR.

12. LICENSOR has conducted a patentability search on the concept of the PRODUCT as presently contemplated, and has been advised that the PRODUCT includes features which may be patentable. LICENSOR agrees to file at LICENSOR'S expense and to prosecute a United States patent application covering the PRODUCT as developed in the prototype submitted to LICENSEE and to provide to LICENSOR complete copies of said patent application and of any and all communications to and from the United States Patent and Trdemark Office relating to said patent application upon their filing in or receipt from the United States Patent and Trademark Office. Upon receipt of itemized statements therefore, LICENSEE agrees to pay during the life of this agreement the expenses for prosecution of said United States patent application after the filing thereof through the first appeal, if any, to the Board of Appeals in the United States Patent and Trademark Office and for the filing, prosecution (until LICENSEE notifies LICENSOR in writing that LICENSEE will no longer pay such prosecution expenses) and maintenance of any corresponding foreign patent applications and foreign patents issued thereon covering the PRODUCT and requested by LICENSEE to be filed, which foreign patent applications and foreign patents shall be included in the exclusive license herein granted to LICENSEE. LICENSEE shall notify LICENSOR in writing approximately nine months after the filing date of said United States patent application of the foreign countries in which LICENSEE desires LICENSOR to file such corresponding foreign patent applications. LICENSOR agrees to file such foreign patent applications within one year from the filing date of said United States patent applications in the designated foreign countries, to prosecute and maintain those foreign patent applications and any foreign patents issuing thereon and to provide to LICENSEE complete copies of all such foreign patent applications, foreign patents and correspondence to and from the Patent Offices of such foreign countries. LICENSEE may also subsequently notify LICENSOR of other foreign countries in which LICENSEE desires LICENSOR to file corresponding foreign patent applications and in such event, LICENSOR agrees to file prosecute and maintain at LICENSEE'S expense such additional foreign patent applications and foreign patents issuing thereon in accordance with the provisions set forth hereinabove in this paragraph of this agreement. LICENSOR may at his own expense file, prosecute and maintain corresponding patent applications and foreign patents issuing thereon in foreign countries other than those designated by LICENSEE.

13. This Agreement and the license granted herein shall not be assignable by LICENSEE without the writen consent of LICENSOR, which consent shall not unreasonably be withheld. LICENSEE shall provide LICENSOR with a copy of each sub-license granted by LICENSEE, and shall require each sub-licensee to submit to LICENSEE quarterly reports stating the number of the components of said PRODUCT sold by said sub-licensee, and shall pay to LICENSOR, for each component of the PRODUCT sold under each sub-license, royalties in accordance with the schedule set forth in paragraph 8 hereof. LICENSEE shall also include in the written reports provided for in paragraph 9 hereof a report on all royalties payable to LICENSOR under each sub-license for the term covered by each such report. Each sub-license granted hereunder shall provide that LICENSOR has the option to continue said sub-license when and if the license under this agreement is terminated. This agreement shall be binding upon and inure to the benefit of LICENSOR, his heirs, legal representatives and assigns, and LICENSEE, its successors and assigns.

14. After three (3) years, LICENSEE may at any time terminate this agreement by serving written notice of such termination on LICENSOR ninety (90) days before the end of any calendar year throughout the life of this agreement, and in the event of such notice the agreement will automatically expire sixty (60) days after the end of such year but such termination shall not relieve LICENSEE of the obligation to make payments including the minimum guaranteed payments becoming due up to the time of such termination. Notwithstanding such termination, LICENSEE shall have the right thereafter to dispose of any stock of said articles then on hand or in the process of manufacture, but shall pay LICENSOR for the same at the rate and terms provided for by this agreement, such payments becoming due and payable on any licensed articles then on hand or in the process of manufacture.

15. In the event of failure of LICENSEE to perform its part of this agreement, or to make payments of LICENSOR, as provided in this agreement, within thirty (30) days after payments shall become due, LICENSOR shall have the option and privilege of terminating this agreement upon thirty (30) days written notice by registered mail to LICENSEE, which notice shall state the particulars of such alleged failure. If LICENSEE, within thirty (30) days after receipt of such notice, makes full performance of its obligations under the agreement and listed in said notice and makes full payments then due and payable to LICENSOR, then this agreement shall continue in effect as if such notice by LICENSOR had not been sent. Otherwise this license shall, at the expiration of such thirty (30) days after receipt of such notice, be automatically terminated and ended without further notice or action by LICENSOR: but such act shall not prejudice the right of LICENSOR to recover any payments or other sums due at the time of such cancellation or thereafter, and shall not prejudice any cause of action or claim of LICENSOR accrued or to accrue on account of any breach or default by LICENSEE. In the event of termination as provided for in this paragraph, payments shall become due and payable on any of said articles then on hand or in process of manufacture.

16. The term "net sales price", as used in paragraph 8 herein, is defined as LICENSEE'S price to its customers, less cash and/or trade discounts, sales and excise taxes imposed upon

and paid by LICENSEE directly, and for freight and quantity allowances. LICENSEE shall be entitled to take credit for returns of the PRODUCT, if such returns are accepted and credited by LICENSEE.

17. In order to ensure to the LICENSOR the full royalty payments contemplated hereunder, as based upon a percentage of the net sales price the LICENSEE agrees that, in the event that any PRODUCT licensed hereunder shall be sold to a corporation, firm, or association which, or individual who, shall own the controlling interest in the LICENSEE by stock ownership or otherwise, the royalty to be paid hereunder in respect to such PRODUCT shall be based upon the invoice price of such purchaser to its customer rather than upon the invoice price of the LICENSEE: and that, in the event that any PRODUCT licensed hereunder shall be sold to a corporation, firm, or association in which the LICENSEE or its stockholders shall own the controlling interest by stock ownership or otherwise, any deduction or adjustment made by the LICENSEE in fixing the invoice price in respect of such PRODUCT, by reason of such control, shall be disregarded in determining the royalties to be paid hereunder in respect to such PRODUCT.

18. In the event that any patent or patents licensed hereunder shall be deemed by either LICENSOR or LICENSEE to be infringed by a competitive product or process, the bringing of litigation to enjoin such infringement shall be in accordance with the following alternative provisions:

(a) In the event that the parties hereto decide to proceed jointly against such infringer or infringers, they shall be represented in such proceedings by counsel of their joint selection and each shall pay one-half (½) of the costs and expenses of bringing and prosecuting such litigation, it being understood and agreed that any recoveries resulting from such litigation shall be divided equally among the parties hereto.

(b) In the event that only one of the parties hereto shall desire to bring such litigation, then the party desiring to do so may bring suit to enjoin any infringement or infringements at that party's expense and in that party's name and through counsel of that party's choice, retaining all recoveries resulting from such litigation. The party who does not wish to join in such litigation agrees to execute the necessary papers to permit the bringing of such suit, and may be represented by counsel of its own selection and at its own expense, if it desires to do so.

19. In the event that LICENSEE shall be sued for infringement by reason of the manufacture, use or sale of the PRODUCT, then the expense of defending such suit and the payment of any settlement thereof (approved by LICENSOR) or of any judgment thereon shall be borne by LICENSOR to the extent of one-half (½) of the royalties due LICENSOR

under the provisions of paragraphs 8, 9, and 10, hereof beginning with the date on which each suit is brought. In the event a counterclaim is filed by LICENSEE in any such suit, and a money judgment is received in favor of LICENSEE on such counterclaim, LICENSOR shall be credited with the amount of royalty which was deducted to defray the expense of prosecuting said counterclaim. In the event a sub-licensee or customer of LICENSEE shall be sued for infringement by reason of the manufacture, use or sale of the PRODUCT, and LICENSEE intervenes or otherwise defends said suit, the provisions of this paragraph shall apply.

20. LICENSOR agrees to immediately notify LICENSEE in writing of any improvement or modification in the PRODUCT LICENSOR makes or discovers during the life of this agreement; and such improvement or modification shall automatically become part of the exclusive rights granted to LICENSEE in accordance with the terms of this agreement. In the event that any improvement or modification of the PRODUCT is developed or adopted by LICENSEE, and if a United States patent application or applications shall be filed with respect to such improvement or modification, LICENSEE shall forthwith cause such application or applications to be assigned to LICENSOR without cost or charge to LICENSOR. After assignment thereof, LICENSOR agrees to prosecute, at LICENSEE'S expense in accordance with the provisions of paragraph 12 hereof, such application or applications assigned by LICENSEE to LICENSOR. The provisions of paragraph 12 hereof shall apply with respect to the filing, prosecution and maintenance of any and all corresponding foreign patent applications and foreign patents. In the event of termination of this agreement, LICENSEE shall automatically be granted a royalty-free, paid up, non-exclusive license with the right to grant sub-licenses to make, have made, use and sell any product or process under any patent or patent application covering any improvement or modification developed or adopted by LICENSEE, provided however that any such license shall not include a license under any other patent of LICENSOR. During the life of this agreement, LICENSEE shall make the same payments with respect to articles as modified or improved, as it is obligated to make with respect to the unimproved or unmodified articles pursuant to this agreement.

21. A waiver at any one time of any of the terms and conditions of this contract shall not be considered a modification, cancellation or waiver of such term or terms or condition or conditions thereafter.

22. Whenever, under the terms of this agreement, any notice is required or permitted to be given by either party to the other, it shall be deemed to have been sufficiently given for all the purposes thereof, if mailed by registered mail, postage prepaid, to the party or parties to be notified at the address given for such party or parties at the beginning of this agreement, or to such other address as such party or parties shall have furnished each to the other by written notice prior thereto.

IN WITNESS WHEREOF, the parties hereto have duly executed this agreement in duplicate originals the day and year above first written.

_____

_____

_____ INC.

By _____
President

LICENSING AGREEMENT:
. . . COMPANY TO COMPANY

AGREEMENT

THIS AGREEMENT, made and entered into as of the _____ day of _____, 19____, by and between _____ _____ (hereinafter referred to as "LICENSOR") and _____ INC., of _____ _____ (hereinafter referred to as "LICENSEE");

WHEREAS, LICENSOR warrants that it has developed and is the owner of the entire right, title and interest in and to a product in the nature of a lawn and garden fertilizer device consisting of a cartridge containing plant nutrients in a gel carrier, and a cylindrical container into which the cartridge is to be removably and replaceably inserted, with the container adapted to be connected to a garden hose, enabling the user to fertilize or otherwise treat lawns and gardens (hereinafter referred to as "PRODUCT");

WHEREAS, LICENSOR is proceeding promptly to file an application for patent of said PRODUCT in the United States Patent and Trademark Office:

WHEREAS, LICENSOR owns and has possession of trade secrets comprising technical and manufacturing information relating to the PRODUCT and in particular to the composition and formulation of the cartridge unit (hereinafter referred to as "TECHNOLOGY");

WHEREAS, LICENSEE desires to obtain, for the United States of America and all foreign countries, the exclusive right and license to manufacture, use, sell and have made and to sub-license others to manufacture, use, sell and have made the PRODUCT and to obtain the TECHNOLOGY related thereto; and

WHEREAS, LICENSOR is willing to grant such licenses and convey such TECHNOLOGY to LICENSEE;

NOW, THEREFORE, in consideration of the promises and mutual covenants herein contained, the parties herein agree as follows:

1. Upon execution of the agreement, LICENSEE agrees to pay to LICENSOR the sum of TEN THOUSAND DOLLARS ($10,000), the receipt of which is acknowledged by LICENSOR. This sum shall constitute consideration for an option of LICENSEE to obtain an exclusive license as set forth in paragraph 3 hereof, and, upon exercise of said option, shall further constitute a credit in like amount for cartridges shipped by LICENSOR, to LICENSEE under the provisions of paragraph 4 hereof. After execution of this agreement, LICENSEE shall have until December 31, 1979 in which to exercise the option, by giving LICENSOR written notice to such effect. If the option is not exercised by December 31, 1979, this agreement shall

automatically terminate. The primary purpose of the foregoing option is to give LICENSEE the opportunity to conduct an infringement study on the PRODUCT, for purposes of which study LICENSOR has given to LICENSEE a full disclosure of the PRODUCT and its manufacture, including trade secrets. Said infringement study shall be conducted by attorneys of LICENSEE'S CHOICE and at LICENSEE'S expense, but upon exercise of said option LICENSEE shall receive a credit of one-half (½) of said expense against royalties payable under the provisions of paragraph 8 hereof.

2. In the event that LICENSEE exercises the option during the time period and in accordance with the provisions designated in paragraph 1 hereof, LICENSEE shall pay to LICENSOR as a forty percent (40%) advance against the pre-paid royalty provision described in paragraph 8 hereof, under the license herein provided, the sum of Two Hundred Thousand Dollars ($200,000), the payment of which shall accompany the exercise of the option by LICENSEE.

3. Upon exercise of said option and payment of the sum of Two Hundred Thousand Dollars ($200,000) in accordance with paragraphs 1 and 2 hereof, LICENSOR shall grant to LICENSEE for the life of this agreement the exclusive right and license to make, have made, use and sell, and to license others to make, have made, use and sell said PRODUCT, and the inventions disclosed and claimed in any patents or patent applications coming under paragraph 13 hereof, throughout the United States of America, its territories and possessions, and all foreign countries, under the conditions hereinafter set forth. LICENSOR further agrees that it shall not assert against LICENSEE, its sub-licensees or customers, during the life of this agreement, any patent owned or controlled by LICENSOR which is infringed by the manufacture, use or sale of said PRODUCT.

4. On or about November 1, 1979, LICENSEE shall purchase the equipment necessary to set up a pilot plant for the manufacture of the cartridges of said PRODUCT at an estimated cost of approximately $62,000, and shall have the equipment shipped to LICENSOR'S plant in   . Upon installation of the pilot plant, LICENSOR will commence to manufacture said cartridges for technical and market testing, and shall ship said cartridges and containers to LICENSEE who shall pay LICENSOR for said cartridges and containers at the rate of cost (including allocable overhead and general administrative expenses) plus ten percent (10%). Shipment will be made upon manufacture and payment will be made upon receipt of billing from LICENSOR.

5. During the time in which LICENSOR is manufacturing the cartridges of said PRODUCT at the aforementioned pilot plant, LICENSOR agrees to train representatives of LICENSEE in the methods of manufacture of said PRODUCT and the composition and requirements thereof, and to furnish and make available to LICENSEE such TECHNOLOGY as is in the possession or control of LICENSOR relating to the manufacture of the PRODUCT.

6. Any and all TECHNOLOGY transmitted by LICENSOR to LICENSEE pursuant to the provisions of this agreement shall be treated as confidential and as a trade secret, and

LICENSEE agrees that it will use its best efforts to prevent disclosure to third parties of any such TECHNOLOGY received by it. LICENSEE agrees that all of its officers and employees who may come into possession of such TECHNOLOGY will be advised as to the obligations and requirements of this particular paragraph, and each will be required to execute an appropriate secrecy agreement prior to receiving any confidential disclosure.

7. LICENSEE intends to conduct, a test-market evaluation program to be completed between December 1, 1979 and June 30, 1980. After the aforementioned training of LICENSEE'S representatives has been completed, and LICENSEE'S test-market program has been implemented, LICENSEE may ship the pilot plant equipment to its plant at   and begin manufacture of the PRODUCT sufficient for its marketing requirements. LICENSOR at its option may not be required to manufacture the PRODUCT beyond one year from the date of this agreement.

8. LICENSEE agrees to pay to LICENSOR a pre-paid royalty of Five Hundred Thousand Dollars ($500,000) which shall be payable at a rate of sixteen and two-thirds percent (16 2/3%) of the net sales price of the PRODUCT, including both the containers and cartridges, shipped by LICENSEE. The forty percent (40%) advance payment in the amount of Two Hundred Thousand Dollars ($200,000) against the entire pre-paid royalty referred to hereinabove made upon the exercise of the option referred to in paragraphs 1 through 3 hereof shall be recouped from the sixteen and two-thirds percent (16 2/3%) of the net sales price of the PRODUCT referred to hereinabove (that is, at the rate of forty percent, 40%, of the royalty obligation). The term "net sales price" is defined as LICENSEE'S price to its customers, less cash and/or trade discounts, sales and excise taxes imposed upon and paid by LICENSEE directly, and for freight and quantity allowances. LICENSEE shall be entitled to take credit for returns of the PRODUCT, if such returns are accepted and credited by LICENSEE. Subject to the termination provisions of paragraph 19 hereof, the aforesaid royalty payments shall be continued until the entire pre-paid royalty has been paid to LICENSOR.

9. After the entire pre-paid royalty, provided for in paragraph 8 hereof, has been fully paid to LICENSOR, LICENSEE shall pay to LICENSOR royalties as follows:

First year	6.5%
Second year	6.0%
Third year	5.5%
Fourth year	5.0%
Fifth year	4.5%
Sixth year	4.0%
Seventh year	3.5%
Eighth year	3.0%
Each following year in which cartridges are sold by LICENSEE	3.0%

(a) For each cartridge constituting one of the two components of the PRODUCT and manufactured in accordance with the TECHNOLOGY transmitted by LICENSOR to LICENSEE, the following percentages of the net sales price of cartridges shipped by LICENSEE during the following years subsequent to the full payment of the aforesaid prepaid royalty:

(b) For ech container constituting one of the two components of the PRODUCT and covered by any pending patent application of LICENSOR, the following percentages of the net sales price of containers shipped by LICENSEE during the following years subsequent to the full payment of the aforesaid prepaid royalty:

First year 3.25%
Second year .... 3.0 %
Third year 2.75%
Fourth year .... 2.5 %
Fifth year 2.25%
Sixth year .... 2.0 %
Seventh year 1.75%
Eighth year .... 1.5 %
Each following year .... 1.5 %

10. The royalties for said containers payable in accordance with the schedule designated in paragraph 9(b) hereof shall be payable by LICENSEE, during the life of this agreement, so long as there exists a pending patent application of LICENSOR which includes one or more claims claiming the container alone or in combination with the cartridge. In the event that the last of LICENSOR'S patent applications shall be finally rejected and all appeals or petitions therefor shall be exhausted, so that it becomes impossible for LICENSOR to obtain a patent covering the container alone or in combination, the royalties payable under paragraph 9(b), but not the rights granted to LICENSEE hereunder, shall automatically terminate. In the event that a period of seven (7) years elapses from the filing date in the United States patent and Trademark Office of the first patent application of LICENSOR disclosing or claiming the container alone or in combination with the cartridge without a United States patent issuing to LICENSOR with claims covering the container alone or in combination with the cartridge, the royalties payable under paragraph 9(b) hereof, but not the rights granted to LICENSEE hereunder, shall automatically cease, subject to resumption in accordance with the following sentence of this paragraph upon the issuance of such a United States patent with claims covering the container alone or in combination with the cartridge. In the event that combination with a cartridge or cartridges, the royalties payable under paragraph 9(b) hereof for sales of said containers shall be doubled to conform to the royalties designated in paragraph 9(a) hereof, and shall be payable to LICENSOR at said doubled rate according to the yearly schedule for the period following the issuance of said patent or patents for the effective life of any patent containing claims covering the container sold by LICENSOR.

11. During the period in which royalties in accordance with paragraphs 8, 9 and 10 shall be payable, LICENSEE agrees to make written reports to LICENSOR quarterly within thirty (30) days after the last day of each quarter during the life of this agreement and, as of such dates, to state in each such report the number of cartridges and/or containers of the PRODUCT sold or otherwise disposed of during such quarter. The reports shall be certified to by an officer of LICENSEE and the first such report shall include all of said articles sold or otherwise disposed of between the date of this agreement and the date of such report.

Concurrently with the making of the foregoing reports, LICENSEE agrees to pay to LICENSOR the total payments due in accordance with paragraphs 8, 9 and 10 hereof for said cartridges and/or containers included in said reports.

12. LICENSEE agrees to pay to LICENSOR a minimum guaranteed royalty under paragraphs 8, 9 and 10 hereof at a rate of Two Hundred and Thirty-Five Thousand Dollars ($235,000) for the first year beginning with payment of the forty percent (40%) advance in the amount of Two Hundred Thousand Dollars ($200,000) against the entire pre-paid royalty of Five Hundred Thousand Dollars ($500,000) provided for in paragraph 8 hereof, and One Hundred Thousand Dollars ($100,000) per year thereafter during the life of this agreement. In the event that royalties payable by LICENSEE during any one year are less than the minimum royalty specified above, LICENSEE shall have the right to pay to LICENSOR an amount equal to the difference between the minimum amount specified and the amount of royalties actually paid to LICENSOR in accordance with the quarterly statements submitted for that year, in order to maintain this agreement and the license granted herein. In the event that such additional amount is not paid to LICENSOR within thirty (30) days from the submission of the last quarterly statement for the aforesaid year, either LICENSOR or LICENSEE may terminate this agreement and the license granted herein, by the sending of written notice to the other party.

13. LICENSOR agrees to file at LICENSOR'S expense and to prosecute a United States patent application or applications on the PRODUCT and to provide to LICENSEE complete copies of said patent application or applications and of any and all communications to and from the United States Patent and Trademark Office relating to said patent application or applications upon their filing in or receipt from the United States Patent and Trademark Office. Upon receipt of itemized statements therefor, LICENSEE agrees to pay during the life of this agreement the expenses for prosecution of said United States patent application or applications after the filing thereof through the first appeal, if any, to the Board of Appeals in the United States Patent and Trademark Office and for the filing, prosecution (until LICENSEE notifies LICENSOR in writing that LICENSEE will no longer pay such prosecution expenses) and maintenance of any corresponding foreign patent applications and foreign patents issued thereon covering the PRODUCT and requested by LICENSEE to be filed, which foreign patent applications and foreign patents shall be included in the exclusive license herein granted to LICENSEE. LICENSEE shall notify LICENSOR in writing approximately nine months after the filing date of said United States patent application or applications of the foreign countries in which LICENSEE desires LICENSOR to file such corresponding foreign patent applications. LICENSOR agrees to file such foreign patent applications within one year from the filing date of said United States patent application or applications in the designated foreign countries, to prosecute and maintain those foreign patent applications and any foreign patents issuing thereon and to provide to LICENSEE complete copies of all such foreign patent applications, foreign patents and correspondence to and from the Patent Offices of such foreign countries. LICENSEE may also subsequently notify LICENSOR of other foreign countries in which LICENSEE desires LICENSOR to file corresponding foreign patent applications and in such event, LICENSOR agrees to file,

prosecute and maintain at LICENSEE'S expense such additional foreign patent applications and foreign patents issuing thereon in accordance with the provisions set forth hereinabove in this paragraph of this agreement. LICENSOR may at its own expense file, prosecute and maintain corresponding patent applications and foreign patents issuing thereon in foreign countries other than those designated by LICENSEE.

14. LICENSOR agrees to assign to LICENSEE all orders it has received or will hereafter receive for sale of the PRODUCT. LICENSEE shall be responsible for the payment of any commissions payable to LICENSOR'S salesmen or agents.

15. LICENSEE agrees to keep accurate records showing the sale of said PRODUCT, including the cartridge and the container (where applicable) under the agreement herein, in sufficient detail to enable the payments payable hereunder by LICENSEE to be determined, and further agrees to permit its books and records to be examined from time to time to the extent deemed necessary by LICENSOR to verify the reports provided for in paragraph 11 hereof, such examinations not to exceed two per year and such examinations to be made at the expense of LICENSOR by an auditor appointed by LICENSOR who shall be acceptable to LICENSEE, or by a certified public accountant appointed by LICENSOR.

16. This agreement and the license granted herein shall not be assignable by LICENSEE without the written consent of LICENSOR, which consent shall not unreasonably be withheld.

17. LICENSEE shall provide LICENSOR with a copy of each sub-license granted by LICENSEE, and shall require each sub-licensee to submit to LICENSEE quarterly reports stating the number of components of said PRODUCT sold by said sub-licensee. LICENSEE shall pay LICENSOR, for each component of said PRODUCT sold under each sub-license, royalties in accordance with the schedule set forth in paragraph 9 hereof. LICENSEE shall also include in the written report provided for in paragraph 11 hereof a report on all royalties payable to LICENSOR under each sub-license for the terms covered by each report. Each sub-license granted by LICENSEE shall require the sub-licensee to comply with paragraph 6 of this agreement and further provide that LICENSOR has the option to continue said sub-license when and if the license under this agreement is terminated. This agreement shall be binding upon and inure to the benefit of LICENSOR and LICENSEE, their successors and assigns.

18. In order to ensure to the LICENSOR the full royalty payments contemplated hereunder, as based upon a percentage of net sales price, the LICENSEE agrees that, in the event that any PRODUCT licensed hereunder shall be sold to a corporation, firm, or association which, or individual who, shall own the controlling interest in the LICENSEE by stock ownership or otherwise, the royalty to be paid hereunder shall be based upon the invoice price of the LICENSEE; and that, in the event that any PRODUCT licensed hereunder shall be sold to a corporation, firm, or association in which the LICENSEE or its stockholders shall own the controlling interest by stock ownership or otherwise, any deduction or adjustment made by the LICENSEE in fixing the invoice price in respect of such PRODUCT,

by reason of such control, shall be disregarded in determining the royalties to be paid hereunder in respect to such PRODUCT.

19. Upon exercise of the option and payment of the forty percent (40%) advance (against the entire pre-paid royalty) in the amount of Two Hundred Thousand Dollars ($200,000) under paragraphs 1 and 2 hereof, LICENSEE may at any time terminate this agreement by serving written notice of such termination on LICENSOR ninety (90) days before the end of any calendar year throughout the life of this agreement, and in the event of such notice the agreement will automatically expire sixty (60) days after the end of such year but such termination shall not relieve LICENSEE of the obligation to make payments including the minimum guaranteed payments becoming due up to the time of such termination. Notwithstanding such termination, LICENSEE shall have the right thereafter to dispose of any stock of said articles then on hand or in the process of manufacture, but shall pay LICENSOR for the same at the rate and terms provided for by this agreement, such payments becoming due and payable on any licensed articles then on hand or in process of manufacture.

20. In the event of failure of LICENSEE to perform its part of this agreement, or to make payments to LICENSOR, as provided in this agreement within thirty (30) days after payments shall have become due, LICENSOR shall have the option and privilege of terminating this agreement upon thirty (30) days written notice by registered mail to LICENSEE, which notice shall state the particulars of such alleged failure. If LICENSEE, within thirty (30) days after receipt of such notice, makes full performance of its obligations under the agreement and listed in said notice and makes full payments then due and payable to LICENSOR, then this agreement shall continue in effect as if such notice by LICENSOR had not been sent, otherwise this license shall, at the expiration of such thirty (30) days after receipt of such notice, be automatically terminated and ended without further notice or action by LICENSOR; but such act shall not prejudice the right of LICENSOR to recover any payments or other sums due at the time of such cancellation or thereafter, and shall not prejudice any cause of action or claim of LICENSOR accrued or to accrue, on account of any breach or default by LICENSEE. In the event of termination as provided for in this paragraph, payments shall become due and payable on any of said articles then on hand or in process of manufacture.

21. LICENSOR agrees to immediately notify LICENSEE in writing of any improvement or modification in the PRODUCT LICENSOR makes or discovers during the life of this agreement; and such improvement or modification shall automatically become part of the exclusive rights granted to LICENSEE in accordance with the terms of this agreement. In the event that any improvement or modification of the PRODUCT is developed or adopted by LICENSEE, and if a United States patent application or applications shall be filed with respect to such improvement or modification, LICENSEE shall forthwith cause such application or applications to be assigned to LICENSOR without cost or charge to LICENSOR. After assignment thereof, LICENSOR agrees to prosecute, at LICENSEE'S expense in accordance with the provisions of paragraph 13 hereof, such application or applications assigned by LICENSEE to LICENSOR. The provisions of paragraph 13 hereof shall apply with respect

to the filing, prosecution and maintenance of any and all corresponding foreign patent applications and foreign patents. In the event of termination of this agreement, LICENSEE shall automatically be granted a royalty-free, paid-up, non-exclusive license with the right to grant sub-licenses to make, have made, use and sell any product or process under any patent or patent application covering any improvement or modification developed or adopted by LICENSEE, provided however that any such license shall not include a license under any other patent of LICENSOR. During the life of this agreement, LICENSEE shall make the same payments with respect to articles so modified or improved, as it is obligated to make with respect to the unimproved or unmodified articles pursuant to this agreement.

22. In the event that any patent or patents licensed hereunder shall be deemed infringed by LICENSOR or LICENSEE by a competitive product or process, the bringing of litigation to enjoin such infringement shall be in accordance with the following alternative provisions:

a) In the event that the parties hereto decide to proceed jointly against such infringer or infringers, they shall be represented in such proceedings by counsel of their joint selection and each shall pay one-half (½) of the costs and expenses of bringing and prosecuting such litigation, it being understood and agreed that any recoveries resulting from such litigation shall be divided equally among the parties hereto.

b) In the event that only one of the parties hereto shall desire to bring such litigation, then the party desiring to do so may bring suit to enjoin any infringement or infringements at that party's expense and in that party's name and through counsel of that party's choice, retaining all recoveries resulting from such litigation. The party who does not wish to join in such litigation agrees to execute the necessary papers to permit the bringing of such suit, and may be represented by counsel of its own selection and at its own expense, if it desires to do so.

23. In the event that LICENSEE shall be sued for infringement by reason of the manufacture, use or sale of the PRODUCT, then the expense of defending such suit and the payment of any settlement thereof (approved by LICENSOR) or of any judgement thereon shall be borne by LICENSOR to the extent of one-half (½) of the royalties due LICENSOR under the provisions of paragraphs 8, 9 and 10 hereof beginning with the date on which such suit is brought. In the event that a counterclaim is filed by LICENSEE in any such suit, and a money judgment is received in favor of LICENSEE on such counterclaim, LICENSOR shall be credited with the amount of royalty which was deducted to defray the expense of prosecuting said counterclaim. In the event a sub-licensee or customer of LICENSEE shall be sued for infringement by reason of the manufacture, use or sale of the PRODUCT, and LICENSEE intervenes or otherwise defends said suit, the provisions of this paragraph shall apply.

24. A waiver at any one time of any of the terms and conditions of this contract shall not be considered a modification, cancellation or a waiver of such term or terms or condition or conditions thereafter.

25. Whenever, under the terms of this agreement, any notice is required or permitted to be given by either party to the other, it shall be deemed to have been sufficiently given for all the purposes thereof, if mailed by registered mail, postage prepaid, to the party or parties to be notified at the address given for such party or parties at the beginning of this agreement, or to such other address as such party or parties shall have furnished each to the other by written notice prior thereto.

IN WITNESS WHEREOF, the parties hereto have duly executed this agreement in duplicate originals the day and year above first written.

_____ INC.

By _____
President

_____ INC.

By _____
President

PRIVATE PLACEMENT:

. . . BUSINESS PLAN AND PRO FORMA

(Company History, Management, and Stockholder Lists Removed)

CONFIDENTIAL MEMORANDUM

PRIVATE PLACEMENT

INDUSTRIES, INC.

160,000 Shares of Common Stock

THIS PRIVATE PLACEMENT INVOLVES A HIGH DEGREE OF RISK
(See "Speculative Aspects")

July 19

The information contained in this Memorandum has been obtained from the management of   INDUSTRIES, INC. No representation or warranty is made, however, as to the accuracy or completeness of such information, and nothing contained in this Memorandum is, or shall be relied on as, a promise or representation as to the future. This confidential Memorandum is submitted in connection with the private placement of securities as referred to herein to a limited number of persons and may not be reproduced, in whole or in part, for any other purpose.

TABLE OF CONTENTS

Industries, Inc., a research and development company, has conceived and developed a unique agricultural product, as well as the prototype machinery to produce it. The product is called an Environmental Seed Cell (ESC) and its use should enable growers of many crops to significantly increase profitability by reducing costly hand labor. Concurrently, it should improve yield and the quality of the harvest. In fact, the use of   product could revolutionize current vegetable farming practices. The domestic market for the Environmental Seed Cell is estimated to be between $75 million and $300 million. Based on its study of the market, management believes that vegetable growers would be highly receptive to a product such as   and appear likely to adopt it relatively rapidly. The Company estimates that it can achieve sales of approximately $18 million and net profit after taxes of about $5 million within five years. In two years, management believes the Company could attain sales of $2 million and net income after taxes in excess of $500,000.

Proposed Private Placement

It is the Company's purpose to raise $1,000,000 through a private placement of 160,000 shares at $6.25 per share for   Industries, Inc. to transform the Company from its current development stage into a profitable production-oriented organization. Funds obtained from this financing will be used to build machines, expand management and staff and market the Company's product (ESC). Each machine unit will cost approximately $20,000 excluding support equipment, and the first unit (excluding the prototype) is scheduled to be producing by April 19 · It is projected that three machines will be in operation by June 19 Thereafter, following a five-month period during which the initial three production machines will be carefully studied and evaluated, two machine units are expected to be added monthly.   believes it could have ninety-one machine units producing in July 19   having sufficient monthly capacity to produce Environmental Seed Cells for over 35,000 acres. This would equal more than $1,750,000 in sales per month based on a currently planned selling price of $50 per acre. In management's opinion, the new funds will permit the Company to reach the stage in its development when internal cash flow generation will be adequate for the Company's foreseeable future expansion requirements. To date, the present share-holders have invested $489,400 in the Company to develop the concept, the Environmental Seed Cell, and the prototype machinery.

Speculative Aspects

The Company is in the developmental stage and has no operating history and accordingly there can be no assurance that it will ever be profitable. Although considerable time and effort have been devoted by management and directors to forecasts, projections and financial planning, there can be no assurance that these plans will be accomplished or carried out within the time periods contemplated.

Background

Advances in mechanization and in the biological sciences have
enabled farmers, over the years, to increase productivity by a lesser
input of manual labor. However, many crops -- particularly small-seed
vegetable crops -- have defied mechanization. The problems associated
with planting, growing, and harvesting of small-seed vegetable crops
are quite different than those experienced in farming the larger feed
grain crops. Until recently, the costs of developing machinery and
making required changes in vegetable cultural practices were considered
prohibitive when compared with the continued use of procedures which
employed abundant, relatively cheap, migratory farm hand labor. The
labor situation has changed dramatically in the past five years and
growers now are quite receptive to methods that might reduce their
dependence on hand labor and its attendant costs.

The factors contributing to this changed attitude are:

1. A change in the United States immigration program in 1964
    prohibiting Mexican farm laborers (braceros) to work in
    this country during the harvest season. Previously, the
    braceros program had been quite liberal;

2. Another change in the United States immigration law in
    1968 restricting to only 120,000 annually the number of
    immigrants allowed to enter the United States from the
    Western Hemisphere (including Mexico). Prior to this,
    there was no quota set upon Mexicans;

3. The inclusion of farm laborers under the minimum wage in
    1967 and the rise in the rate from $1.35 to $1.65 per
    hour; and

4. The increasing unionization of farm labor.

The problem has become further aggravated in that the quality of
the work force also has deteriorated during this period.

The growing scarcity and increasing cost of farm labor has led to
a broadscale search for ways to plant, grow, and harvest vegetables and
other crops with a minimum of hand labor at all stages of crop production.

Currently, there are over three million acres of vegetables planted
in the United States, and almost half are of the small-seed varieties.
California is the United States' largest vegetable producer, harvesting
741,300 acres in 1968, or 23% of the total U. S. vegetable acreage.
Lettuce, the country's fourth largest vegetable crop, accounted for
222,000 acres in 1968, and 60% of the crop (133,000 acres) was harvested
in California alone. About 85% of the nation's lettuce is grown in
California and Arizona.

The lettuce crop provides insight into the vegetable grower's
predicament. Because of the lettuce seed's small and irregular shape,
no mechanical planter has yet been developed that can accurately plant
raw seed individually. Consequently, the grower has been forced to use
mechanical planters which traverse the field slowly dribbling out seed
in rows. The farmer thus sows between 400,000 and 500,000 seeds per acre,
although the theoretical maximum crop per acre is generally thought to be

only 26,000 heads[1]. The resulting oversupply of seedlings must be hand thinned (the removal of excess plants by hand) so that, hopefully, 26,000 plants remain. Hand thinning often "shocks" many of the remaining plants, causing a setback in their growth. The lack of uniformity in raw seed (current seeding rates make preselection of seed for a higher degree of uniformity prohibitively expensive), combined with the variations in the degree of thinning shock to the remaining plants, means that the lettuce crop will not mature uniformly. Thus, the grower has to harvest the crop manually in two or three passes through the field.

The ultimate solution for the grower is to plant more uniform high-quality seed "to stand" -- that is, to sow only one seed in the exact place where the grower desires a plant to mature. To do this, the grower must be able to sow mechanically individual seeds with great precision, and perhaps more importantly, he must create more favorable conditions to ensure that most of the seed planted will grow into mature plants. If this is achieved, hand thinning will be eliminated and the crop will have more uniform growth, thereby permitting, for the first time, machine harvesting. It should also enable the farmer to increase his yield, which now averages only 12,000 heads per acre out of a potential of 26,000, while improving the quality of the harvest.

The Product

Industries, Inc. has, over the last three years, developed a product which satisfies the criteria of planting to stand. It is comprised of a seed, preselected for vigor, which is surrounded by organic and inorganic environmental materials. The construction of the tablet allows for the adjustment of Ph (acidity/alkalinity) levels to take account of the needs of various varieties of seeds. In addition, the environment includes certain nutrients and other ingredients beneficial to the seed, and is compressed to form a multilayered tablet similar in size and shape to a large aspirin. This tablet, called an Environmental Seed Cell, is highly water-absorbent. A relatively minor adaptation (developed by   ) to a type of mechanical planter now in wide use enables the planting of Environmental Seed Cells with a very high degree of precision. As a result, vegetable growers using   product will be able to eliminate costly hand labor while improving yield and uniformity of harvest.

plans to operate as a converter - taking the grower's choice of seed type and incorporating a single seed into a tablet along with required nutrients and environmental materials conducive to uniform germination and growth. To the best of the Company's knowledge, its

----

[1]   management believes that it can increase the theoretical maximum yield to approximately 31,000 heads of lettuce per acre.

ESC is the only precision planted product containing nutrients and other growth-inducing materials. In addition, the ESC's specially prepared matrix of organic and inorganic materials is recognized as excellent mulch.

To date, growers have expressed a major concern with the method by which precision planted products are placed in the ground. They have been extremely reluctant to get involved with sophisticated and intricate machines which require skilled labor.

ESC can be planted with a modified Deere #71 Flexi Planter (a unit used by many West Coast growers). The modification basically involves the use of a new dispensing plate which, because of its low cost,   plans to provide at little or no cost to the grower. A prototype of this planter has been field tested in California by the Company and, with minor modifications now being made, should perform successfully in future field tests.

Product Performance

has been engaged in a continuous product testing program since it first developed the capability of manufacturing tablets by hand in 19 . Working in its own laboratory, germination and emergence tests have enabled the Company to identify (a) those materials and conditions which materially affect the growth of lettuce seed from within an environmental tablet, and (b) the variables which must be accommodated in automated tablet production.

In April 19. the Company conducted its first product test under field conditions in Salinas, California. Using tablets produced on single station manual machinery and planted by hand, the Company determined that its product more than satisfied minimum criteria for expected grower use. With this knowledge, the Company then focused its energies on its automatic prototype machine in an effort to ensure that it could replicate product as manufactured on single station machines. Product testing in the laboratory was continued.

In April 19 , the Company conducted its second field test in Salinas, using product manufactured by its multi-station working proto-type machine. In addition, the Company's planter modification was tested for the first time.

The results of this test indicated the following:

1. An additional manufacturing process was needed to screen out tablets of improper size which occasionally jammed the planter modification.

2. Additional modifications were needed in the tablet maker to better control pressure.

Because of the sizing problem associated with the planter, it was impossible to measure emergence rates with accuracy.

A third field test, as part of a continuing field program, using accurately sized tablets and employing modified pressures, should be completed by early Fall, 19 . For all three tests, the Company has, or will, work closely with   a large California lettuce grower, who has maintained high interest in the Company's product.

Market and Sales Potential

The potential market for Environmental Seed Cells is substantial -- in excess of 3.2 million acres of harvested vegetables in the U. S. Their most practical and immediate use will be for small-seed vegetable crops such as lettuce, tomatoes, cabbage, onions, carrots, celery, broccoli, and peppers where hand labor has become a serious problem. The total annual crop acreage for these vegetables in the United States alone is in excess of 1.4 million acres*, as documented in the following table:

1968 Small Seed Vegetable Crops

Crop	1968 Acreage for Harvest
Artichokes	9,600
Beets	22,960
Broccoli	42,950
Brussel Sprouts	6,800
Cabbage	108,565
Carrots	71,995
Cauliflower	26,800
Celery	33,580
Cucumbers	201,120
Lettuce	222,255
Onions	106,420
Peppers	51,780
Spinach	39,160
Tomatoes	512,615
Others	19,810
Total Small Seed Crop	1,476,420
Total Vegetables	3,244,165

Source: U.S.D.A. Crop Reporting Service

---

*Two crops from a 20-acre field are considered 40 acres for harvest.

Other crops for which Environmental Seed Cells may ultimately be used are sugar beets and tobacco (small seeds), cotton (to provide more uniform maturity for machine harvesting), and high-priced seed crops such as hybrid corn and hybrid barley (systemic poisons placed in the outer layer of Environmental Seed Cells could protect these seeds from rodents and vermin). Commercially grown flowers, such as petunias (small seeds), represent another potentially large market. In addition, a sizeable consumer market may exist. These markets have not been explored in any detail nor are they included in Company estimates of near term sales potential.

will be directing its initial marketing efforts toward the commercial lettuce market -- the second largest small-seed crop and the one considered to be the most difficult to plant with precision. Lettuce growers produce annually approximately 220,000 crop acres of lettuce having a consumer market value, according to the U. S. Department of Agriculture, of approximately $200,000,000 F.O.B. the shipping point. It is estimated that 75% of the crop is produced by fewer than 50 - 60 growers situated in California and Arizona. These growers are among the most progressive farmers in the country. Direct conversations with many of them, as well as with government agents serving them, indicate that these growers are highly receptive to any new methods, particularly those which promise labor savings.

estimates that the near term sales potential for its product is as follows:

1. <u>Minimum</u>: 50% of U. S. lettuce acreage at a price of $50.00 per acre for   product
   (222,000 acres) (50%) ($50/acre)   = $ 5.55 million

2. <u>Possible</u>: 60% of U. S. lettuce acreage
   (222,000 acres) (60%) ($50/acre)   = $ 6.66 million

   50% of remaining small-seed vegetable acreage
   (1,254,000 acres) (50%) ($50/acre)   = $31.35 million

                                             $38.01 million

The Company expects to begin marketing its ESC for other vegetable crops in approximately two years. The Company also believes that the overseas vegetable potential for the ESC may be at least as great as that available in the United States.

Economic Benefits to Growers

The realizable economies to the farmer of using Environmental Seed Cells are striking. The use by the grower of Environmental Seed Cells will eliminate his cost of raw seed (approximately $10 - $12 per acre) and the cost of hand thinning (approximately $75.00 per acre). Also, it is anticipated that Environmental Seed Cells will enable farmers to cut planting time by 50%, thereby halving the cost of planting (direct savings of $1.50 per acre). These calculations of direct savings do not include the dollar value derived from improved yield which should result from the elimination of thinning shock to, and laborer trampling of, small seedlings.

In arriving at its price estimate of $50.00 per acre, the Company has considered available competitive product alternatives:

1. Raw Seed Growers

   Currently pay $10.00 - 12.00 per acre for good quality seed plus $75.00 for thinning.

2. Coated Seed Growers

   Currently pay $5.50 - 8.00 per acre for coated seed (requires less seed per acre) plus $45.00 for thinning.

3. Seed Tape Growers

   Currently pay $35.00 per acre for seed tape plus $20.00 - 30.00 for thinning.

The following table illustrates the risk/reward possibilities facing the grower if he uses the   Environmental Seed Cell, keeping in mind that the current general estimate of the optimal yield per acre is 26,000 heads or 1,083 cartons. The table correlates various loss factors with harvestable yields. Two possibilities have been explored: 26,000 tablets per acre, spaced twelve inches apart; and 28,400 tablets per acre, spaced about eleven inches apart.   believes that its ESC lettuce tablets can be planted ten to eleven inches apart.

Harvestable Heads of Lettuce			Loss		Loss
Cartons*	Heads	% of 26,000	Factors	% of 28,400	Factors
850	20,400	78	22	71	29
800	19,200	74	26	67	33
750	18,000	69	31	63	37
700	16,800	65	35	59	41
675	16,200	62	38	57	43
650	15,600	60	40	54	46
625	15,000	58	42	52	48
600	14,400	55	45	50	50
500	12,000	46	54	42	58

*There are 24 heads of lettuce per carton.

It can be seen that, if only 46% of the tablets result in harvestable heads when planting 26,000 to the acre, the grower's yield would still equal the average of 12,000 heads now being harvested per acre. If he increases the number of seeds to 28,400 per acre, a 58% loss factor would still yield almost a carload of lettuce per acre, the expressed goal of most growers.

If ESC can consistently maintain an average stand of 70%, a target management expects to exceed, then, average yields would be increased by 50% to 65% when compared to results now being obtained with existing cultural practices.

In addition, the proper spacing of plants will increase the effectiveness and use of herbicides, thereby reducing the need for hand hoeing to eliminate weeds. Thinning shock, which can severely set back plant growth will also be eliminated. Preselection of seed and elimination of thinning shock should allow the crop to develop and mature uniformly and hold the promise of machine harvesting in one pass through the field, as opposed to the present system of manual harvesting in two or three passes. The potential savings of machine harvesting could exceed the aggregate of all of the other cost savings. Lastly, it should be noted that preselection of seeds and more effective use of nutrients and herbicides should result in a better crop and increased yield.

Mass Production Capability

Many studies have been done to verify the practicality and need for a plant to a stand product. However, mass production of such a product has been difficult to achieve so as to make it economical for a grower to use. Although information confirming the success of a plant to stand tablet (made and planted by hand) has been available for at least three and a half years, machinery to singulate raw seed and to incorporate it into a tablet has not yet been developed. As simple as a tablet maker might appear to be, one synchronized with a singulator which also (1) handles materials, (2) incorporates one seed, and (3) makes a multi-layered tablet has not been developed by others to the best of   knowledge.

It has been assumed by some that nutrients and other chemicals can be easily incorporated into an environmental seed tablet. However, the toxic effects of chemicals upon raw seed have to be eliminated, indicating that an effective environmental "planting to a stand" vehicle has to provide protection for the seed from these desired chemicals. The technique of isolating and protecting the seed is a difficult one to develop and master.   has successfully accomplished this. To the best of   knowledge, no other company has yet achieved this technology.

expects to have the capability of mass-producing Environmental
Seed Cells at low cost. It has designed, developed, and manufactured a
full-scale prototype machine which incorporates a number of variable
components to enable experimentation prior to resolving the final design
of a production machine. The prototype machine is to be used to produce
all test planting product necessary prior to implementation of a full-
scale market program derived from regular production machinery. The
machinery is comprised of a singulator which takes an individual seed
from a mass of seeds with great speed and accuracy and then transports
the seed to a second machine (the Tablet Maker) which tabletizes it in
its multilayered environment.

The Company expects each production machine to be capable of
producing 388 acres per month based on operations continuing six days
a week for fifteen hours per day and allowing for 15% downtime and 10%
rejects. With the assumption that by December 19   on average two
machines can be brought on stream per month, the Company will have a
monthly production capability of 35,335 acres by July 19   (See
Exhibit I, Page 17.)

Management presently plans that   will retain ownership of all
production machines and in its role as converter will concentrate on
the manufacturing and marketing of its disposable proprietary product.

The Company's offices. design and manufacturing facilities are
located at   Approximately 2,000 square feet of leased space includes offices, drafting
room, a completely equipped machine shop, a laboratory, raw materials
storage, and production and support equipment.

The existing space can accommodate the operating prototype machine
and support equipment, as well as one production unit which is currently
being designed. Commencing with the second production machine, the Company
will need larger quarters. Management anticipates that during the
Fall of 1971 manufacturing facilities will also be established in the
Salinas Valley -- the heart of the fresh vegetable growing area of
California.

believes that both the Singulator and Tablet Maker are
unique. The Singulator is capable of handling a wide variety of seed,
including the smallest and most irregularly shaped seed which have
heretofore defied individual mechanical handling. The Tablet Maker
can produce the multilayered Environmental Seed Cell with great speed.
A multilayered tablet has several advantages, one of which is to permit
the use of nutrients and other substances beneficial to the seed while
not bringing these ingredients into direct contact with the sensitive
seed.

Patents

Since its inception, the Company has been engaged in an active
patent application program. To date, applications have been filed

covering the <u>Environmental Seed Cell</u>, the <u>Singulator</u> and <u>Tablet Maker</u>, and the Company is in the process of filing for its planter modification.

Competition

In addition to   others have recognized the potential of the small seed market and are trying to satisfy it. However, in management's opinion, the Environmental Seed Cell offers unique and important advantages over the products of   competitors. Specifically, it can provide cost savings in all phases of the growing process as well as the prospects for improved yield and harvest. Because of these advantages, should be able to obtain an important share of the market and be relatively free from competition based solely on price.

The competition to   product may be divided into three categories:

1. Raw Seeds
2. Coated and Taped Seeds
3. Seed Cells

1. <u>Raw Seeds</u>

   Raw seeds are grown and marketed by several small to inter-mediate sized companies. Leaders in the sale of raw vegetable seeds to West Coast growers are Asgrow Seed Company, Ferry-Morse Seed Company, and Niagara Seed & Chemical Company. It is estimated that between 30% and 50% of lettuce acreage is still planted with raw seed. The Company believes that this segment of the market has not converted to precision planted products because those currently available have not offered sufficiently signifi-cant cost savings to offset the risks inherent in a reduction of seeds planted.

2. <u>Coated and Taped Seeds</u>

   To meet the farmer's increased demand for labor savings in planting, three companies have marketed products which offer the grower the ability to plant seed with greater precision. None of the products offered by these companies improve the environment of the seed.

   a. <u>Germaine Seed Company</u>

      This Company acts as a converter, taking raw seeds and coating them with clay to increase size and create a more uniform shape. Clay-coated seed, while helping to resolve the handling problem associated with small, irregular seeds have four distinct disadvantages in the opinion of   management:

1. Clay contributes nothing to the environment in
    which seeds grow.

2. Clay is more impervious than soil to water, and
    as a result, often prevents or retards growth.

3. The coating process is imprecise, so that often
    either two seeds or no seed end up inside the
    clay pellets, which frequently vary in size.

4. Existing planters still cannot plant coated seed
    with absolute precision.

Use of coated seed does, however, allow the grower to
reduce the amount of overplanting, thereby reducing his
thinning costs. Mechanical planters can handle coated
seeds more effectively than raw seeds, but still not
with complete precision. The grower plants about
150,000 coated seeds per acre (at a cost of approximately $5.50 per acre, including coating cost) as
opposed to 400,000 raw seeds (at a cost of approximately $10.00 - $12.00 per acre). This limited
advantage over raw seed enabled Germaine's coated seed
to capture approximately 50% of the lettuce-seed market
in the five years prior to the introduction of Asgrow's
competitive product.

b. Asgrow Seed Company

Asgrow, the largest vegetable seed grower and marketer,
recently completed a plant with capacity to coat seeds
with vermiculite rather than with clay. The product
was first marketed early in 1969 and is superior to
Germaine's product because vermiculite is a more water-
absorbent substance than clay. However,
management believes that Asgrow's product has all of
the other disadvantages of coated seed. The price of
the product is $6.00 - $8.00 per acre.

c. Creative Agricultural Systems (Division of Union Carbide)

This Company places raw seed on strips of water-soluble
plastic tape. The tape with the seeds placed at specified intervals is then folded and sealed. The Union
Carbide product is called seed tape, and it provides a
means of accurately spacing raw seed.

Even the spacing problem is not completely solved, as
occasionally two seeds are placed together on the tape.
Use of seed tape requires very carefully prepared
fields. Seed tape does not improve the environment of

the seed. Thus, the chances that each seed planted
will mature into a harvestable plant are not significantly increased. Union Carbide, therefore, relies on
overplanting (104,000 seeds per acre spaced three
inches apart, as opposed to 26,000 seeds per acre
spaced twelve inches apart). Hand thinning is still
required, but is reduced below that of coated seed.
Union Carbide is selling seed tape at $35 per acre.
               management believes that Union Carbide's
cost of producing seed tape per acre is significantly
higher than   projected per acre cost of producing its product because of the high cost of water-
soluble tape.

3. <u>Seed Cells</u>

   One Company appears to be proceeding in a direction similar
   to   . It is management's understanding that the
   Niagara Seed & Chemical Company, a Division of FMC Corporation, has developed and is undergoing test plantings of a
   tablet similar in concept to   except that (a) it is
   not multilayered, (b) its environment is pure vermiculite,
   and (c) it is substantially larger than Aptek's Environmental Seed Cell. Each of these distinctions is important.
   First, as the FMC tablet is not multilayered, nutrients and
   herbicides cannot be introduced into the environment without
   the risk of injuring the seed through direct contact. Second,
   vermiculite stratifies when compressed during the production
   process and, therefore, the FMC tablet must be planted so
   that its strata will be perpendicular to the surface of the
   soil. Third, the larger size of the FMC tablet places it at
   a cost disadvantage and makes it more difficult to handle
   in the field.

It appears that only   Environmental Seed Cell offers both
precise mechanical planting and significantly improved environment.
     is in an excellent competitive position by reason of the unique
proprietary features of its Environmental Seed Cell and the Company's
expected ability to mass-produce it at low cost.

<u>Pro Forma Sales and Earnings Projection</u>

   The forecasts contained herein have been prepared by management of
the Company. They represent management's judgment at this time, based
on presently foreseeable conditions and requirements and are subject to
change, depending on future events.

   The Company has projected revenues and expenses (Exhibit II, Page 18)
based on the following assumptions:

   1. Production of the ESC will commence with one machine unit in
      April 19 .. In each of the next two months, one machine unit
      will be added to the Company's production capability. Follow-

ing that, there will be a five-month period during which
the initial production machines will be carefully evaluated and any necessary modifications made for subsequent
units. Starting in December 19 , machine units will be
added at the rate of two per month;

2. Once normal production levels are reached, machines are
   scheduled to be run for fifteen hours a day, six days a
   week (and assuming four weeks per month). Management
   is allowing for 15% downtime and 10% rejects.

3. Salaries are estimated to increase at an annual rate of
   10% except for certain executive personnel whose salaries
   will increase at a rate of 15%.

4. Projections are based on a selling price for the ESC to
   growers at $50.00 per acre. The projections in Exhibit II
   on Page 18 assume the schedule of machine emplacements as
   set forth in Exhibit I on Page 17.

Projected Cash Flow

Exhibits III and IV on Pages 20 and 21 show the Company's projected
cash flow for operations from August 19   through July 19 .. It should
be noted that cash flow is negative through March 19 ., after which time
it is expected that the Company will operate on a positive and rising
monthly cash flow basis.

Capitalization

As of June 30, 19 ., the total capitalization of
Inc. consisted of 500,000 shares of $.01 par value common stock authorized
and 331,300 shares of common stock issued and outstanding. To date, the
total cash investment by the present investors is $489,400. Of this,
approximately $375,000 has already been spent to bring the Company to its
present stage. There is no debt outstanding.

On a pro-forma basis, reflecting the completion of the private placement of 160,000 shares of common stock at $6.25 per share, the ownership
of   will be as follows:

	Shares Outstanding	% of Total
Present Shareholders	331,300	67.43
New Shareholders	160,000	32.57
	491,300	100.00

Exhibit I

Schedule of Machine Emplacements and Potential Acreage Served

	August	September	October	November	December	January	February	March	April	May	June	July	Year Total
19 - 19													
Machines in shakedown	0	0	0	0	0	0	1	2	2	1	0	0	0
Machines in operation	0	0	0	0	0	0	0	0	1	2	3	3	3
Acres produced	0	0	0	0	0	0	43	172	430	645	774	774	2,838
Sales $	0	0	0	0	0	0	2,150	8,600	21,500	32,250	38,700	38,700	141,900
19 - 19													
Machines in shakedown		3	2	3	4	4	4	4	4	4	4	4	4
Machines in operation	3	3	3	3	5	7	9	11	13	15	17	19	19
Acres produced	774	774	903	1,291	2,067	2,843	3,619	4,395	5,071	5,847	6,623	7,399	41,606
Sales $	38,700	38,700	45,150	64,550	103,350	142,150	180,950	219,750	253,550	292,350	331,150	369,950	2,080,300
19 - 19													
Machines in shakedown	4	4	4	4	4	4	4	4	4	4	4	4	4
Machines in operation	21	23	25	27	29	31	33	35	37	39	41	43	43
Acres produced	8,175	8,951	9,727	10,503	11,279	12,055	12,831	13,607	14,383	15,159	15,935	16,711	149,316
Sales $	408,750	447,550	486,350	525,150	563,950	602,750	641,550	680,350	719,150	757,950	796,750	835,550	7,465,800
19 - 19													
Machines in shakedown	4	4	4	4	4	4	4	4	4	4	4	4	4
Machines in operation	45	47	49	51	53	55	57	59	61	63	65	67	67
Acres produced	17,487	18,263	19,039	19,815	20,591	21,367	22,143	22,919	23,695	24,471	25,247	26,023	261,060
Sales $	874,350	913,150	951,950	990,750	1,029,550	1,068,350	1,107,150	1,145,950	1,184,750	1,223,550	1,262,350	1,301,150	13,053,000
19 - 15													
Machines in shakedown	4	4	4	4	4	4	4	4	4	4	4	4	4
Machines in operation	69	71	73	75	77	79	81	83	85	87	89	91	91
Acres produced	26,799	27,575	28,351	29,127	29,903	30,679	31,455	32,231	33,007	33,783	34,559	35,335	372,804
Sales $	1,339,950	1,378,750	1,417,550	1,456,350	1,495,150	1,533,950	1,572,750	1,611,550	1,650,350	1,689,150	1,727,950	1,766,750	18,640,200

Notes:
1. Shakedown time per machine is estimated to be two months.
2. During the first month of shakedown, machine production will be 1/6 of normal production. During the second month, it will be 1/2 of normal production.
3. The first three machines are projected to run 10 hours a day, 6 days a week (4 weeks per month). Management is allowing for rejects of 12.5% and downtime of 12.5%. Assumed monthly output per machine is 258 acres.
4. All other machines are projected to run 15 hours a day, 6 days a week (4 weeks per month). Management is allowing for rejects of 10% and downtime of 15%. Assumed monthly output per machine is 388 acres.
5. California operations will commence in the second year.

Exhibit II

Projected Pro-Forma Profit and Loss Statements
For the Years Ended July 31, 19__ to July 31, 19__

	19__	19__	19__	19__	19__
Revenue					
Product Sales	$141,900	$2,080,300	$7,465,800	$13,053,000	$18,640,200
Interest Income(a)	47,000	13,850			
	188,900	2,094,150			
Expenses					
Bad Debts & Collection Expenses(b)	$ 1,419	$ 20,803	$ 74,658	$ 130,530	$ 186,402
Salaries	251,083	717,555	1,490,425	2,405,864	3,466,616
Fringe Benefits	50,217	143,511	298,085	481,172	693,323
Consultants	12,000	15,000	18,000	24,000	30,000
Mix and Material(c)	7,095	104,015	373,290	652,650	932,010
Seed(d)	4,257	62,409	223,974	391,590	559,206
Packaging Cost(e)	1,419	20,803	74,658	130,530	186,402
Shipping Cost(f)	5,676	34,735	74,658	130,530	186,402
Rent, Heat, Light & Power(g)	14,800	40,400	78,800	117,200	155,600
Office Supplies	3,600	6,000	9,000	15,000	21,000
Maintenance Supplies	3,600	6,600	12,000	18,000	30,000
Telephone & Telegraph	3,000	4,500	7,500	10,500	15,000
Laboratory Supplies	1,800	4,200	9,000	15,000	20,000
Travel and Entertainment	15,000	21,000	30,000	45,000	60,000
Insurance	9,000	15,000	24,000	33,000	45,000
Sales Promotion(h)	15,000	62,409	223,974	391,590	559,206
Legal Fees	7,500	6,000	9,000	13,500	18,000
Accounting Fees	4,500	6,000	9,000	12,000	15,000
Patent Processing & Protections	9,000	9,000	7,500	7,500	7,500
Miscellaneous	15,000	21,000	36,000	54,000	75,000
Contingencies	15,000	27,000	45,000	75,000	100,000
Cost of Moving to California(i)	---	35,000			
Research & Development	12,000	24,000	75,000	150,000	250,000
Depreciation Machinery	5,000	40,000	105,000	175,000	245,000
Depreciation Other Assets	1,500	3,500	6,000	10,000	15,000
	468,466	1,450,440	3,314,522	5,489,156	7,871,667
Net Income Before Taxes	(279,566)	643,710*	4,151,278	7,563,844	10,768,533
Federal Taxes	---	60,000	1,846,530	3,370,000	4,800,573
State Taxes	1,500	10,000	290,590	529,469	753,797
Net Income After Taxes	$(281,066)	$ 573,710	$2,014,158	$3,664,375	$ 5,214,163

*Net loss carry forward of approximately $500,000

Footnotes for
Projected Profit and Loss Statements

(a) Interest income has been computed at a rate of approximately ½% per month (6% per annum) on the cash float less $50,000. Interest income has only been assumed for the first two years.

(b) Bad debt and collection expenses have been computed at 1% of sales.

(c) Mix and material expenses have been based on a cost of $2.50 per acre.

(d) Seed expenses have been based on a cost of seed at $1.50 per acre.

(e) Packaging expenses have been computed at a rate of 50¢ per acre.

(f) Shipping costs have been computed on the basis of $2.00 per acre for East Coast manufacturing for shipment to the West Coast.

(g) Rent, heat, light and power expenses are computed at a rate of $4.00 per square foot. Each machine, including support equipment and other ancillary space requirements, needs 400 square feet. Cost estimates assume that all space, etc. will be available and leased at start of year during which it will be required. In addition, 2,500 square feet are also included for administrative and research offices and laboratories.

(h) Sales promotion expenses have been computed at $10,000 in the first year, and thereafter at a rate of 3% of sales.

(i) Cost of moving to California includes actual moving costs as well as start-up costs.

Exhibit IV

Statement of Projected Sources and Application of Funds
August 1, 19 — July 31, 19

Cash Sources	Aug.	Sept.	Oct.	Nov.	Dec.	Jan.	Feb.	Mar.	Apr.	May	June	July	Year Total
Accts. Rec. Collected	$38,700	$38,700	$38,700	$45,150	$64,550	$103,350	$142,150	$180,950	$219,750	$253,550	$292,350	$331,150	$1,749,050
Interest Income	2,800	2,300	1,800	1,500	1,000	500	500	500	250	450	1,000	1,250	13,850
Total Cash Receipts	41,500	41,000	40,500	46,650	65,550	103,850	142,650	181,450	220,000	254,000	293,350	332,400	1,762,900
Cash Uses													
Expenses													
Bad Debts & Collection Costs	387	387	387	452	646	1,034	1,422	1,810	2,198	2,536	2,924	3,312	17,495
Salaries	37,379	37,379	47,865	49,533	53,870	56,454	62,146	65,721	72,632	74,210	79,304	80,973	717,466
Fringe Benefits	7,476	7,476	9,573	9,907	10,774	11,291	12,429	13,144	14,526	14,860	15,861	16,195	143,512
Consultants	1,250	1,250	1,250	1,250	1,250	1,250	1,250	1,250	1,250	1,250	1,250	1,250	15,000
Mix & Materials	1,935	1,935	2,258	3,228	5,168	7,108	9,048	10,988	12,678	14,618	16,558	18,498	104,020
Seed	1,161	1,161	1,355	1,937	3,101	4,268	5,429	6,593	7,607	8,771	9,935	11,099	62,414
Packaging Costs	387	387	452	646	1,034	1,422	1,810	2,198	2,536	2,924	3,312	3,700	20,808
Shipping Costs	1,548	1,548	1,613	1,807	2,195	2,583	2,971	3,359	3,697	4,085	4,473	4,861	34,740
Rent, Heat, Light & Power	3,367	3,367	3,367	3,367	3,367	3,367	3,367	3,367	3,367	3,367	3,367	3,367	40,404
Office Supplies	550	550	550	550	550	550	550	550	550	550	550	550	6,600
Maintenance Supplies	550	550	550	550	550	550	550	550	550	550	550	550	6,600
Telephone & Telegraph	375	375	375	375	375	375	375	375	375	375	375	375	4,500
Laboratory Supplies	350	350	350	350	350	350	350	350	350	350	350	350	4,200
Insurance	1,750	1,750	1,750	1,750	1,750	1,750	1,750	1,750	1,750	1,750	1,750	1,750	21,000
Travel & Entertainment	1,250	1,250	1,250	1,250	1,250	1,250	1,250	1,250	1,250	1,250	1,250	1,250	15,000
Legal Fees	500	500	500	500	500	500	500	500	500	500	500	500	6,000
Accounting Fees	500	500	500	500	500	500	500	500	500	500	500	500	6,000
Patent Processing & Protection	750	750	750	750	750	750	750	750	750	750	750	750	9,000
Miscellaneous	1,750	1,750	1,750	1,750	1,750	1,750	1,750	1,750	1,750	1,750	1,750	1,750	21,000
Contingencies	2,250	2,250	2,250	2,250	2,250	2,250	2,250	2,250	2,250	2,250	2,250	2,250	27,000
Research & Development	2,000	2,000	2,000	2,000	2,000	2,000	2,000	2,000	2,000	2,000	2,000	2,000	24,000
Sales Promotion	1,161	1,161	1,355	1,937	3,101	4,265	5,429	6,593	7,607	8,771	9,935	11,099	62,414
Cost of Moving to California	5,000	10,000	10,000	5,000	5,000								35,000
Federal Taxes											60,000		60,000
State Taxes			2,500			2,500			2,500			2,500	10,000
Inventory													
Spare Parts	2,000	2,000	2,000		2,000			2,000					10,000
Material for Product	2,000												
Fixed Assets													
Misc. Shop Equipment			1,000	1,000	1,000	1,000	1,000	1,000	1,000	1,000	1,000	1,000	10,000
Machines		40,000	40,000	40,000	40,000	40,000	40,000	40,000	40,000	40,000	40,000	40,000	440,000
Support Equipment		20,000			20,000			20,000			20,000		80,000
Laboratory Equipment			2,000			2,000			2,000			2,000	8,000
Office Equipment				1,000			1,000			1,000			5,000
Truck													5,000
Total Cash Outlays	(75,576)	(142,576)	(139,500)	(132,589)	(167,031)	(150,064)	(160,826)	(191,548)	(184,623)	(190,917)	(233,444)	(270,879)	(2,039,573)
Cash Flow	(34,076)	(101,576)	(99,000)	(85,939)	(101,481)	(46,214)	(18,176)	(10,098)	35,377	63,083	59,906	61,521	(276,673)
Balance	$598,501	$496,925	$397,925	$311,986	$210,505	$164,291	$146,115	$136,017	$171,394	$234,277	$292,383	$355,904	

Exhibit III

Statement of Projected Sources and Application of Funds
August 1, 19 — July 31, 19

	Aug.	Sept.	Oct.	Nov.	Dec.	Jan.	Feb.	Mar.	Apr.	May	June	July	Year Total
Cash Sources													
Accts. Rec. to be Collected								2,150	8,600	21,500	32,250	38,700	103,200
Interest Income	5,000	4,850	4,700	4,500	4,400	4,000	3,750	3,500	3,250	3,100	3,000	2,950	47,000
Total Cash Receipts	5,000	4,850	4,700	4,500	4,400	4,000	3,750	5,650	11,850	24,600	35,250	41,650	150,200
Cash Uses													
Expenses													
Bad Debts & Collection Costs								22	86	215	323	387	1,033
Salaries	12,958	15,875	18,250	18,417	18,417	18,461	21,292	23,625	25,958	25,958	25,958	25,959	251,128
Fringe Benefits	2,592	3,175	3,650	3,683	3,683	3,683	4,258	4,725	5,192	5,192	5,192	5,192	50,217
Consultants	1,000	1,000	1,000	1,000	1,000	1,000	1,000	1,000	1,000	1,000	1,000	1,000	12,000
Mix & Materials							108	430	1,075	1,613	1,935	1,935	7,096
Seed							65	258	645	968	1,161	1,161	4,258
Packaging Costs							22	86	215	323	387	387	1,420
Shipping Costs							86	344	860	1,290	1,548	1,548	5,676
Rent, Heat, Light & Power	1,233	1,233	1,233	1,233	1,233	1,233	1,233	1,233	1,233	1,233	1,233	1,233	14,796
Office Supplies	300	300	300	300	300	300	300	300	300	300	300	300	3,600
Maintenance Supplies	300	300	300	300	300	300	300	300	300	300	300	300	3,600
Telephone & Telegraph	250	250	250	250	250	250	250	250	250	250	250	250	3,000
Laboratory Supplies	150	150	150	150	150	150	150	150	150	150	150	150	1,800
Travel & Entertainment	1,250	1,250	1,250	1,250	1,250	1,250	1,250	1,250	1,250	1,250	1,250	1,250	15,000
Insurance	1,000	1,000	1,000	1,000	1,000	1,000	1,000	1,000	1,000	1,000	1,000	1,000	12,000
Sales Promotion	1,000	1,000	1,000	1,000	1,000	1,000	1,000	1,000	1,000	1,000	1,000	1,000	12,000
Legal Fees	625	625	625	625	625	625	625	625	625	625	625	625	7,500
Accounting Fees	375	375	375	375	375	375	375	375	375	375	375	375	4,500
Patent Processing & Protection	750	750	750	750	750	750	750	750	750	750	750	750	9,000
Miscellaneous	1,250	1,250	1,250	1,250	1,250	1,250	1,250	1,250	1,250	1,250	1,250	1,250	15,000
Contingencies	1,250	1,250	1,250	1,250	1,250	1,250	1,250	1,250	1,250	1,250	1,250	1,250	15,000
Research & Development	1,000	1,000	1,000	1,000	1,000	1,000	1,000	1,000	1,000	1,000	1,000	1,000	12,000
Federal Taxes													
State Taxes	375			375			375			375			1,500
Inventory													
Spare Parts						2,000	1,000	1,000	1,000				5,000
Material for Product		1,500		1,500							1,000		4,000
Fixed Assets													
Misc. Shop Equipment	1,500	1,500			1,000				1,000				5,000
Machines						20,000	20,000	20,000					60,000
Support Equipment						20,000							20,000
Laboratory & Experimental Equip.	1,000					2,000				1,000			4,000
Office Equipment					500		500			500			1,500
Truck			5,000										5,000
Total Cash Outlays	(30,158)	(33,783)	(38,633)	(35,708)	(35,333)	(77,877)	(59,439)	(62,223)	(47,764)	(49,167)	(49,237)	(48,302)	(567,624)
Cash Flow	(25,158)	(28,933)	(33,933)	(31,208)	(30,933)	(73,877)	(55,689)	(56,573)	(35,914)	(24,567)	(13,987)	(6,652)	(417,424)
Balance	1,024,842	995,909	961,976	930,768	899,835	825,958	770,269	713,696	677,782	653,215	639,228	632,576	

COMPANY LOAN APPLICATION
(Management Resumes Removed)

INTRODUCTION

, a new and unique product, was developed to satisfy established consumer needs in the fertilizing of house plants. The product provides an "idiot proof" method of accurately feeding plants for an extended period of time without handling, mixing, or storing chemicals, or recordkeeping of previous feedings.

The house plant market has experienced very rapid growth in the last five years due to increased consumer interest in ecology and horticulture and the awareness that house plants represent an inexpensive but attractive means of home decorating.

As a result of consumer demand, distribution of house plants and ancillary materials and products has expanded from the traditional channels, such as florists and lawn and garden stores, to include most forms of mass merchandising as well as many specialty outlets such as gift shops and department stores.

It was the objective of   Inc. to develop a method of precisely releasing or dispensing a specific amount of fertilizer to a plant over a specific period of time. Although we speak of fertilizer as the substance to be released, it must be kept in mind that this product can also be used to release other water-soluble substances such as insecticides, fungicides, bactericides, etc. It was also our objective to make a device that required no prior measurement or handling on the part of the user and, in addition, provided an almost "idiot proof" method of dispensing difficult substances with accuracy and convenience.

PRIOR ART

For purposes of this description, the prior art will concentrate on the field of fertilizer. At present, to our knowledge, there is *no* commercially available or in-use automatic method of dispensing fertilizer in specific quantities over a specific period of time to individual plants by either the consumer or the commercial grower. Every method presently used requires continuous measurement, mixing, or periodic dispensing and, because of this, is subject to error all along the line, particularly in the mixing and dispensing. There is also the problem of recordkeeping in relation to the time between applications. One more problem related to prior art is that, except in one case, it is extremely difficult to know exactly how much fertilizer has been dispensed to an individual plant. This case is the application of water-soluble fertilizer mixed into the watering tank and applied during watering by the commercial grower. Even in this case, according to our information, the commercial grower has difficulty in calculating the exact amount of fertilizer each plant receives.

The primary thrust of this argument relating to prior art is that there does not exist any automatic method of dispensing specific quantities of fertilizer over a specific period of time without prior mixing or measurement that provides the user with specific knowledge pertaining to the amount of fertilizer dispensed over a long and continuous perod of time.

Argument may be made for tablets and resin-coated particles; however, it is extremely difficult to know, without precise recordkeeping, when these products have been exhausted and, also, how much fertilizer has actually been released per watering per use period of time.

OBJECTIVE OF PRODUCT

The objective of the product is to provide a method by which water-soluble fertilizer can be released in very specific quantities over a specific period of time. These quantities will be *uniformly* released during that period so that the user will know how much fertilizer is dispensed with each watering. In addition, the objectives are to provide the user with a product that requires no prior mixing, handling, or storage. A further objective is to enable the user to determine when the product is depleted.

DESCRIPTION OF PRODUCT

The product consists of a water-soluble fertilizer incorporated into a gel substance. When the gel is in contact with water, the fertilizer will be released from the gel through diffusion in direct proportion to the amount of gel surface available to the water. Therefore by making a container that will permit variable amounts of the gel surface to be in contact with water, the amount of fertilizer (assuming at all times that we are working with a saturated solution) to be released can be specifically controlled. We, therefore, made a container that will have several orifice openings for water contact, these orifice openings being of specific size in relation to the desired amount of fertilizer to be released per size of plant. In addition, we included with the gel and the fertilizer, a water-soluble dye that is released with the fertilizer (the gel remaining in the container) so that the consumer will be aware when the fertilizer has been depleted from the container.

INGREDIENTS

In summary, the ingredients of this product consist of fertilizer, trace elements, water, gel, catalyst and dye. These are mixed in specific proportion so that, in the end, gelation occurs, and we have a semisolid fertilizer-incorporated substance. The primary benefit pertains to the fact that after gelation, the water-soluble substance in the gel will remain stable in the gel for a long period of time, as long as the gel is incorporated in an airtight container.

BACKGROUND

At present, the commercial-greenhouse method of applying fertililzer is via liquid feed tubes supplying water-soluble fertilizer or resin-coated particles, which are mixed with the potting mix (soil is rarely used), or the placing of tablets on top of the pot. Greenhouses generally force-feed their crops. This is the reason that when a plant is purchased at a garden supply center, it looks full and lush. Generally speaking, no further feeding takes place by the retailer or the consumer—the retailer primarily because of fast turnover, the consumer, we have found, for many reasons, such as . . .

☐ ignorance
☐ fear of mishandling
☐ fear of having chemicals in the home

☐ does not wish to be bothered with mixing
☐ fear of touching chemicals
☐ uncertainty as to timing of application. etc.

Because the plant is no longer fed, it generally returns to a normal state of appearance and growth rate and in a relatively short period of time, and, therefore, does not look anywhere near as good as when originally purchased.

There are a number of fertilizer products now on the market for potted plants. They are as follows:

☐ dry mix (various standard fertilizers)
☐ soluble dry mix (Grow Well & Peters)
☐ liquids (Ortho and Hy-Trous)
☐ tablets (Planttabs and Minipill)
   —for liquid mix
   —for insertion
☐ resin-coated particles (Osmokote and Rain Bird)
☐ dry fertilizer in polyethelene bags (Easy Grow)
☐ coated liquid droplets (3M)

Each of the above listed products has several major drawbacks which are:

☐ Mixing for either dry or liquid fertilizers is considered a serious drawback on the basis of reluctance to handle the product and, in addition, because of the potential error factor in mixing and application.
☐ Tablets. The primary difficulty is that it is difficult to know when these products are depleted or used up, and in addition, it's extremely difficult to measure the amount of fertilizer released per day or per watering. Also, handling is considered a problem because the fertilizer is actually touched. These factors are also true for Osmokote. Insofar as Easy Grow is concerned, the major problem is an inability to know when the product is depleted.
☐ Storage is considered a major difficulty primarily by consumers in that they believe that they have dangerous chemicals around the house.
☐ Temperature sensitivity is a factor with Osmokote, and presumably also with Rain Bird, in that the amount of fertilizer released is also dependent on temperature.
☐ 3M. The primary drawbacks to this product are (1) that you cannot remove the depleted product and the depleted product does not dissolve, and (2) it is impossible to tell when the product is depleted if the product is mixed with the soil rather than being sprinkled on top of the pot. The 3M product is made by coating a droplet of liquid fertilizer with a water-penetrable wax or plastic.

To reiterate, the primary difficulties are that there is no way of knowing how much fertilizer has been released per watering or the time period required to replenish. In addition, release is not consistent over the specified time period for various reasons. This is a particular complaint made by the commercial grower.

OUR PRODUCT

When we started the development of our product, we were looking for a method to not only overcome the above stated shortcomings of present products, but also a method of specifically fulfilling the functional needs of both the consumer and the commercial grower. In the pursuit, we ended up with a general product that can be applied to many market areas. The product we ended up with is a method of releasing water-soluble substances at a specific rate and quantity over a specific period of time.

As can be seen, such a function can be used in many market areas. For example:

- ☐ fertilizers
- ☐ aquariums
- ☐ swimming pools
- ☐ toilet bowls, etc.

We have chosen to develop an automatic dispenser utilizing this function for the fertilizer use first. Essentially, what we have accomplished is the gellation of a water-soluble substance that can be released through diffusion when the gel is in contact with free water. By restricting or predetermining the area of contact with free water by the gel, we can control the amount of fertilizer to be released over a specific period of time. (We can also control this by the amount of concentration of the fertilizer in the gel. However, by assuming the use of a fully concentrated solution in the gel, control is maintained by the area of release.) It is, therefore, logical that the container becomes an important factor in the total functioning of this product. We have developed these containers and also determined the diameter of the release areas required for various functions.

It should be noted that when the gel is in contact with free water, the gel does not dissolve. (In fact, although biodegradable and nonthermal affected, the gel remains intact.) The water-soluble ingredients within the gel are dispersed through the surface of the gel. By using a water-soluble dye in the ingredients (fertilizer), the user can see when the gel is depleted. The dye is dispersed with the fertilizer (when the gel is in contact with free water through the release area of the container). The gel itself remains in the container and loses its color when the ingredients are depleted.

MARKETS AND PRODUCTS

Each of the product areas listed below represents a full product line. In order to start somewhere, we started with a general fertilizer formulation and also restricted (for ease of production) the container sizes we would use. Once we have marketed the general formula, we intend to develop specific formulas and containers with specific release areas to meet the needs of various plant varieties such as:

☐ african violets
☐ geraniums
☐ poinsettias, etc.

In other words, each of the products listed below represents a total production line of between eleven and fourteen products. It is our plan to develop separate products for various plant varieties and pot sizes.

At present we have developed the technology required to manufacture and market the following products:

1. Consumer—Single Dispenser. This product is designed for use in potted plants ranging in size from 4″ to 6″ in diameter. Its duration and release rate is as follows:

Pot Size	Approx. Duration	Release Rate
4″	3 Years	25 mg.
5″	2 Years	32 mg.
6″	1 Year	42 mg.

2. Consumer—Two-Pack. This product is also designed for use in potted plants ranging in size from 4″ to 6″ in diameter.

Pot Size	Approx. Duration	Release Rate
4″	202 days	25 mg.
5″	158 days	32 mg.
6″	120 days	25 mg.

Please note that the duration is based on watering once every 3½ days.

3. Greenhouses (commercial growers). For the greenhouse market, we will develop a different container for each pot size. The size of the container will be dependent on the quantity of gel required for various periods of time. In addition, formulas will vary according to commercial growers' needs. The greenhouse product will be packaged 1,000 units per carton and will be manufactured in such a manner so that all the greenhouse worker need do is insert the dispenser into the pot without cutting the tip.

MARKET SIZE AND POTENTIAL

In 19 ____, approximately 750,000,000 house plants were sold in the U.S. market. Market growth rate in 19 __ is estimated to have been at least 10%-15%, which translates into unit sales of between 800 and 900 million plants. Approximately 60%-70% of these plants were sold or transplanted into 4″-6″ pots. Sales of ancillary materials and product such as fertilizers, chemicals, soils, pots, and associated hardware amounted to approximately two billion dollars. *House plant* fertilizers represented about 10% of sales or approximately 200 million. Future growth for plant supplies is expected to be at a rate at least equal to that of the plants and could be significantly higher as consumers become more aware of the necessity for plant care and maintenance. Indications are that the house plant market is maturing and well past the fad stage and that growth will continue at an annual rate of at least 8%-10% for the next several years. Healthy growth seems assured with continued high consumer interest, fueled at least in part by increased media attention to the house plant market as well as continued promotion on the part of retailers and manufacturers.

The number of retail outlets selling plants and plant supplies has been increasing for the past five years in all channels of distribution (including supermarkets, mass merchandisers, discounters, lawn and garden outlets, hardware stores, florists, department stores, and specialty retailers and service organizations).

It is conservatively estimated that at present there are some 35,000 to 50,000 retail outlets selling either plants, plant supplies or both. In the recent past the market has attracted numerous individual retailers with little or no experience in merchandising house plants. Many of these retailers have dropped out of the market only to be replaced by others eager to try their hand.

In the case of mass merchandisers, most sell plants (and in many cases, plant supplies as well) on the basis of a rack/plant jobber or leased space arrangement. The jobber is responsible for inventory and plant maintenance, thus relieving the retailer of the responsibility of plant care prior to sale as would be the case with a florist or lawn and garden retailer.

There is every indication that the mass merchandisers will continue to allot significant space to plants and plant supplies at least as long as sales and profit maintain their present high levels.

MARKETING STRATEGY

_____ will be marketed as a mass merchandise product line with initial sales effort directed to supermarkets and variety chains in order to build sales volume as quickly as possible. It is estimated that approximately 65% of sales will be through these types of outlets, with 45%-50% through supermarkets, and the remainder through variety chains. It should be noted that discounters will not be an initial target for distribution in order to ensure some semblance of price maintenance until distribution is established and sales patterns, through the various channels, can be charted.

The specialty retail market (i.e., lawn and garden supply, hardware stores, florists, etc.) will have second priority in the establishment of distribution. This market, while vast in the aggregate number of outlets, is more difficult to reach and basically more conservative in its approach to new products. Thus, this market will develop more slowly in terms of selling outlets and sales volume. It is estimated that sales through specialty retailers will amount to about 15%-20% of the retail sales of

In addition, sales to the consumer through mail order, direct mail and premium promotions, will be pursued, but primarily as product promotion devices to generate consumer awareness.

DISTRIBUTION

Sales to mass merchandisers will be accomplished using a combination of direct effort and the use of outside sales organizations such as manufacturers representatives, rack/plant jobbers, and food brokers and distributors. To a degree, local or regional market conditions will dictate which type of sales organization will be used.

The specialty retail markets will be sold through stocking distributors enlisted either on a direct basis or through the use of manufacturers representatives.

It is our present intention to handle mail-order sales directly and perhaps, to some extent, premium sales as well. However, to generate any signigicant impact in the premium and mail-order markets, outside sales and/or service organizations will be used.

PRICING

The suggested retail pricing for the initial product line is as follows:

- ☐ Single unit 1.89
- ☐ Two pack (120 day unit) 1.39

Based on the product features offered (ease of use, duration of product life, and fertilizer concentration and formulation),   is judged in the marketplace to be competitively priced vis-a-vis the competition.

Discount structures will vary by channel of distribution but will be at least comparable with present industry norms.

ADVERTISING AND PROMOTION

, because of its unique design and method of function, is judged to be a highly promotable product, particularly when compared to competitive items now on the market.

The degree to which we can promote   will be governed by the dollars available. Assuming minimal dollars available, we would plan to promote the product using a variety of relatively inexpensive means, including:

- ☐ Self-liquidating mail-order advertising in newspapers and magazines (regional placement following retail distribution)
- ☐ Premium sales
- ☐ Selected magazine advertising on regional basis (again to correspond with regional retail distribution)
- ☐ Placement in existing catalogue and direct-mail vehicles
- ☐ Promotional giveaways and accompanying product literature to consumer and trade media.
- ☐ Point-of-sale displays and promotional literature.

While it is recognized that television represents the best potential promotion vehicle, the cost would prove prohibitive, at least in the early stages of product introduction. However, potential exists for a joint venture television mail-order campaign, and this will be investigated at an early stage of product introduction.

TEST MARKET PROGRAM

Initial production of   commenced in August 19   . The units were produced by hand in limited quantities for test market purposes. There were several objectives of the test market:

1. To determine consumer and retailer acceptance of the product   concept
2. To test the packaging in terms of eye appeal and sale effectiveness
3. To determine if the initial pricing structure was acceptable
4. To expose   to a number of different retail environments to test the product's saleability as a stand-alone item and on an unaided sales basis

The first   cases were placed with retailers in late September 19   . By December, approximately 100 stores were displaying and selling   . Retailers included supermarkets, variety stores, lawn and garden centers, florists, hardware stores, and specialty shops. The retailers are all located in the Northeast—from Massachusetts to Maryland. Stores were regularly checked by   Inc. personnel or by distributor salesmen to count stock and to assess retailer and consumer reaction to the product. It should be noted that the test marketing was conducted with no advertising or promotional support except for point-of-purchase cards.

TEST MARKET RESULTS

Test market results were positive in terms of retail and consumer acceptance of the product. The product was recognized as being unique and fulfilling a consumer need not otherwise provided by competitive plant foods. The testing also indicated that the packaging and display carton needed to be revised in terms of graphics to more clearly state what the product is and what the product does.

PRODUCT CONCEPT

Retailers and consumers both consider the   concept to be a great step ahead of competitive timed-release plant food products. The ease of use was the most common reason stated by the consumers for purchasing the product. The second most frequently given reason for product purchase was the quality of the fertilizer formulation and the inclusion of trace elements, indicating that the product has appeal to the serious plant grower as well as the casual plant owner. A number of retailers reported considerable repeat business among customers who had purchased a two-pack, used the product for several weeks, were delighted with the results, and returned to purchase additional units.

PRODUCT PACKAGING

It has been determined, as a result of the testing, that the graphics on the package and the display carton needed revising to more clearly state what the product is and what it does. It was found that the present packaging graphics tend to blend when viewed on the shelf and are difficult to read and understand in the short time that the consumer's eye passed down the shelf.

PRODUCT PRICING

In general, present product pricing levels appear acceptable, especially in the case of the K-2 pack. Some price resistance was encountered with the K-1 long-term unit, but it is thought that such resistance can be overcome by proper product packaging and advertising. It was found that a number of retailers increased the prices above the suggested retail with no measurable loss of sales; in fact, several experienced higher sales than those retailers selling at the suggested price levels. It should be noted that while the price testing to date is not definitive, there is every indication that present price levels should be maintained, at least for the foreseeable future.

RETAIL OUTLETS

Although the   was sold in the various type of retail outlets indicated above, the highest sales rates were attained by retailers selling on an aided basis . . . that is, where the retail sales people could discuss the product with the consumer. Slowest sales were recorded in some of the supermarkets where the display cartons were simply placed on the shelf among all the other fertilizer products. It is in this retail environment that the problems with the packaging graphics became apparent. In total, however, all the retail outlets in which   was placed sold some product. A number have reordered product already, and more are expected in the near future, once the house-plant market emerges from the post-holiday doldrums.

To summarize, it should be noted that objectives of the test market were attained—limited though they have been—and they clearly show that the
can be successfully marketed on a national basis. Introducing a new product is a difficult task at best, but for a new company to introduce a new product concept into a competitive market, obtain valuable shelf space for the testing, and to successfully sell to consumers who have zero awareness of the product without benefit of any advertising is a true indication of   's potential market acceptance on a national basis. With improved packaging and an effective advertising and promotional campaign to generate consumer awareness,   Inc. is confident of reaching the sales and profit goals we have set for ourselves.

PRODUCT METHODOLOGY

In the course of producing product for test marketing, a number of production difficulties were encountered and overcome. Much was learned in terms of production procedures and methodology, and changes in product formulation and handling techniques were instituted.

As a result of this experience, we solved many of the problems inherent in the start-up production of any new product. We now have a proven production methodology which can be expanded to meet future production requirements without the necessity of remethodizing our entire production process.

BENEFITS OF LOAN

By obtaining a loan in the amount of $150,000,   Inc. will be assured of adequate capital for the purchase of necessary production equipment and the rental and maintenance of a suitable production facility. Perhaps of most importance, however, will be the adequate supply of working capital that will allow the company to pursue its goals with a maximum flexibility, particularly in the marketing program that will be crucial to the success of the company.

In the dynamic houseplant accessory market, to be successful a company must have the resources to respond to market conditions quickly and effectively, be it with more products or additional advertising and promotional activity. Thus, adequate working capital becomes crucial if the Company is to successfully gain and hold a significant share of the houseplant market.

With adequate capital for growth,   Inc. will expand its works force to approximately 12 people at the end of the first year, and by the end of the second year, the company should employ over 30 people. It should be noted that the majority of the employees will be drawn from the local pool of unskilled or semiskilled labor force, thus benefiting the community as a whole.

CAPITAL EQUIPMENT TO BE PURCHASED:

ITEM	Estimated Costs
K-2 24 cavity mold from Techniplast	$18,000.00
Filling equipment from Nat'l Instrument Co.	4,412.00
Sonic sealer with rotary table and unit holder from Branson Sonic Power Company	12,281.00
Mixing equipment	1,500.00
Benches and shelves	300.00
Blister packager from Packaging Industries	3,500.00
Blister packaging mold from Ambrozy	1,500.00
Dodge delivery van	6,000.00
TOTAL	$47,493.00

EXHIBIT "A" TO MEMORANDUM

--------, INC.
STATEMENT OF INCOME, PROFIT AND LOSS
FOR THE PERIOD FROM INCEPTION, JUNE 22,
19--, TO DECEMBER 31, 19--

INCOME
SALE $3,881

COST OF SALES:
Packaging $11,247
Supplies   236
        Total   11,483

Less: Estimated Inventory
       at December 31, 19--   8,612

Cost of Sales - Estimated   2,871

GROSS PROFIT - ESTIMATED $1,010

EXPENSES:

Salaries - Packaging   871
Salaries - Office   250
Consulting & Design Fees   2,185
Insurance   306
Auto & Trucking   587
Shipping Supplies   155
Travel & Entertainment   248
Office Stationary & Printing   234
Licenses   840
Amortization - Patents   1,151
Depreciation - Equipment   1,688
Payroll Taxes   71
Miscellaneous   511

        Total Expenses   9,097

        NET LOSS FOR PERIOD   ($8,087)

EXHIBIT "A" TO MEMORANDUM

--------, INC.
BALANCE SHEET
DECEMBER 31, 19--

ASSETS
Current Assets:
Cash in Bank	$ 377	
Accounts Receivable	1,913	
Inventory - Estimated	8,612	
Unexpired Insurance	306	
Total Current Assets		$11,208

Fixed Assets:
Equipment	6,750	
Less: Accumulated Depreciation	1,688	
Net Fixed Assets		5,062

Other Assets:
Product Development Expenses	78,250	
Less: Amortization of Product Development Expenses	1,151	
Net Other Assets		77,099
TOTAL ASSETS		$93,369

LIABILITIES AND NET WORTH
Current Liabilities:
Accounts Payable and Accrued Expenses	12,841	
Payroll Taxes Payable	115	
Loan Payable (due 2/20/--)	1,000	
Total Current Liabilities		13,956

Long Term Liabilities:
Note Payable - Apredel, Inc. due July 26, 19--	75,000	
Loan Payable - G.P. due August 1, 19--	2,500	
Total Long Term Liabilities		77,500

Net Worth:
Capital Stock Issuede and Outstanding 76 shares	10,000	
Operating Deficit	(8,087)	
Net Worth		1,913
TOTAL LIABILITIES AND NET WORTH		$93,369

EXHIBIT "A" TO MEMORANDUM

--------, INC.
NOTES TO FINANCIAL STATEMENTS
DECEMBER 31, 19--

Note Payable - due July 26, 19-- to Apredel, Inc.
    In payment of patent and related costs $75,000
    Payment of principal due at maturity except
    for on account payments to be made each July 31
    of 50% of net income after taxes of --------, Inc.
    No interest due until maturity

Loan Payable - to G.P.   2,500
    due August 1, 19--. Convertable into Capital
    Stock at $625 per share or at a lower price if
    corporation subsequently sells stock to a
    controlling shareholder at such a lower price.
    No interest due until maturity

Accounts Receivable Ageing -
    31 days (December 19--)   709
    61 days (November 19--)   949
    92 days (October 19--)   255

                      TOTAL $ 1,913

Accounts Payable Ageing -
    31 days (December 19--)   123
    61 days (Novemebr 19--)   1,446
    92 days (October   19--)   1,658
   122 days (September 19--)   1,404
   153 days (August   19--)   4,245
   184 days (July   19--)   3,965

                      TOTAL $12,841

Business Equipment
    Molds and Cutter at Cost
    (August - September 19--) $ 6,750

------ Inc. Summary Sheet
January 19--

ITEM / Months	Jan.	Feb.	March	April	May	June	July	August	Sept.	Oct.	Nov.	Dec.	Jan.	Feb.	Total
Revenue as Income	---	2878	5762	11573	19477	29458	43978	49508	54955	66204	77401	91577	104816	126392	683979
Expenses															
Fixed	---	8343	8918	8768	8768	8768	8268	7268	8468	8268	7518	8468	7918	---	99741
Admin. & Marketing	---	5258	5258	5508	5508	5508	5508	5508	5758	5758	5758	5758	5758	---	66846
Facilities & Services	---	3085	3660	3260	2760	3210	2760	1760	2710	2510	1760	2710	2160	---	32345
Variable	---	10255	16379	17660	25576	25870	24579	27265	28195	36350	39141	32023	47915	---	331208
Production Personnel	---	3948	4555	4555	5162	5769	5769	6376	6376	6376	6376	6376	6376	---	68014
Advertsng & Promotion	---	6000	10500	8500	11500	9000	6000	7000	5500	11000	11000	0	10500	---	96500
Packaging	---	307	268	2646	4478	8098	9378	10137	11960	13581	15516	18288	22169	---	116826
Containers	---	0	1050	1888	11320	2813	3216	3517	4082	5253	5858	6898	8314	---	54209
Ingredients	---	0	0	71	116	190	216	238	277	340	391	401	556	---	2796
Payments Due Vendors	---	2844	4700	1535	1600	0	1000	0	0	0	0	0	0	---	11679
Capital Expenditures	---	19627	32804	4620	200	11040	200	200	200	200	200	200	200	---	69691
Total Expenses	---	41069	62801	32583	36144	45678	34047	34733	36863	44818	46859	40691	56033	56033	556352
Profit or " " Loss	---	-38191	-57039	-21010	-16667	-16220	9931	14775	18092	21386	30542	50886	48783	70359	115627
Cumulative	---	0	-95230	-116240	-132907	-149127									

Sales and Shipments

Item / Month	Jan.	Feb.	March	April	May	June	July	August	Sept.	Oct.	Nov.	Dec.	Jan.	Total
Cases	83	159	285	515	840	1390	1565	1715	2025	2450	2800	3300	4000	0
K12														
at 50+10+10	78	109	170	310	480	795	920	995	1150	1450	1700	2000	2400	
at 50+10	10	34	75	125	225	375	410	470	550	700	850	1000	1200	
Catalogue 50+10	18	75	95	135	255	420	460	525	600	700	850	1000	1200	
	50			50			50			50				0
K20														
at 50+10+10	5	50	115	205	360	595	645	720	875	1000	1100	1300	1600	
at 50+10	5	25	65	105	185	305	330	360	450	500	550	650	800	
at 50+10	0	25	50	100	175	290	315	360	425	500	550	650	800	0
Nursery Sales -- Units				200		400		600		800		1000		
Mail Order Sales -- Units			1250	1500	1500				1250	1500	1500			
Revenues	2878	5162	11507	19477	29458	43978	49508	54955	66204	80801	91577	104876	126392	686773
K12 at 50+10+10	319	1084	2391	3985	7173	11955	13071	14984	17534	22316	27098	31880	38256	
at 50+10	638	2651	3365	4782	9032	14876	16293	18596	21252	24794	30107	35420	42504	
Catalogue	1771			1771			1771			1771				
K20 at 50+10+10	150	676	1750	2837	4999	8241	8917	10268	12159	13510	14861	17563	21616	
at 50+10	0	751	1501	3002	5254	8706	9456	10807	12759	15010	16511	19513	24016	
Nursery				100		200		300		400		500		
Mail Order			2500	3000	3000				2500	3000	3000			

_____, Inc.   January 19--

Item / Month	Jan.	Feb.	Mar.	Apr.	May	June	July	Aug.	Sept.	Oct.	Nov.	Dec.	Jan.	Feb.	Total
Administration	0	5258	5258	5508	5508	5508	5508	5508	5758	5758	5758	5758	5758	0	66846
President	0	2000	2000	2000	2000	2000	2000	2000	2000	2000	2000	2000	2000	0	24000
Marketing	0	2000	2000	2000	2000	2000	2000	2000	2000	2000	2000	2000	2000	0	24000
Sec/Bkpr	0	758	758	758	758	758	758	758	758	758	758	758	758	0	9096
Travel & Entr.	0	500	500	750	750	750	750	750	1000	1000	1000	1000	1000	0	9750
Facilities & Services	0	3085	3660	3260	2760	3210	2760	1760	2710	2510	1760	2710	2160	0	32345
Rent		1700	850	850	850	850	850	850	850	850	850	850	850		11050
Heat, Light & Power		325	200	200	200	200	200	200	200	200	200	200	200		2525
Telephone		400	300	300	300	300	300	300	300	300	300	300	300		3700
Office Supplies		250	250			500				750					1750
Insurance			750			750			750			750			3000
Accounting			400			200			200			200	400		1400
Legal -- General				1500											1500
Patent			500		1000		1000								2500
Waste Disposal		60	60	60	60	60	60	60	60	60	60	60	60		720
Maintenence Supplies		150	150	150	150	150	150	150	150	150	150	150	150		1800
Contingency		200	200	200	200	200	200	200	200	200	200	200	200		2400
Accounts Payable as of End of January	0	2844	4700	1116	2019	0	1000	0	0	0	0	0	0	0	11679
Jon	0		500		419										919
Tech		1000	2000	1116											4116
Harold			600		1000		1000								2600
Arthur			600		600										1200
Graphics		1731	1000												2731
Quarter		113													113

————, Inc.   January 19——

Item	Jan.	Feb.	Mar.	Apr.	May	June	July	Aug.	Sept.	Oct.	Nov.	Dec.	Jan.	Feb.	Total
Advertising & Promotion	0	6000	10500	8500	11500	9000	6000	7000	5500	11000	11000	0	10500	0	96500
Production & Make Up		5000	5000					3000							
Campaign															
1			3000						3000	3000	3000		2000		
2				3000	3000	3000				3000	3000		2000		
3				3000	3000	3000	3000			1500	1500		2000		
4					3000	3000	3000	3000		1000	1000		2000		
Mailorder															
Production		1000						1000							
Space			2500	2500	2500				2500	2500	2500		2500		
Production Personnel	0	3948	4555	4555	5162	5769	5769	6376	6376	6376	6376	6376	6376		68014
Machine & Maintenence		1040	1040	1040	1040	1040	1040	1040	1040	1040	1040	1040	1040		
Production Supervisor		1000	1000	1000	1000	1000	1000	1000	1000	1000	1000	1000	1000		
Production		694	694	694	694	694	694	694	694	694	694	694	694		
1		607	607	607	607	607	607	607	607	607	607	607	607		
2		607	607	607	607	607	607	607	607	607	607	607	607		
3			607	607	607	607	607	607	607	607	607	607	607		
4					607	607	607	607	607	607	607	607	607		
5						607	607	607	607	607	607	607	607		
6								607	607	607	607	607	607		
Shipping			607	607	607	607	607	607	607	607	607	607	607		
Capital Expenditures	0	19627	32804	4640	200	11040	200	200	200	200	200	200	200		69711
K2 Mold (24 Cavity)			9000			9000									18000
Filling Machinery		2206	2206												4412
Sonic Sealer & Rotary Tbl		6000	5781												11781
Unit Holder for Rtry Tble		500													500
Mixing Equipment		500	1000												1500
Benches & Shelving Etc.		300													300
Hookup & Set Up		500													500
Blister Packager				3500											3500
Blister Package Design		6000													6000
Blister Pack Mold			3000												3000
Delivery Van			6000												6000
Misc.		350	350	350	200	200	200	200	200	200	200	200	200		2850
Contingency 20%		3271	5467	790		1840									11368

————, Inc.   January 19——

Costs*

Item / Month	Jan.**	Feb.	Mar.	Apr.	May	June	July	Aug.	Sept.	Oct.	Nov.	Dec.	Jan.	Feb.	Total
Containers	0		1056	2030	4552	3193	3648	3993	4636	5733	6640	7818	9368		172087
K1 $.10 per unit					1152	1908	2208	2388	2760	3480	4080	4800	5760		52667
K2 $.055 per unit			1056	1888	3168										
$.0095 per unit						905	1008	1129	1322	1573	1778	2098	2554		
Ingredients	0		0	71	116	190	216	238	277	340	391	460	527		2826
K1 $.005				37	58	95	110	119	138	174	204	240	258		
K2 $.001				34	58	95	106	119	139	166	187	220	269		
Packaging & Printing	81		268	2646	4478	8098	9372	10137	11960	13581	15516	18288	22169		116594
Shipping Cases $187.50 M				254		260	293	355	380	459	525	619	750		
Display Cartons $350 M				250	588	973	1090	1215	1418	1715	1960	2310	2800		
Display Sleeves															
K1 $140 M					179	268	268	334	161	203	238	280	336		
K2 $135 M				259			298		392	466	527	621	756		
Packages															
K1 $50 M					576	954	1104	1194	1380	1479	1734	2040	2448		
K2 $42.50 M				858	1440	2382	2652	2970	3480	3519	3978	4692	5712		
Vacuum Forming															
K1 $27.62 M					795	1316	1465	1640	1922	2287	2585	3049	3712		
K2 $22.73 M				474	262	434	502	543	627	791	927	1091	1309		
Information Sheets															
Pkg Inserts $13.75 M	81		188	339	554	917	1033	1145	1337	1617	1848	2178	2640		
Distr Sheets $45 M					63	63	70	78	91	110	126	149	180		
Shpg Label $156.50 M			212	212	217	217	245	272	317	383	438	516	626		
Retail Insert $25 M			40		42	70	78	87	101	123	140	165	200		
Retail Suplmt $25 M			40		42	70	78	87	101	123	140	165	200		
POP Cards $125 M					174	174	196	217	253	306	350	413	500		

* Note: For purposes of this Pro Forma Blister Packaging costs are assumed to be the same as regular packaging costs

** Note: Beginning month blanks indicate inventory on hand

------, Inc.   January 19--

Month	Jan.	Feb.	Mar.	Apr.	May	June	&July	Aug.	Sept.	Oct.	Nov.	Dec.	Jan.	Total
Unit Requirements														
Plastic Containers														
K1 Units	1872	2616	4080	7488	11520	19080	22080	23880	27600	34800	40800	48000	57600	301416
K2 Units	4224	10512	19200	34320	57600	95280	106080	118800	139200	165600	187200	220800	268800	1427616
Shipping Cases	83	169	285	515	840	1390	1565	1735	2025	2450	2800	3300	4000	21157
Display Cartons & Sleeves														
K1	78	109	170	312	480	795	920	995	1150	1450	1700	2000	2400	12559
K2	88	219	400	715	1200	1985	2210	2475	2900	3450	3900	4600	5600	29742
Package & Vacuum Form Sets														
K1	1872	2616	4080	7488	11520	19080	22080	23880	27600	34800	40800	48000	57600	301416
K2	2112	5256	9600	17160	28800	47640	53040	59400	69600	82800	93600	110400	134400	713808
Information Sheets														
Package Insert	3984	7872	13680	24648	40320	66720	75120	83280	97200	117600	134400	158400	192000	1015224
Distributor Sheet	83	169	285	515	840	1390	1565	1735	2025	2450	2800	3300	4000	21157
Shipping Label	83	169	285	515	840	1390	1565	1735	2025	2450	2800	3300	4000	21157
Retail Inserts	166	328	570	1027	1680	2780	3130	3470	4050	4900	5600	6600	8000	42301
Retail Supplement	166	328	570	1027	1680	2780	3130	3470	4050	4900	5600	6600	8000	42301
POP Cards	83	169	285	515	840	1390	1565	1735	2025	2450	2800	3300	4000	21157

TIMING PLAN FLOWCHART

_____, Inc. 19--

	Week Month Week Ending	1 June 3	2 June 10	3 June 17
1. PLANT LAYOUT				
a. Layout				----X-X-
b. Lights - purchase/installation				
c. Electric sup. for each machine				
d. Storage production separ. wall				
2. MIXING AREA & EQUIPMENT				
a. Tile drainage installation		X-X-X-X-X-X		
b. Sink & Plumbing Installation			X-X---------	
c. Double Jacketed SS Tank purchase			X-----------	
d. Double Jacketed SS Tank/Install				-----X-X-XX-X-X-X-X-X
e. Mixing Equipment purchases				X-X-X-X----
f. Mixing Equipment/Install				X-X-X-X----
3. CAPITAL EQUIPMENT				
3.1 -FILLING-				
a. Review Filling Machinery at Mfr.		X-X-X-X----		
b. Review & Preliminary Test		X-X-X-X----		
c. Order Placement		------X----		
d. Prep. of Material for final test				X-X-X-X----
e. Final test prior to delivery				
f. Delivery				X-X-X-X-----
g. Installation				X-X-X-X----
				X-X-X-X-X-X

NOTE: "X" = ONE DAY

-------, Inc. 19--

	Week	1	2	3	4	5	6	7	8	9
	Month	June	June	June	June	July	July	July	July	July
	Week Ending	3	10	17	24	1	8	15	22	29

CAPITAL EQUIPMENT (cont'd)

3.2 -SONIC SEALER-

	1	2	3	4	5	6	7	8	9
a. Review Models for Capacity	X-X-X-X----								
b. Order Placement	----X-X---								
c. Seal Testing on Containers			X-X-X-X----						
d. Delivery						X-X-X-X----			
e. Installation						----X-X----X-X-X-X-X-X-X-X			

3.3 -CONTAINER MOLDS-

	1	2	3	4	5	6	7	8	9
a. Mold Modif. for Sonic Sealing	- - - -x X-X-X-X-X----								
b. Mold Modif. - material removal on tip for easier cutting			X-X-X-X----						
c. Review bids of large Mold for small containers	- - - - - - - - - - - - - - -						X-X-X-X----		
d. Place order for Large Mold	- - - - - - - - - - -			-					

3.4 -PACKAGING-

	1	2	3	4	5	6	7	8	9
a. Review various methods of pkg	X-X-X-X----								
b. Adapt pkg Design to Skin Pkg	X-X-X-X----X-X-X-X---								
c. Review Packaging Machinery for Blister, Vac Forming & Skin	X-X-X-X-X----X-X-X-X---								
d. Purchase Vac Form & Die Cutter	X-X---------								
e. Delivery					X-X-X-X----				
f. Installation & Dry Runs						X-X-X-X-X-X-XX-X-X-X-X-X			

NOTE: "X" = ONE DAY

-------, Inc.   19--

	Week	1	2	3	4	5	6	7	8	9
	Month	June	June	June	June	July	July	July	July	July
	Week Ending	3	10	17	24	1	8	15	22	29
CAPITAL EQUIPMENT (cont'd)										
3.5	-CONTAINER HOLDERS - ROTARY TABLE									
	a. Design		--X-X-X-X----							
	b. Subcontract or Make			X-X-X-X----	- - - -					
	c. Installation				- - -	X-X-X-X----				
3.6	-ROTARY TABLE PURCHASE-	X-X-X-X----								
3.7	-PRODUCTION FURNITURE PURCHASE-				- - - -	X-X-X-X----				
4.	PRODUCTION LINE SET UP									
	a. Layout		X-X-X----X-X-X-X----							
	b. Rotary Table Installation				X-X-X-X-X-X					
	c. Adaption of Container Holders to Rotary Table				--X-X-X----X-X-X-X-X-X-X					
	d. Alignment & Installation of Filling Equipment						X-X-X-X----			
	e. Alignment & Installation of Sonic Sealer to Rotary Table						X-X-X-X----			
	f. Electrical Hook up for Above						X-X-X-X----			
5.	PRINTING									
	a. Design of Camera Ready Art	X-X-X-X-X----X-X-X-X----								
	b. Competitive Bids	X-X-X-X----X-X-X-X----								
	c. Selection of Printer for Sheets 20 cards per, 3 color front, Back copy only, die cut		------X-X----							

NOTE: "X" = ONE DAY

------, Inc.   19--

	Week	1	2	3	4	5	6	7	8	9
	Month	June	June	June	June	July	July	July	July	July
	Week Ending	3	10	17	24	1	8	15	22	29

PRINTING   Continued

d. Placement of Order

e. Delivery   --X------- (wk 4)

f. Display Carton Design   X-X-X-X----- (wk 4)

g. Shipping Case Design   X-X-X-X----- (wk 4)

h. Placement of Order for display
    cartons & shipping cases
    estimated delivery date   X-X-X----- (wk 5)

i. Purchase of Packaging Film   -----X-X----- (wk 3)

6. RAW MATERIAL

a. Mfg. of Plastic Containers   ----X-X-X-X----X-X-X-X---X-X-X-X----X-X-X-X----X-X-X-X----X-X. X-X-X-X---X-X. X-X-X----- (wk 3-9)

b. Delivery of Plastic Containers   -X-X----- (wk 5)   -X-X----- (wk 8)

c. Purchase Gel & Other Chemicals   X-X-X-X----- (wk 4)

d. Purchase Fertilizer   X-X-X-X----- (wk 2)

7. INGREDIENT TESTING

a. Review & Testing of Formula re:
    hard gel & large batches   ----X-X-----X-X-X----X-X-X----- (wk 3-4)

8. PRODUCTION PERSONNEL HIRING

a. Plant Manager   X-X-X-X----- (wk 6)

b. Shipping & Receiving   X-X-X-X----- (wk 4)

c. Production Personnel - 3 or 4   X-X-X-X-X----X-X-X-X----- (wk 6)

NOTE: "X" = ONE DAY

----, Inc. 19--

	Week	1	2	3	4	5	6	7	8	9
	Month	June	June	June	June	July	July	July	July	July
	Week Ending	3	10	17	24	1	8	15	22	29

9. PRODUCTION
   a. Learning Period
   b. Limited Production - based on
      limited supply of containers
      from small mold   X-X-X-X-X-X- - - - -
   c. Full production estimated to start 1st week of August   X-X-X-X-X-XX-X-X-X-X-X

10. ACCOUNTING
    a. Interview with new CPA   X-X-X------
    b. Accounting procedures set up   X-X-X-X----X-X-X-X----

NOTE: "X" = ONE DAY

PRO FORMA

-------, Inc.

November 19--

Item / Month	Jan.	Feb.	Mar.	Apr.	May	June	July	Aug.	Sept.	Oct.	Nov.	Dec.	Total
REVENUE AS INCOME - 30 day delay	3000	70200	10000	145000	39000	119500	62000	63000	184000	93000	103000	43000	934700
FIXED EXPENSES	31075	25170	27507	25962	26273	23124	26504	24524	24924	26079	24049	23049	308240
Administration & Marketing	7350	7350	7050	6850	6850	6850	7050	7650	7650	6850	6850	6650	
Facilities & Services	4005	3450	2925	4030	6250	2925	4105	3525	2975	4180	3600	3050	
Consultants	6000	1000	5500	2050	50	50	50	50	1000	500	50	50	
Debt Maintenence & Fees	13720	13370	12032	13032	13123	13299	15299	13299	13299	14549	13549	13299	
VARIABLE EXPENSES	23479	94684	28564	100947	24024	24419	54369	50219	23094	19644	23944	18844	486231
Production Personnel	12284	13284	14367	14367	14974	16144	16144	16144	16144	16144	16144	16144	
Materials & Indredients	10745	79000	11697	81930	5100		32975	24275	5100				
Advertising & Promotion		500	1000			500	1500	5500	500		5100		
Selling Costs	450	1900	1500	4650	3950	7775	3750	4300	1350	3500	2700	2700	
PACKAGING DESIGN			2000	2000	3000	2000	1000						10000
CAPITAL EXPENDITURES Pro rated 5 years													32870
TOTAL EXPENDITURES	54554	119854	58071	128909	53297	49543	81873	74743	48018	45723	47993	41893	804471
PROFIT or "-" LOSS	-51554	-49654	-48071	16091	-14297	69957	-19873	-11743	135982	47277	55007	1107	130229
Accounts Payable	17623	17623	17623	17623	17623								88115
Accounts Receivable	7930												7930
PROFIT or "-" LOSS TOTAL	-61247	-67277	-65694	-1532	-31920	69957	-19873	-11743	135982	47277	55007	1107	50044
CAPITAL EXPENDITURES	7250	86200	42000	3500	2200		8800	14400					164350
CUMMULATIVE CASH FLOW	-68497	-221974	-330668	-335700	-369820								

_____, Inc.

November 19--

Item / Month	Jan.	Feb.	Mar.	Apr.	May	June	July	Aug.	Sept.	Oct.	Nov.	Dec.	Total
ADMINISTRATION													
President	2100	2100	2100	2100	2100	2100	2100	2100	2100	2100	2100	2100	25200
V.P. Marketing	2100	2100	2100	2100	2100	2100	2100	2100	2100	2100	2100	2100	25200
Office Manager	1000	1000	1000	1000	1000	1000	1000	1000	1000	1000	1000	1000	12000
Clerk Typist	650	650	650	650	650	650	650	650	650	650	650	650	7800
Travel & Entertainment	1500	1500	1200	1000	1000	1000	1200	1800	1800	1000	1000	800	14800
	7350	7350	7050	6850	6850	6850	7050	7650	7650	6850	6850	6650	85000
FACILITIES & SERVICES	4005	3450	2925	4030	3450	2925	4105	3525	2975	4180	3600	3050	42220
Rent	975	975	975	975	1050	1050	1050	1050	1050	1050	1050	1050	12300
Heat/Power & Light	700	700	700	650	600	600	650	650	650	700	700	700	8000
Telephone	500	500	500	500	500	500	500	500	500	500	500	500	6000
Office Supplies	50	100	50	50	100	50	50	100	50	50	100	50	800
Postage	75	75	75	75	75	75	75	75	75	75	75	75	900
Insurance	200	200	200	200	200	200	200	200	200	200	200	200	2400
Office Copier	130			130			130			130			520
Truck Maint. & Fuel	75	100	75	100	75	100	100	100	100	100	100	100	1125
Accounting	1000			1000			1000			1000			4000
Legal	100	500			500			500			500		2000
Maint. Supplies	100	100	150	150	150	150	150	150	150	175	175	175	1775
Contingency & Misc.	200	200	200	200	200	200	200	200	200	200	200	200	2400
CONSULTANTS	6000	1000	5500	2050	50	50	50	50	1000	500	50	50	16350
Horticultural	1000	1000	500	50	50	50	50	50	1000	500	50	50	4350
Laboratory Product Testing	5000		5000	2000									12000
DEBT MAINTENENCE & FEES	13720	13370	13032	13123	13299	13299	15299	13299	13299	14549	13549	13299	163137
Debt Maintenence	10000	10000	10000	10000	10000	10000	10000	10000	10000	10000	10000	10000	120000
License Fees	1000	500								1250	250		3000
Membership							2000						2000
Payroll Taxes	2720	2870	3032	3123	3299	3299	3299	3299	3299	3299	3299	3299	38137

————, Inc.

November 19—

Month / Item	Jan.	Feb.	Mar.	Apr.	May	June	July	Aug.	Sept.	Oct.	Nov.	Dec.	Total
REVENUE													
Feeder Meter (own label)	3000	70200	10000	145000	39000	119500	62000	63000	184000	93000	103000	39000	930700
Feeder Meter Private Label	3000	8000	10000	8000	5000	3000	3000	4000	9000	14000	18000	14000	99000
Fuller Brush		55200		75000					150000				280200
BACO		7000		7000						14000			28000
Other Private Label										40000	60000		100000
Vacuum Formed Feeder													
Gro Craft *							25000	25000	25000	25000	25000	25000	150000
Lawn Feeder													
Nat'l Gar.Spply,Can.**				55000		82500							137500
Other (U.S.)					34000	34000	34000	34000					136000
ADVERTISING & PROMOTION	0	0	1500	0	0	500	1500	5500	500	0	0	0	9500
Trade Shows			1000					1500					2500
Publicity								2000					2000
Media							1500	2000					3500
Printing, Sell Sheets etc.			500			500			500				1500
Adver. Production Make-up													
PACKAGING DESIGN	0	0	2000	2000	3000	2000	1000	0	0	0	0	0	10000
Feeder Meter Redesign			2000	2000	1000								5000
Flower Formula					2000	2000	1000						5000
SELLING COSTS	450	1900	1500	4650	3950	7775	3750	4300	1350	3500	2700	2700	38525
Commissions 10 %	300	1500	1000	1500	2000	1800	1900	2400	900	2800	1800	1800	19700
Shipping 5 %	150	400	500	3150	1950	5975	1850	1900	450	700	900	900	18825

Notes: * Estimated Revenue 1st year of $500,000 2 year Contract Sales
       ** Remaining $192,500 on P.O. to be shipped March/April 19—

-------, Inc.

November 19--

Item	Jan.	Feb.	Mar.	Apr.	May	June	July	Aug.	Sept.	Oct.	Nov.	Dec.	Total
PRODUCTION PERSONNEL (9 Hour Day)	12284	13284	14367	14367	14974	16144	16144	16144	16144	16144	16144	16144	182284
Plant Manager	2100	2100	2100	2100	2100	2100	2100	2100	2100	2100	2100	2100	25200
Weighing & Mixing Super (1)		1000	1000	1000	1000	1000	1000	1000	1000	1000	1000	1000	11000
Weighing & Mixing Asst.(2)	607	607	607	607	1214	1214	1214	1214	1214	1214	1214	1214	12140
Shipping/Receiving (2)	520	520	1040	1040	1040	1040	1040	1040	1040	1040	1040	1040	11440
Machinery Maintenence	867	867	867	867	867	867	867	867	867	867	867	867	10404
Quality Control Super.	607	607	607	607	607	607	607	607	607	607	607	607	7284
Quality Control Helpers (2)	563	563	1126	1126	1126	1126	1126	1126	1126	1126	1126	1126	12386
Production Personnel	7020	7020	7020	7020	7020	8190	8190	8190	8190	8190	8190	8190	92430
MATERIAL & INGREDIENTS	10745	79000	11697	81930	5100	0	32975	24275	5100	0	5100		255922
Indredients	1435	47000	1897	47350	1000		4275	2765	1000		1000		107722
Plastic Containers	4305		5691	1100			9850	8350					29296
Cards - Skin Wrap	600		820				7560	6250					15230
Display Trays	555			525				3200					4280
Headers	400			375				750					1525
Display Boxes	2620	5000	3034	5000			6800						22454
Plastic Sheet					4000		4000		4000		4000		16000
Plastic Bottles		7000		7000									14000
"Y" Top Connectors		11000		11000									22000
Caps		1700		1700									3400
Cup - Water Gauge		4000		4000									8000
Labels		800		800									1600
Shipping Cases	830	2500	255	3080	100		490	2960	100		100		10415

------, Inc.   PART "A"

November 19--

Item / Month	Jan.	Feb.	Mar.	Apr.	May	June	July	Aug.	Sept.	Oct.	Nov.	Dec.	Total
CAPITAL EQUIPMENT "A" and "B"	7250	86200	42000	3500	2200		8800	14400					164350
Feeder Meter (Own Label)													
Dies (3)					900								
Striker Plates (3)					300								
Flower Formula F-M													
Dies (2)							600						
Striker Plates (2)							200						
Vacuum Form Tray Mold								6000					
Tray Die Cutter (2 ea)								400					
F-M Private Label (Fuller)													
Mold Modification	1000												
Dies & Strikers (2 ea)	1000												
Gro Craft vac-formed product													
Heated Tanks SS Water Jacketed (3)			2400										
Motionless Mixers with Bypass			8000										
Pumps			4800										
Controls			8500										
Motors			5000										
Agitators (4)			1400										
Misc. Tubing, fixtures, Fittings, Heaters, Filling Heads, etc.			6000										

Item / Month	Jan.	Feb.	Mar.	Apr.	May	June	July	Aug.	Sept.	Oct.	Nov.	Dec.	Total
CAPITAL EQUIPMENT --- CONTINUED													
Automatic Lawn Feeder													
Tanks (3) Heated, SS Water Jacketed	9000												
Catalyst Tank	900												
Motionless Mixers (8)	4800												
Pumps (5)	7500												
Motors & Controls	6000												
Bottom Filler	3000												
Synchronizer	2000												
Bottle Feed Equipment	6000												
Strip Heat Sealer	4500												
Label Equipment	2000												
Connector Mold (8 up)	25000												
Gauge Mold	10000												
General Equipment													
Weighing Equipment	2500			2500									
Blender, High Speed	1150												
Mixing & Holding Tank			400										
Catalyst Tanks (2)			3000										
Fork Lift (Used)			1500										
Air Compressor	600												
Vacuum Form Blow Off							8000	8000					
Auto Capper & Auto Feeder													
Jigs, Fixtures, Tables, Storage, Misc.Tubing Fittings, & Tools	1000	1000	1000	1000	1000								
Leasehold Improvements													
Electrical Contracting		2500											
Plumbing Contracting		2000											

Index